THE LAST DAYS OF NAPOLEON'S EMPIRE

Frontispiece: Napoleon on the *Bellerophon*, by Orchardson

THE LAST DAYS
OF
NAPOLEON'S EMPIRE

From Waterloo to St. Helena

———————

HENRY LACHOUQUE

TRANSLATED BY LOVETT F. EDWARDS

ORION PRESS · NEW YORK
1967

To the proud, fiery and loyal Corsicans, my friends
To the memory of General de Carbuccia
Colonel of the 2nd Regiment of the Foreign Legion
died of cholera at Gallipoli, July 10, 1854
To Horace de Carbuccia

CONTENTS

———

CONTENTS

ILLUSTRATIONS

PRELUDE

The Emperor returned to Paris from Elba on March 20, 1815. At the Congress of Vienna, the sovereigns of Europe declared Napoleon an outlaw and agreed to unite their forces against France. War was inevitable. Both sides prepared for it.

France: Napoleon brought his army up to strength, formed army corps on the frontiers and concentrated five of them and a reserve of cavalry on the northern frontier: in all 124,000 men and 374 guns.

The Coalition: Five armies, two of them in Belgium:

The *Army of the Netherlands* under the Duke of Wellington: 96,000 English, with Dutch and German mercenaries. 219 guns, from the sea to Mons.

The *Army of the Rhine* under Marshal Blücher. 123,000 Prussians with 124 guns, from Charleroi to Givet.

Length of front was 150 kilometres.

On June 15th Napoleon secretly massed his forces around Beaumont, in a rectangle thirty kilometres wide and ten kilometres in depth, and moved towards Charleroi, where the English and Prussians were to meet.

It was a strategy of surprise; first the Prussians, then the English, had to be destroyed. Napoleon kept control of the situation with what he called this 'brilliant stroke' with a ninety-nine to one chance of success. But there were obstacles and delays from the very start. Blücher concentrated his forces between Ligny, Bry and Sombreffe. Wellington pushed on towards Quatre-Bras.

This led to two battles on June 16th. Ney, too weak, could not break through the English lines. The Emperor defeated the Prussians at Ligny and forced them to retreat, but did not crush them. Blücher withdrew on Wavre.

It was only about noon on the 17th that Napoleon sent Grouchy (32,000 men and ninety-six guns) to pursue them, with the aim of holding them while he dealt with the English . . . who withdrew to Mont-Saint-Jean, fifteen kilometres west of Wavre.

Sunday, June 18th. The battle began at midday. The Emperor opened with a violent cannonade of the English positions, and then attacked with his infantry, badly formed, which failed to break Wellington's battalions. A Prussian army corps then appeared on his right flank. Heavy cavalry charges by Ney, even though carried out unsystematically, managed to shake the British squares.

That evening, while Grouchy attacked a Prussian corps and forced it back towards Brussels, the Emperor held firm at Plancenoit against the Prussians who were threatening his right flank and, in order to finish with the English, launched an attack on their centre at Mont-Saint-Jean with the battalions of the Imperial Guard, supported by artillery and reinforced by such units as were available. The clash took place about half-past seven.

'All's well!' reported General Friant, senior colonel of the 1st Grenadiers, wounded in the hand, when passing by the Emperor . . .

. . .when the five Dutch battalions and the Belgian battalion of General Chassé, who had served with distinction in the French army in 1814, rushed down the slopes in a bayonet charge . . .

Chapter 1

WATERLOO

THE GUARD RETREATS

A quarter past eight in the evening. Night was falling on the field of Waterloo. Victory, which an hour before had smiled on the Emperor, now passed over to the enemy. The attack of the Imperial Guard on the centre of the English line had just failed. In twenty minutes, sixty officers and 1,200 grenadiers and infantrymen of the Moyenne Garde had fallen; the rest of the six battalions engaged withdrew, more or less in disorder, in the smoke, under a hurricane of steel.

Near the farm of La Haye Sainte, a hundred yards from the orchard, Napoleon tried to stop the rout. Calmly, he ordered the three battalions of the Old Guard which were by then near him to form square in the small valley, with its right on the Brussels road. Sheltered by these 'granite blocks', commanded by Cambronne, Roguet and Christiani, whose veterans had made the Austrians retreat at Marengo, the mauled units would re-form and the divisions of the 2nd Army Corps, supported by the artillery, the cuirassiers, the chasseurs and Piré's lancers, which had not given way, would be able to overwhelm, on the slopes beyond the Chemin de la Croix, the English centre, already decimated and crushed on the bloody field. The battle might yet be won.

Then, dominating the tumult, the cry rose: 'The Guard retreats!' The men of Reille, of Bachelu, of Foy, who had been launched once more against the battalions of Colin Halkett, the 'old hands' of Milhaud and Kellermann, the cavalry of the Guard who were supporting them, all halted in confusion. To the right, d'Erlon's line gave way as far as Papelotte, where the 2,000 men under General Durutte who had survived, worn out by four hours of fighting against the regiments of Saxe-Weimar and Bülow, were wiped out by odds of ten to one when Ziethen's

Prussian corps entered the line from d'Ohain. They retired quickly.

Halted a hundred yards in front of La Haye Sainte, whose solid walls were still standing, the Emperor, impotent to mend the situation, watched the collapse of his battle line.

Some of Vivian's hussars, reinforced by Adam's Scotsmen, clattered down the slopes; the Old Guard opened fire, the dragoons charged, but were quickly pulled back.

About two hundred yards from the Emperor, whom he was never to see, Wellington, mounted on his horse Copenhagen, had just raised his hat — legendary too — and from Hougoumont to Papelotte the battalions rose. There were not many, the units were reduced and the men at the end of their tether. However, to the sound of the drums, the fifes and the bagpipes, the Guards of Maitland and Byng, the thinned battalions of Alten and Chassé and a thousand Scotsmen, flags unfurled, advanced shouting. Cavalrymen advanced between the units. English, Germans, Dutch and Prussians poured on to the field; the Emperor's 'big battery' fired into the thick of them, answered by Wellington's and Blücher's guns. On the left, the French battalions and squadrons toiled upwards towards the crests of La Belle-Alliance, pursued by the yelling mass which could no longer be halted either by the few stoic squadrons of the Guard, or by the weak battalions of Belcourt placed there as 'expendable' by the Emperor himself, south of the present Butte du Lion, or by those of Cambronne, of Roguet or of Christiani.

In reply to the British cries of 'Hurrah!', 'Forever!', 'No quarter!' and the Prussian 'Vorwärts!' there were shouts of 'Trahison!' Cartridges were found filled with bran and iron filings; one general, two colonels and a number of officers deserted to the enemy. Captain du Barail of the 2nd Carabineers had told the English that the Guard was going to attack and thus given Wellington time to load his guns with grape-shot. 'Trahison! Sauve qui peut!' The Emperor went on up the road to La Belle-Alliance, followed by the staff, escorted by Soult, d'Erlon, Drouot and a number of cavalrymen which increased every minute; Ney, unshaven and in tatters, shouted to the square of the 95th: 'Come and see how a Marshal of France dies!'

There was need for haste. A red line, weakly supported, was to be seen; Adam's Scotsmen. General Durutte passed by, streaming with blood; he had galloped, pell-mell, with the Brandenburg Hussars who had cut at him in passing, slicing his face and severing a wrist. West of the road, the cavalry of the Guard was retreating before Vivian's men; the light brigade, lancers and riflemen, now consisted only of two and a half squadrons. Lefebvre-Desnoëttes, Lallemand and Colbert were wounded. Generals Mouton and Poret de Morvan with a number of officers were trying to re-form the regiments; sword in hand, they halted the flying troops, forcing them to re-form their ranks, but, no sooner rallied, they scattered once again.

Night fell; it was half-past eight, perhaps a little later. The moon shone fitfully, lighting up fantastic scenes. In burning Plancenoit 600 bearskins still held out with General Pelet, Lt.-Colonels Golzio and Colomban, the Tirailleurs, the Paris and Lyon Voltigeurs. In the church, in the cemetery and in the nearby houses, and at the Cuvenier farm, they were exchanging fire with the 11th Pomeranian Corps in successive waves in the smoke and flame of the burnings, where dead and wounded alike were roasting.

Then the companies of the Guard disappeared in the darkness, mingled with Lobau's men, overrun by Steinmetz and hammered at by fifty guns. On the extreme right, Duuring's chasseurs, guarding the Emperor's headquarters, were fighting hand to hand with the 25th Prussians in the woods.

It was the end! England's victory, Wellington's apotheosis, Blücher's vengeance, France's ruin, Napoleon's downfall, the end of a world!

Much has been written on mass hysteria. These men shouting and swearing, drunk with fear, rage, frenzy and blood, expressed this epitome of history by cries of mad joy, blasphemies, insults and threats of revenge which, hurled in four languages, struck like bullets, soothed the mutinous, encouraged the faint-hearted, excited the victors, consoled the vanquished, so that the eloquent symbol of all that must have been said on the evening of that June 18th might well have been summed up in the imprecation that posterity has attributed (wrongly) to General Cambronne.

The thin squares of the Guard, sometimes made up of less than 400 men and fifty metres to a side, had for the past half-hour mustered the fugitives, and fired several salvoes at the English; then, willy nilly, overrun, shot down, sabred and hard pressed, they beat a retreat. The 2nd battalion of the 2nd Grenadiers had broken from the start; 'the two battalions of the 3rd Chasseurs had held the English with their fire and, after nightfall, had joined the torrent'; the only remaining battalion of the 4th Chasseurs, wiped out in terrible fighting around the Hougoumont orchard, no longer existed. The 2nd battalion of the 2nd Chasseurs (Lt.-Colonel Mompez) retreated in good order, halted at La Belle-Alliance, and then, reduced to about thirty men, dispersed, probably the last of the battalions of the Guard. That of Cambronne (the 2nd of the 1st Chasseurs) had already disappeared. Sent to the left by General Morand, at the moment of the English counter-attack, it had clashed with W. Halkett's Hanoverians; after a murderous combat and a charge of the British 10th Hussars, it arrived, greatly diminished, near the inn of La Belle-Alliance. It was there that Cambronne fell, struck in the head by a ball.

The other grenadier battalions were already dispersed. The 1st battalion of the 3rd, thrown back on the slopes, 'rallied for a moment by the 1st Chasseurs, were decimated by the fire of a battery . . . ' as its commander, Lt.-Colonel Guillemin, wrote. When this brave man and a few more of the 3rd Grenadiers reached the crest only 'Père Roguet', second-in-command of the Grenadiers of the Guard, the 'Belcourt Battalion '(2nd of the 3rd Grenadiers), posted west of La Haye Sainte by the Emperor, was holding fast. The glory of his retreat has been reflected on the whole corps. Attacked by the British cavalry of Vandeleur and the infantry to the north of Hougoumont, its square surrounded, decimated by grape-shot and ball, little by little reduced to a meagre triangle, it fired a last salvo, shouted 'Long live the Emperor!' and then broke into small groups which reached the heights of Rossomme.

Near the farm, which today is no longer there, the drums of the 1st Grenadiers beat the *Grenadière* and the *Carabinière* to muster the stragglers. The two battalions commanded by General Petit, left by the Emperor before the attack on either side of the road as supreme reserve, with a battery of twelve-pounders, had not budged. The two squares were crammed with generals, officers and soldiers; near them were Lt.-Colonel Combes, later killed in the breaches of Constantine, Colonel Petit of the 'Farewells of Fontainebleau', Soult, Bertrand, Drouot, who had foundered fifteen horses in four days . . . Flahaut, Gourgaud, La Bédoyère, Chief of Staff, Ney, supported by a grenadier . . . and the Emperor. Tears were rolling down his cheeks.

Before them, on foot, on horseback, men fled southward. Who was on the right? . . . the left? . . . friend? . . . enemy? Doernberg's squadrons, driven back towards Hougoumont by the French cuirassiers, sabred by mistake the companies of the British 95th, who fired into the mass. Near La Haye Sainte, Adam's Scotsmen and Chassé's Dutchmen were brutally halted by a hail of bullets from the west. And those cavalrymen yelling there . . . Hussars? the 10th? Vivian's brigade? To the west of Hougoumont a line of lancers showed up on the crest of the ridge; it was Piré, retreating before the light dragoons halted by a fusillade from . . . the Imperial Guard? They were the lost Hanoverians!

The rout was reddened by the fires of Plancenoit where for the past quarter of an hour not a Frenchman had been left alive. Confusion everywhere. The German Legion charged through the British dragoons! The bullets of three nations struck at random!

Petit's grenadiers fired a last volley. They could no longer see anything in the smoke and the darkness. The Emperor tried to check the fugitives . . . perhaps to get killed. The twelve-pounder battery fired a last salvo, one ball of which carried away the leg of Lord Uxbridge, commanding the English cavalry.

It was time to leave, if they were not to be taken prisoner, for everything in front of them was in the hands of the enemy. The Emperor summoned General Petit and ordered him: 'Sound the retreat.'

*　　　*　　　*

Solemn singing rose from flaming Plancenoit. Shako on musket barrel, the Prussians were intoning Luther's hymn, sung fifty-seven years before at Leuthen by Old Fritz's veterans:

> *Herr Gott, Dich loben wir!*
> *Herr Gott, wir danken Dir!*

Down in front of La Belle-Alliance, that roadside inn where

there used to be dancing every fairday, the bands played 'God Save the King', the 'Yorkshire March' and the *'Pariser Einzugs-Marsch'*.

Wellington and Blücher had just met. They congratulated one another. For the Prussian the victory would be known as 'Belle-Alliance', a symbol. But Wellington preferred 'Waterloo', where his field headquarters had been.

'My soldiers are dog-tired', he said to the Marshal. 'I will leave the task of pursuit to Your Excellency . . . '

Alone, followed by five officers, he set off for Waterloo, across the field of carnage and horror, filled with the incessant and mournful wailing of those who were to die without prayers or attention. The moon lit up this misery with a dull, heavy light; the wounded asking for water, the mutilated, some of them stripped and others finished off, the prisoners plundered or, if they belonged to the Guard, shot. All the drama of those men dead and dying on the crests and valleys, soon to become ceme-teries; 4,000 at the sand-pit of La Haye Sainte, 1,000 cavalrymen at the Chemin de la Croix, masses, they said, at Hougoumont. How many in all? No one knew. So many corpses had been burnt, so many wounded men had become corpses; perhaps 50,000 men in all . . .

*   *   *

Ten o'clock at night. In his little room, Wellington, ex-hausted, began his report to Lord Bathurst: 'My Lord, Napoleon had mustered, between the 10th and the 14th of this month, his 1st, 2nd, 3rd, 4th and 6th Army Corps, as well as the Imperial Guard and almost all his cavalry on the Sambre . . . I have the pleasure of telling Your Lordship that the army has never behaved better . . . '

At Belle-Alliance, in his two-room billet at the inn, Blücher, worn out, wrote on June 19th at two o'clock in the morning, to his old companion Knesebeck, the reorganizer of the Prussian army: 'The finest battle has been fought, the proudest victory won . . . we are now mopping up the stragglers. I had thought to shake up Bonaparte's gang, but now it is almost over. I can write no more, for I am trembling all over; the effort has really been too great . . . '

After which, he mounted and went to supervise the pursuit.

' . . . as long as there is a man and a horse able to stand upright', he had said a moment before. 'Bülow, Ziethen, under Gneisenau's orders, to Genappe: Pirch to Mansart to cut off Grouchy's retreat.'

From three in the afternoon Grouchy had been at grips with the 3rd Prussian Corps left at Wavre by Blücher to guard the crossing of the Dyle during his movement towards Mont-Saint-Jean. Why?

Let us go back to June 17th, at three o'clock in the afternoon. The Prussians, beaten but not crushed on the 16th, had not been pursued and were able to go there unhindered. The Emperor, who knew nothing of these movements, thought Blücher, much weakened, was retreating towards Liège or Namur, or even farther, and had ordered Grouchy to go on to Gembloux with 32,000 men to follow or pursue him. He had thought he would be able to crush the English between Grouchy and Ney at Quatre-Bras and to march on Brussels with 70,000 men. Meanwhile, Ney had not moved and Wellington left Quatre-Bras and established himself at Mont-Saint-Jean to get into touch with Blücher and to accept battle there if he had his support.

Soult, for his part, considered Grouchy's contingent to be too large. If the Prussians had been knocked out of the battle, why launch against them a third of the army (62 battalions, 49 squadrons and 96 guns)? But the Emperor's orders could not be disputed. Grouchy set off with this detachment from the right wing of the army. It was a difficult task, an indefinite mission, carried out too late and bedevilled by false and preconceived ideas, entrusted to a recently appointed marshal; forty-nine years old, thirty-six in service, Order of the Grand Aigle in 1807, commander of a cavalry corps and 'The Holy Squadron' in 1812, famous for his skill on the battlefield and his rapid and decisive decisions, his loyalty and devotion. But it was the first time he was acting as a commander-in-chief and he was filled with doubts. Would he be able to make Vandamme (3rd Corps), that intractable character, obey him? What about Gérard (4th Corps), forty-two years old, brilliant, fiery and ambitious?

Had Grouchy made any comments to Napoleon on the deployment of the troops placed under his command, or on Blücher's advance? The Emperor had replied: 'Do you think you know better than I do?' and then: 'Aim for Namur and the Meuse.

That's where you will find the Prussians.' Grouchy agreed. General Baudrand, who was with the Emperor during this conversation, confirmed it later in a letter.

General Flahaut, Napoleon's aide-de-camp, present at the scene, left a note kept by his grandson, the Marquis of Lansdowne: 'Come along, Grouchy,' the Emperor had said about eleven that morning, 'stay close on the tails of the Prussians and keep in constant touch with me through your left . . . . ' This, because of the terrain and the circumstances of the fighting, was very difficult! But there have been discussions about this for the past fifty years.

In fact, despite the unwillingness, the delays, the floods of rain, Grouchy was at Gembloux on the evening of the 17th and learned that the Prussians were in very open formation moving towards Wavre or Perwès. At about ten o'clock he let the Emperor know that he would move in that direction the following day. The Namur-Brussels road via Gembloux crosses the Dyle at Wavre (4,000 inhabitants). The river has steep banks, from six to nine yards across, very deep, and runs from south to north; a marshy valley and wooded country, very broken and difficult. There is another bridge up-stream at Limal (four miles) and yet another a mile away at the Bierges mill.

At daybreak on the 18th Marshal Blücher sent three army corps towards Plancenoit and Mont-Saint-Jean, leaving General Thielmann (3rd Corps) at Wavre to defend the crossing if he were attacked; if not, he was to join up with the others.

11 o'clock. At Sart-à-Walhain (four leagues from Wavre) Grouchy wrote to the Emperor: 'I am marching on Wavre and will attack the Prussians.'

12.30. The guns could be heard from Mont-Saint-Jean to the westward. There was a lively squabble between Gérard and Grouchy; the first wanted to march on the guns, the second to carry out the mission entrusted to him by the Emperor, namely to pursue the Prussians.

From four till eleven in the evening Grouchy's men were engaged in very stiff fighting on the steep banks of the Dyle between Limal and Wavre; the 4th Corps bivouacked opposite Stulpnagel's infantry camped in the Rixensart woods and Kemphen's in the Beaumont woods; the Teste division and the 3rd Corps were before Bierges. The guns at Mont-Saint-Jean fell silent. It was believed that the Emperor's army was on the heels of the English in the forest of Soignes, but not the smallest scrap of news had been received. None of the officers sent by Pajol to the battlefield had returned. In any case, it had been Grouchy's intention to throw back the Prussians on Louvain at daybreak and then to join up with the Emperor at Brussels . . . Ordering Vandamme to take the 4th Corps under his orders, for their leader, the young Gérard, had been wounded, the Marshal went on: ' . . . Reports from prisoners here show that Blücher and Bülow are opposite us . . . I have my doubts . . . '

He was right! At that time both of them were at Genappe with the 5th Brigade Corps of Pirch (1st Corps) and the head of the column of the 4th. The patrols of Röder and Jürgass and Brunswick's hussars had halted near Caillou. The farm, completely pillaged, was burning from top to bottom, because it had sheltered Napoleon. The flames reached the barn and grilled the wounded who were in it.

Gneisenau gave orders to storm Genappe, for there had been firing from the town. 'The enemy has entrenched himself with wagons and guns', he wrote. 'We could hear a great rattling of wagons in the town and on entering we were exposed to very sharp musket fire, to which we replied with several cannon shots followed by a cheer and in a moment the town was ours . . . '

There was inextricable confusion there; they were killing one another to avoid death; General Radet, Provost-Marshal of the Army, became entangled in the wagons and was mercilessly thrashed. The Emperor too had been there, and a way had been cleared for him by blows with the flat of sabres. Having entered Caillou for an instant he had left again hurriedly by the orchard, where a young page, Gudin, was holding a fresh horse for him. Then he took to the road with the 1st battalion of the 1st Chasseurs (Lt.-Colonel Duuring); his rear was protected by the 1st Grenadiers and a few cavalrymen. Sombre and dry-eyed, he spoke little . . . the Chasseurs heard him muttering: 'After today, there is nothing left . . . I must be in Paris . . . Where is Ney? . . . Grouchy? . . . '

It took an hour to get through the village, whose single street was not more than 700 yards long and sloped steeply down to the Dyle which it crossed by a bridge eight feet wide. If any sort of defence had been organized, this bottleneck could have been held, the fugitives halted and the paths leading to Ways and Thy marked in order to show the way to the regiments and wagons; but nothing had been done. Soult, a bad chief-of-staff, had foreseen nothing. However, some units had welcomed Gneisenau's squadrons with shots and gunfire. On reaching the bridge over the Dyle, a carriage was halted by the 15th Prussian Musketeers (Major Keller). The Emperor just had time to get out, leap on a horse and disappear in the crush.

The postilion Horn unharnessed his horses and had his arm torn off by a ball; the outrider Archambault carried off the Emperor's portfolio and *necessaire* under the very noses of the Prussians, who were busy making an inventory of the contents of the *dormeuse* and the 'blue landau': one of the Emperor's hats, a gold sword, all his diamond-studded orders, a silver-gilt service, a frock-coat, a coat and a cloak. In the upholstery were found diamonds sewn there by the Princess Pauline Borghese, worth at least a million. Keller did well out of it; the Hohenzollerns too . . . the last German Empress was to wear the most beautiful of these jewels mounted in her necklace. Several generals' carriages and those of the imperial suite, very modest however, were seized; also the coach that had been used at the coronation at Milan and which had been intended for the entry into Brussels, and the wagon containing the library. Proclamations printed in French were scattered to the four winds. They had been intended for the Belgians and for the people on the left bank of the Rhine—after the victory!

'The God of Battles has decided the fate of your beautiful provinces . . . Napoleon is amongst you . . . you are worthy of being Frenchmen. Rise in your masses, rejoin my invincible hosts to exterminate the rest of these barbarians who are your enemies and mine . . .

'Brussels, at the Imperial Palace of Laeken,

'NAPOLEON.'

DISASTER

Quatre-Bras, a scene of horror. On an area about the size of the Champ-de-Mars 800 horses and 4,000 men were awaiting burial after the battle of the 16th. The heat was suffocating, the air oppressive. On the edges of the Bois-Bossu, Dutch, Scotch, French ghosts, the Death's Head Hussars, grinned in the flames of the bivouac fires lit by the grenadiers. The Emperor dismounted, approached them and said a few words. Little by little units began to appear in good order, the Chasseurs of the Guard, the crack gendarmes, Jacqueminot and the 5th Lancers, the men at the end of their tether, the horses dead-beat.

Standing in the middle of the crossroads, arms folded, a tragic phantom in his grey riding-coat, Napoleon looked fixedly towards Waterloo. Occasionally fugitives recognized him, slipped out of his way and passed. In the distance could be heard those Pomeranian drums whose high-pitched beat had pursued the French since Genappe. Gazing into the distance, the Emperor suddenly noticed 150 horsemen drawn up along the roadway.

'Who are you?' he asked the riders.

'The Lancers of the Guard, Sire,' replied Colbert.

'Ah, yes . . . the Lancers of the Guard! Where is Piré?'

Silence. Piré had commanded the 2nd Cavalry Division, which had not taken part in the battle.

'Sire, we do not know,' said Colbert.

'Why not? . . . And the 6th Lancers?'

'They were not with us.'

Then, sharply: 'But who are you?'

'Sire, I am Colbert and these are the Lancers of your Guard.'

'Ah, yes. And the 6th Lancers? And Piré? Piré! . . .'

Depression? Worry? Bewilderment?

Certainly the results of that terrible melée at Mont-Saint-Jean were not so much a retreat as a rout. No longer believing in its officers or its generals, fevered by political hatred for the enemy and 'the traitors', exalted by love for the Emperor, the army had lost all control. The cool courage of the veterans of Austerlitz, the methodical endurance of those of Auerstädt, the enthusiasm of the entries into the capitals, had been replaced by fever, rage, delirium, which had put an end to all discipline.

There were shots ahead of them. It was high time to leave! Once more that devilish drum which, certainly, was marching at the head of a column of infantry. No one could have known that that drum was alone, or almost alone, mounted on a horse from the imperial carriage!

And Grouchy? Soult considered that it was useless to send him a message; his corps must have been destroyed, or taken prisoner. The Emperor insisted, and ordered that he be told of the defeat; that he should withdraw on Namur, Givet, towards France. Captain Demonceau, aide-de-camp to General Gressot, deputy Chief-of-Staff, was given the order to go—alone, in the darkness, with an exhausted horse. He had to cover twenty or twenty-five miles, perhaps more, across a region he did not know and infested with enemies. However, the lives of 32,000 men depended on him! Had everyone lost their head? The Emperor put his foot in the stirrup and slumped heavily into the saddle. The horsemen made their way towards Charleroi.

At Gosselies, the Dumont house, Rue Saint-Roch, was a fine mansion in mellowed brick with a nailworks separated from it by a wide passage, whence a monumental staircase led to the floors above. It had wide and symmetrical casements, and a high carriage gateway opening into the forecourt. Behind the building a garden stretched down to the Street of the Tanners, giving access to the Courcelles highway.

Three o'clock in the morning. Several generals, their faces half-covered by their regimental cloaks, arrived on horseback; they were accompanying a man of short stature. 'All bowed respectfully as he passed. He asked if there was anything to eat. There was nothing left in the larder except a cold chicken,' wrote Madame Drion in a manuscript account. 'They replied that that would do very well. After the meal, they asked if there were a gate in the garden wall, so that they could get out without having to go back into the street. There was one; it opened almost outside the town. The mysterious person was taken there, through the garden, while the horses were led around there from the street. He went out by the wicket gate and they all mounted. They went on to Philippeville.'

*　　　　*　　　　*

Meanwhile in Paris the guns thundered out in honour of the victory at Ligny. 'There's no hurry,' Prince Joseph said to his brother Lucien . . . doubtfully. In the *Moniteur* the townspeople read glowing accounts of military events and the names of the generous Frenchmen who had sent money for the uniforms of the Garde Nationale: the High Court at Amiens 1,540 francs, the magistrates' court at Rion 300, the pupils of the Lycée Napoléon 1,000, the Calvados workhouse 390, etc. At Lyon the students of the Veterinary School drilled in artillery practice and formed a company which was assigned to the Garde Nationale. The players of the Théâtre-Français of Her Majesty the Empress decided to take over the administration of the Odéon. 'They hoped to gather around them the leading authors.'

The electors and deputies of the Gironde dined together at the 'Rocher de Cancale'.

'To the Emperor, whose interests are those of the nation, which sees in him the defender of its liberty,' said M. Grammont, mayor of Bordeaux, raising his glass.

'To the army, essentially national,' replied the deputy, Bory de Saint-Vincent.

'To the girls of Bordeaux,' the gallant General Faucher drank.

Mlle. George was applauded in the role of Clytemnestra in *Iphigenia in Aulis*.

Meanwhile the House of Representatives was discussing the measures to be taken against seditious shouts of 'Long live the King!', 'Long live Louis XVIII!', etc., and the excesses of the press. Fouché drafted a proposal that gave him the right to control the seventeen political newspapers, one of which was called the *Old Republican*. Life went on.

*   *   *

At Brussels, cavalrymen arrived about ten o'clock from the battlefield shouting 'Victory!' After the anxiety caused by the sight of fugitives, the sight of the artillerymen with harness cut yelling 'Every man for himself' and the rapid exodus westward of Wellington's baggage, there was an outburst of joy. The city was illuminated, the people congratulated one another and kissed in the streets and the French prisoners were led past and taken to the Petit Chateau barracks. The wounded, heaped on the setts of the Charleroi highway, were in a bad way. Help was being organized. The countesses of Merode and Robiano prepared the departure of convoys which would arrive at Mont-Saint-Jean the following day. Here and there heartrending scenes took place; wives of officers and soldiers trying to find out the fate of their husbands. The casualty lists were untrustworthy; it seemed that everyone had fallen. The priests collected money and bed linen.

At Ghent, where 'legitimacy rested like an old broken-down wagon', everything was in confusion; the city gates were closed.

'Monsieur', coming from Brussels, announced that 'the first battle lost leaves nothing to hope for from a second . . . ' This news confirmed the message sent the day before by the Duke of Wellington: 'Be ready to leave at the first signal.' Louis XVIII held council in his mansion in the Rue des Champs. Blacas, Richelieu, General Clarke, the Marshals of the Empire, Marmont, Victor, etc. were present; the wagon with 'the crown diamonds' was harnessed and ready.

Chateaubriand, as he wrote, was unable to hear the guns at Waterloo, but he gauged the consequences with remarkable foresight. 'Listening at the foot of a poplar to the echoes, a silent and solitary witness to the mighty judgment of destiny . . . ' he asks: 'Will Wellington triumph? Will legitimacy re-enter Paris in the wake of these redcoats who have once more dyed their purple in the blood of Frenchmen? Will royalty have for its coronation coaches the ambulances filled with our wounded grenadiers? What sort of a restoration will it be, if accomplished under such auspices?'

At one o'clock in the morning a letter from Pozzo di Borgo, sent by relay, announced that 'Bonaparte has lost the battle of Waterloo'.

*   *   *

About five o'clock in the morning of June 19th Napoleon crossed the Sambre to Charleroi, where the crush and the disorder were the same as at Genappe. There were dramatic scenes at the bridge, where the parapet had been broken. The town was chock-a-block with wounded and the prisoners from Ligny, with baggage trains, guns captured from the Prussians, wagons of the Great Park, bridging trains and carriages sent from Caillou about five the evening before. Everything was plundered. Loaves rolled about the streets, wine and brandy flowed in rivers. The soldiers squelched in a reddish mud as though stained with blood. The treasury limber had been pillaged of its millions of gold, the papers of the portfolio blazed . . . Such was the last vision of war carried away by the Emperor, fleeing swiftly from this pandemonium to stop on the right bank of the Sambre in a field near Marcinelle.

Sitting near a great fire, he bit into a crust and drank a glass of wine. Near him, silent, dog-tired, broken by this misfortune,

were those of his suite who had followed or rejoined him :
Gourgaud, thirty-two years old, trained at the Military
Academy, general since Ligny, first orderly officer to the
Emperor, an upstanding man, bluff, zealous, touchy, passionately
loyal to his master; Bertrand, Marshal of the Household, scrupu-
lous, a good general; Drouot, son of a Nancy baker, first scholar
of the Artillery School at Châlons, commander-in-chief of the
Guards Artillery, honest, straightforward, unprejudiced, 'the
sage of the Grande Armée'; General Dejean, a brilliant cavalryman, thirty-five years old, aide-de-camp to the Emperor; Honoré
de la Riboisière, second son of the general who had died exhausted by the Russian campaign: Juvénal Corbineau, cavalry
general, who had saved Napoleon's life the year before at
Brienne; de Bussy; La Bédoyère, etc. All these men were eager,
of undoubted loyalty and devotion, watching the Emperor's
words, expressions, gestures, twitches . . .

Head lowered, hands behind his back, he walked around the
fire, searching for inspiration to lessen the deadly check that he
could not understand : 'An incomprehensible day, a run of
unheard of bad luck', he was to say a little later. Had there been
treason? Was it only bad luck?

No! In an extraordinary letter,[1] little known or unknown,
unsigned and probably addressed to Marshal Drouot, an important military personage coming from the battle, one who had
gone through the recent campaigns and 'whose duties allowed
him to approach the Emperor', sums up the events and points
out the causes of the disaster with as much intelligence as
perspicacity :

'. . . On the 18th, towards evening, a Prussian corps appeared
on our right flank and was able to take the village of Plancenoit,
while the Emperor, instead of leaving the battlefield and taking
up a new position by withdrawing his right wing, threw all the
Guards rashly at the enemy centre, an operation which was
unsuccessful and which led to the most complete and precipitous
rout, since there were no troops remaining which had not been
engaged . . .

'It could not be said, as is often done, that the results of this
rout were incalculable and were bound to lead to the loss of the

[1] *Archives de la Guerre.*

Emperor's throne and the downfall of France . . . Even though from then on there may have been little hope of being able to prevent these results, something should have been done to examine the causes of the disaster and to remedy them.

'The causes of this disaster and of all those that preceded it, from 1812 onward, were of two types:

'*First Type*. The Emperor, carried away by the memory of former victories, thinks only of how to profit from his victory before making sure of it, and without even taking any precautions in the event of misfortune.

'The Emperor no longer visits the battlefield, gives few and disjointed commands, in such a way that there is no overall plan in the order of battle, nor in its execution.

'There are also several causes of a similar type that I omit to mention, not knowing how they may be corrected, nor indeed do I know how those preceding may be corrected and, for that reason, I might have kept silent . . . '

Amongst the causes of the *second type*, the writer stresses that 'the infantry and cavalry corps each have independent commanders so that on the battlefield each does as he thinks fit and it is therefore impossible to carry out any movement which requires co-operation, still less to carry out a retreat.

'The cavalry divisions are independent, so that when the infantry needs support, this is only provided after discussions, and often not at all, or too late.'

He points out that the regimental uniforms are of such a type that it is impossible to recognize regiments and rally them. 'It is essential to vary the collars and the shoulder tabs.

'Each battalion should have colours, without which it cannot be rallied. If the enemy should capture them, more can quickly be made. Nothing is worse than the usual habit of leaving the eagles in the rear with the baggage train.'

He insists especially on the terrifying lack of discipline of the troops, 'the cause of all our misfortunes', and the comments submitted to the minister by a combatant at Waterloo could, it seems to him, be of value to refresh the memory of those who come after him:

'The bonds of discipline are completely destroyed between

soldiers and officers, between officers and generals. Each is distrustful of his neighbour; they look on themselves as crusaders who have the same aims, but without obligations one to another.

'There is no way to punish the soldiers; one must bring back the stake or the wooden horse. There is much talk of honour and sentiment, but these are imaginary factors and so rare that no regulations may depend on them.

'Pillage has become so universal that the soldiers regard it as one of their rights. Officers and generals are in no position to prevent this, even should they wish it. It is this that has produced this habit of "stampede" which is endemic in the army and makes us, with good reason, the object of the scorn and hatred of other nations.

'My position permitted me to approach the Emperor and I had enough courage to point out to him several times the vices of his army, but always without success. He is lost in his memories, but since France must not perish with him it is essential to take prompt and vigorous measures to reorganize the army and restore military honour, without which all is lost.'

The remedies follow. Amongst them are:

'To form divisions out of twelve battalions, four squadrons, two batteries; to place the cavalry divisions under the orders of the commander-in-chief . . . to diversify the uniforms; to provide colours and leave the eagles, if so desired, in store; to punish ignominiously officers who behave badly; to establish a system of field punishments, above all when in camp, in fact everywhere, for breaches of discipline; to compel soldiers to halt and salute officers; to enforce with the greatest rigour the regulations against pillage. It is only harsh discipline which can give us an army capable of saving the country. This is the opinion of all those who may truly be called fighting men . . .

'The country must be saved and everyone must make sacrifices; one of mine will be to displease the ruler by sending this letter to a minister . . .

'Avesnes and Beaumont have already been sacked, as if they were enemy territory. Can one imagine anything of the sort happening in Champagne or in Picardy? This will make the people put up even with the Russians, who are no greater barbarians, and love the English who, by their discipline, have made themselves respected in the Midi, while the disorder in the French army has made it hated and despised there . . . '

*   *   *

Wellington's men buried their dead, evacuated their wounded to Brussels and settled down to eat and sleep in their bivouacs, set up on each side of the road from Nivelles to La Louvière. After a visit to Brussels to get news of the Prince of Orange, who had been wounded on the 18th, the Duke, narrowly victorious but uneasy and in dread of a French counter-offensive, wrote to his elder brother, Baron Marlborough, and asked for reinforcements:

Brussels
June 19th.

'My dear William,

'You will see the account of our life and death battle and of our victory over Boney. It was the most desperate struggle I have ever seen. I have never been so worried about the outcome of a battle and I have never been so nearly beaten. Our losses are immense, particularly among our best British infantry units. I have never seen infantry behave so well. I am leaving here immediately. May we have some cavalry reinforcements? . . . Or infantry? . . . Or both? . . . We need Lord Combermere, for Lord Uxbridge has lost a leg . . . He was wounded while talking to me, at the moment of the final attack, almost by the last ball.

'Always yours,
'WELLINGTON.'

After returning the same evening to his headquarters at Nivelles, Wellington acknowledged his debt to his best military adviser, General Dumouriez, who had in his time been adviser to Moreau, the Tsar, etc. . . . a real blackguard, traitor to his country and who called himself 'your humble servant'.

'What reliance can be placed on the Belgian officers' corps, who by inclination and habit belong to the French system?' the victor of Jemappes had written to him!

Wellington replied:

Nivelles, June 20, 1815.

'My dear General,

'I began my letter on the 19th, but since it was not a post day, I did not finish it then.

'I got yours of the 15th, for which I thank you. You will have seen what I have done and I hope you will be satisfied. I have never before seen such a battle as that of the day before yesterday, nor even won such a victory, and I think now that this is the end of Bonaparte. We are hard on his heels . . . '

Neither hard nor soft!

Before the inn known as 'the Emperor's', two leagues south of Quatre-Bras, Gneisenau called off the pursuit; some scouts advanced cautiously towards Gosselies, preceding Blücher who had narrowly missed Napoleon at Genappe. 'The hotel of the King of Spain', where he halted, was 'a picture of desolation', fences broken, windows smashed, rooms piled with wounded heaped one upon another like 'salted herrings' and running with blood. The hospital was in a barn, where four French surgeons, with embroidered coats and bloodstained instruments, were performing operations. One poor wretch implored them to spare his leg, but a deep incision below the knee had already been made. 'It is gangrenous', replied the patrician, as he finished his work, heedless of the cries of the patient. In a nearby room General Duhesme, commander of the Young Guard, seriously wounded at Plancenoit, was in his death throes. He was to die the next day. Blücher sent him his own surgeon, Brieske, to try and save him before setting out for Gosselies, where he took up his quarters at the Dumont mansion. 'I have kept my promise,' he wrote to his wife. 'On the 16th I was forced to retreat before superior forces, but on the 18th, in accord with my friend Wellington, I exterminated Napoleon's army . . . ' His troops entered Charleroi, Marchienne and Le Châtelet that evening; the 1st and 4th Corps bivouacked on the left bank of the Sambre.

However, the two commanders, who had met for an instant on June 19th, could scarcely believe in their victory. They certainly thought that Napoleon would be overwhelmed by the immense forces of the Allies and that he would be beaten at the end of the unequal struggle. But that the colossus should be overthrown after a single battle and his army so decimated that not

33

a trace of it could be found; the vast military state of France destroyed; the Emperor in flight to Paris, abandoning his carriages, his baggage train, his treasure and his soldiers . . . all this was beyond imagination! 'A hundred and fifty guns have already fallen into the hands of the Duke of Wellington; Prince Blücher, for his part, has captured sixty', stated the communiqué published at midday on June 19th at Brussels by the Secretary of State, Baron Capellen. 'Bonaparte's army?' said Blücher. 'It is a huge discouraged mob of fugitives, each accusing the other of treason! . . . None of the French fortresses is provisioned; even those in the front line have only weak garrisons . . . Napoleon has exaggerated on paper his means of resistance, which are practically nil . . . '

They decided to cross the frontier without waiting for the armies in the second line and to push on towards Paris.

But Wellington dared no impetuous moves; all his actions were carefully calculated; furthermore, his soldiers, calm and unmoving under arms, showed no great enthusiasm, whereas the Prussians were ardently eager to conquer what their diplomacy had refused them the year before. The Englishman had the greatest trouble in restraining Blücher who wanted to rush on Paris.

RETREAT TO LAON

General Dupuy de Saint-Florent, forty years old, from Limoges, as was also Jourdan whose aide-de-camp he had been with the Army of the Sambre-et-Meuse, had been cut to pieces with countless wounds; fourteen at Ulm in 1805, one at Jéna, one at Eylau. Since then, attached to the General Staff of the Grande Armée, as deputy commander, he had served in Russia and in Saxony and was now in command of the fortress at Philippeville.

On June 19th, about nine o'clock in the morning, the Emperor arrived at the outposts with his suite and an escort of cavalry 'of all sorts and conditions'. He had pulled himself together. Seeing at the gates of Charleroi fewer stragglers and larger disciplined detachments, Napoleon thought he might be able to rally his troops behind the fortresses of Givet, Philippeville, Mézières, Marienbourg, Landrecies, Avesnes, etc., take them in hand and halt the enemy. It was reported that Prince Jérôme with 2,000 men, a battalion and a squadron in battle trim, had crossed the Sambre and was on his way to Beaumont.

He ordered Gourgaud to send to Avesnes the pioneer companies who were in the park on the right bank of the Sambre, and told the orderly officers to assemble the baggage train and get supply centres organized to prepare for his departure for Philippeville. He was so exhausted that he demanded a travelling-carriage. Those around him objected that this was most unwise. The road was congested. It would be hard to escape the enemy's cavalry which might appear at any moment. Prussian troops had been sighted near Beaumont.

At about six o'clock the Emperor rode off for Philippeville by way of Leuverval and Somzée. The retinue was so shabby that they had trouble in getting the suspicious National Guards to open the French Gate. At last they stopped at the Golden Lion inn; the innkeeper, Vessié, a former officer of the Grande Armée, had room No. 4 opened. It was furnished with peasant furniture and overlooked the Place d'Armes and the Rue de la Roche. The maidservant, Gilliard, brought bread, eggs, butter and wine. Dupuy de Saint-Florent, Colonel Casergue commanding the fortress, the sub-prefect and the mayor came to pay their respects, were received and quickly dismissed. Ali the Mameluke himself undressed the Emperor, who lay down to get a little rest. In four days he had spent thirty-seven hours on horseback and twenty-four without eating. He had, so to speak, not slept, had just covered nearly forty miles and was suffering from cystitis.

Alone, he calmly reviewed the situation. The defeat had destroyed his plan of campaign. The Allies would not stop at the frontiers. The Flemish strongpoints could not hold back the invasion. Paris was now the central point of the defence system. The main worry was Paris. He kept thinking of it as he had done before, at Vienna, at Moscow, at Leipzig, in his victories and in his defeats, above all in his defeats. He must concentrate his forces in the basins of the Marne and the Seine.

While he was sleeping, Soult, Bassano and the secretary Fleury de Chaboulon arrived from Charleroi; from dawn onward orders flew in all directions:

'To General Reille,

'The Emperor places you in command of all the corps of the

Army of the North which are coming, one after the other, to the Philippeville glacis. It is of the utmost importance that work should begin at once on their re-formation and reorganization. Companies, regiments and brigades must be created. The field officers, staff officers and administrators, etc. must take over their duties and be directly under your orders. We shall thus be able to re-form the army swiftly. The material is there, but it needs organization.

'It is the Emperor's intention that you distribute per day to every soldier two rations of bread, one of brandy, one of meat and one of rice, with thirty rounds of ammunition to each infantryman and ten to each cavalryman. The governor will provide food and munitions . . . '

'The Emperor is rallying the army at Philippeville and at Avesnes,' Soult wrote to Davout. 'The corps will then be reorganized and its needs satisfied; you can imagine that after such a disaster they are immense . . . '

Order to the generals commanding the 2nd and 16th military divisions (Dumonceau at Mézières and Frère at Lille) to beat the countryside for stragglers, form them into detachments and supply them with food, munitions and arms; in case of need bring into the strongpoint every possible means of defence, 'everything lacking to sustain a siege, by any means you can employ'.

Order to Gazan, Inspector of Fortresses, and to Frère to 'try to arrange for the flooding of places where it may be possible; take all police and defensive measures that the circumstances may suggest. Hold out everywhere to the last.'

Order to General Rapp, commanding the Army of the Rhine, to General Lecourbe commanding the Jura Corps, and to General Lamarque commanding the Army of the Loire, 'to move by forced marches to Paris'.

'Nothing is lost,' said the Emperor. 'There are still 300,000 men in France; in a couple of months there will be twice that number . . . ' Then he dictated to Fleury de Chaboulon two letters addressed to his brother Joseph.

One 'to be read to the Council of Ministers' gave only an imperfect account of the outcome of the battle; the other, for the prince's eye alone, gave a faithful account of the rout, but ended like this:

' . . . All is not yet lost. I estimate that, by reuniting my forces, I shall have a hundred and fifty thousand men. The Federals and those National Guards who have guts will provide a hundred thousand men; the supply battalions another fifty thousand. I will therefore have three hundred thousand soldiers ready to oppose the enemy at once. I will harness thoroughbreds to the guns. I will call up a hundred thousand conscripts. I will arm them with rifles taken from the royalists and the untrust-worthy National Guards. I will make a mass levy in Dauphiné, Lyons, Burgundy, Lorraine and Champagne . . . I will overwhelm the enemy. But I need men to help me. I must not be knocked out again . . . The English march slowly; the Prussians are afraid of the peasants and dare not advance too far . . . All may yet be set right. If Grouchy has not been taken I can have fifty thousand men in three days . . . '

Soult had just sent him (Grouchy) a letter, dictated by the Emperor, which 'M. Cousin, spy' took with him towards Namur-Gembloux.

'The army has withdrawn to the fortresses; I wrote to you yesterday evening to re-cross the Sambre. I assume you have done this. You can move on Philippeville or on Givet, but you must not lose time. You must march in close formation.'

Meanwhile Grouchy was near Rosierne, on the road from Wavre to Brussels. That morning, at daybreak, von Marwitz's cavalrymen had tried to surprise the sleepy squares of the French 4th Corps and drive them into the river. The attempt failed. The infantry of Vichery and Pêcheux counter-attacked, threw back the enemy and reached the Templiers farm, four leagues from Brussels. Even though forced to retreat, Thielmann could have reached the capital, the more so, logically, since he had learnt at nine o'clock about the victory of La Belle-Alliance, but Blücher had told him the day before on leaving: 'In case of a check, retreat on Louvain.' So, having met with a check at Wavre, the Saxon withdrew to Louvain! Relentless reasoning, but absurd. Moreover the Chief of the General Staff of the 3rd Corps was the great strategist Clausewitz. It was Grouchy, still ignorant of the outcome of the battle, who was preparing to reach Brussels . . . by pursuing the Prussians with a few squadrons!

Half-past ten. A horseman arrived, hatless, with coat and

trousers torn to shreds, unshaven; his exhausted horse trembling on its feet . . . This was Demonceau. He mumbled alarming news, incoherently: ' . . . Rout, the Emperor, the dead, rout! The Guard! . . . ' There was no sense to be made of it.

On the road, Grouchy, La Sénécal, Chief of Staff, the aides-de-camp Colonel Bloqueville, Bella, Pont-Bellanger, etc., argued and listened.

Was he drunk? Or mad? Had he the password? Demonceau had no orders! Had he been given any? No one knew. Given a drink, he gave his message: the army was routed . . . The Emperor had lost the battle. He had been at Quatre-Bras about one in the morning . . . among the fugitives, pursued by the Prussians.

Marshal Grouchy must retreat to the Basse-Sambre, to Namur, to France.

Could he be a spy? A traitor? There were so many of them! A gendarme officer was ordered to keep watch on him.

Grouchy listened with tears in his eyes to the terrible tale which, by certain indications, seemed to be true. His situation was dramatic; he was alone with his small corps behind the enemy armies who could and must cut off his retreat and annihilate him.

For Wellington and Blücher it was child's play.

The generals were summoned: Vandamme, Vichery, Pêcheux, Hulot, Exelmans. The Marshal's voice quavered. What did they think? Vandamme proposed to follow up Thielmann's retreat to Louvain and to march on Brussels; Enghien, Valenciennes and Lille could be won. Fifty leagues through a country occupied by 200,000 of the enemy! Madness.

Moreover, the officer sent by Marshal Soult had added: 'Retreat to the Basse-Sambre.' Very well, then . . .

Half-past eleven: Order to Exelmans, commanding the dragoons:

'Leave Wavre at midday; make all haste to Namur (twenty-five miles). A well-mounted advance party must go ahead of the column; it must seize the bridges over the Sambre and Meuse. The main body must follow in two columns, the 3rd Corps on the left, the 4th on the right, covered by the cavalry of Pajol and Vallin.'

Thielmann was sure of himself. He did not sound the boot-and-saddle until the 20th at five in the morning, at the same time as an advance brigade (Sohr) of the 2nd Prussian Corps (General von Pirch 1st) was sent with a special mission to cut off the retreat of the French.

In his works, Clausewitz avoids any judgment on these operations 'in which he took part'. Damitz considers them 'of no great credit . . . ' but no German critic regards the Prussian generals as traitors . . . Whereas Thiers and many others overwhelm Marshal Grouchy with their reproaches. The Marshal, provided with vague and uncertain instructions, perhaps paralyzed on June 18th by fear of transgressing his orders, was, when he was left to himself on the 19th, able to overcome the difficulties into which his chief had plunged him and to take unhesitatingly one of his boldest decisions. 'It is my intention to push on without stopping as far as Temploux, passing through Gembloux,' he wrote to General Vichery commanding the 4th Corps. 'General Vandamme will keep his men at Wavre until nightfall.'

The execution of these movements was carried out with un-flagging energy by troops heavily engaged during the fighting of June 16th, 17th and 18th, exhausted, with little or no food, morally stricken by the news of the disaster and the certainty of being cut off. The will, the endurance, the sense of duty of the soldiers and their leaders, with Grouchy at their head, are worthy of the highest admiration.

About two o'clock in the afternoon the Bonnemains Brigade (4th and 12th Dragoons) halted at Gembloux for a breather; the advance-guard of the 12th then carried on towards Namur.

Built on the left bank of the Sambre, the town stretches in an ellipse northward from its confluence with the Meuse. The approach is picturesque, along a paved road bordered by four rows of poplars and deep ditches. The men and women of Namur, seated on benches, awaited the French . . . or the Prussians, since, according to a soldier who arrived there at seven o'clock, the townspeople knew of the disaster.

A civil guard of forty leading citizens which had set out towards Bellegarde met the French dragoons about three o'clock; shortly afterwards, Colonel de Puzy, commanding the 12th, entered the Brussels Gate. General Bonnemains ordered the Sambre bridge to be held, as well as the bridge over the Meuse which linked the citadel to the suburb of Jambes. Squadrons were stationed at the various gates. About seven o'clock the whole corps of Exelmans' dragoons entered the town, crossed the bridges and, well supplied with food and good cheer, disappeared before nightfall in the direction of Givet.

Meanwhile Grouchy and the 4th Corps, the wounded and the baggage train, were at Temploux (six miles west of Namur). The Teste division, acting as rearguard, arrived only at midnight. Vallin's cavalry held the Orneau cutting at Mazy. The troops were exhausted; not an enemy was in sight.

Naturally, Vandamme had not carried out his orders. After a night march his divisions reached Gembloux in disorder at five o'clock on the morning of the 20th without having seen a Prussian cavalryman. As for Vandamme himself, no one knows what happened. Did he sleep at Gembloux? Or at Namur? Even more uneasy after receiving the letter sent by Soult from Philippeville, Grouchy decided to push on, earlier than he had foreseen, towards Namur with the 4th Corps, Teste, the wounded and the baggage train, while officers were sent out in all directions to look for the 3rd Corps.

Ten o'clock. Alarm from the west. Prussian cavalry near Mazy; on the east the road to Namur had been cut. There were sounds of gunfire from near Rhisnes (on the Gembloux road).

And the Emperor was awaiting him impatiently.

*   *   *

The Emperor had left Philippeville.

According to all reports, so great was the disorder in the army that it was not possible to re-group the units so near the frontier. After an exchange of views with his entourage, especially Soult, Bertrand and Drouot, the Emperor, after long consideration and hesitation, decided to rally the regiments around Laon, to reorganize the artillery at La Fère, the cavalry at Reims and Saint-Quentin, the Guard at Soissons. He gave the necessary orders to the staff.

But to reconstitute an army able to halt the invasion, other and more important measures were needed; appeals for men, acquisition of material, horses, etc. Before, when he had been 'the Emperor', able to act on his own authority alone, he had wrought miracles with the French; now, as a constitutional sovereign, he had to take account of the Chambers, which were hostile to him. Besides, he had always been suspicious of assemblies, 'those lawyers who lose themselves in futile speeches and sterile debates and provoke catastrophes'.

'Write me what effect this horrible affray has had on the Chamber,' he wrote to Joseph. 'I believe that the deputies will be convinced that their duty, in the circumstances, is to stand by me to save France. Make them ready to support me worthily . . .' And he added in his own hand: 'Courage and firmness.'

Then, on June 19th, about midday, he left for Laon in Soult's travelling carriage, with other carriages bearing his aides-de-camp, orderly officers and secretaries. At the posting-station of Maubert-Fontaine (near Rocroy), where there were no horses available and the postmaster was trying to find them in the nearby villages, the Emperor was shaved in a room at the Grand Turk hotel, while his aides-de-camp got some refreshment in the main hall. 'We were in a piteous state,' wrote Fleury de Chaboulon, 'our eyes were swollen with tears, our faces distorted, our clothes covered with blood and dust.'

'The Emperor,' said General La Bédoyère, 'must go at once, without stopping on the way, to the heart of the national representation; he must openly avow his misfortunes and (like Philip Augustus) offer to die like a soldier and relinquish his crown to the most worthy. The two Chambers will revolt at the idea of betraying Napoleon. They will join forces with him to save France . . .'

La Bédoyère was a young romantic, twenty-nine years old, a former military policeman, aide-de-camp to Lannes, then to Prince Eugène, colonel of the 7th of the Line and devoted to the Emperor; he had brought his regiment from Grenoble on March 7th and won his stars and the position of aide-de-camp.

'Don't forget,' Fleury de Chaboulon replied, 'that we are no longer in the days when misfortune was regarded as a divine chastisement. Far from being sorry for Napoleon and coming nobly to his aid, the Chamber will accuse him of losing France and will try to save the country by sacrificing him.'

'May God preserve us from such a misfortune!' retorted La Bédoyère. 'If the Chambers break away from Napoleon, then all is lost. In a week our enemies will be in Paris. A day later, we shall see the Bourbons again; then what will happen to freedom and to all those who have embraced the national cause? As for me, there is no doubt about it; I will be the first to be shot.'

'The Emperor is a lost man if he sets foot in Paris,' broke in General de Flahaut. 'There is only one way to save him and France, that is to treat with the Allies and for him to cede his crown to his son. But in order to treat, there must be an army and perhaps, even as we are talking now, most of the generals are planning to send their submission to the king.'

Fleury and Flahaut were right. Fleury, or Fleury de Chaboulon, or Chaboulon de Fleury, for the name is uncertain, was an official of the State Council, sub-prefect of Château-Salins, a careerist, familiar with the world of politics. He had visited Napoleon on the island of Elba, had forced himself upon the Duke of Bassano and been given the rank of fourth secretary to the Emperor . . . who seemed to have no great appreciation of his services, whereas Flahaut was among his favourites. He was, in fact, the bravest, the gayest, the most charming and irresistible of all the knights of that epic. At thirty years of age, he had crossed Europe at the head of his squadrons and been wounded nine times. He was a divisional general and aide-de-camp to His Majesty. Son of Madame de Souza, a woman of great wit, good taste and talent, and perhaps of Talleyrand, lover of Queen Hortense and father of the future Duke of Morny, generous, diplomatic, elegant in appearance and witty, this gentleman of heart and character was the faithful companion of the Emperor in his evil days; riding stirrup to stirrup with him the previous day he had supported him when he was staggering from lack of sleep, even as he had supported him morally during the agony of Fontainebleau.

'At Paris the Emperor is lost,' he insisted to his companions. 'He will never be forgiven for having abandoned his army in Egypt, in Spain and at Moscow; he will be forgiven still less for having left it in the heart of France.'

*   *   *

June 20th, about six o'clock in the morning. The people of Laon, walking on the northern ramparts (Rempart Saint-Rémy) saw on the main Marle road, running straight ahead for four leagues, a mass of men unusual at that hour. It moved slowly. It was soon seen to be soldiers in disorder. The alarm was sounded in the suburb of Vaux and the National Guard was called to arms. They were infantrymen, dismounted cavalrymen, without weapons, ragged, bleeding, wounded, hungry and terror-stricken. 'All is lost,' they said. 'The army was destroyed last night near Brussels.'

General Radet, who had arrived shortly before with gendarmes, some carriages and a body of soldiers, began to muster them by corps and regiments. A dragoon officer, covered with mud, arrived. He dismounted before the posting-station where the Reims and Marle roads crossed; a carriage gateway opened on to each of them and gave onto an inner courtyard, surrounded by outbuildings: stables, barns, etc. 'The Emperor is just behind me,' the officer said to the postmaster, M. Lecat. 'He will stop here; be ready to welcome him.'

A few moments later a broken-down travelling carriage stopped. Napoleon stepped out and, as the gates were shut, made his way to the house.

'Your soldiers are on the run,' a passer-by remarked to him.

Very tired, despondent and irritable by turns, he was greeted by Radet; a detachment of the National Guard presented arms.

'Sire,' said the commandant, 'our brothers and our children are in the fortresses, but use us; we are ready to die for our country and for you . . . ' Greatly moved, Napoleon thanked him warmly and raised his hat to a few persons who had stopped in the court-yard crying: 'Long live the Emperor!'

'It was heartrending,' wrote an eye-witness.

Then Baron Micoud d'Umons the prefect, General Langeron the provincial commandant, the mayor and the 'leading men of the city' arrived. The Emperor walked and chatted with each one of them. A messenger brought a letter from Jérôme, headed Avesnes. The Prince gave an account of his 'efforts to re-form the corps . . . ' The Guard was mustering at Chivy (near Laon); 2,400 infantrymen (General Morand) and 1,000 cavalrymen (General Lefebvre-Desnoëttes) were already there. An officer reported that Marshal Soult and Generals Petit and Poret de Morvan were on their way to Laon and would arrive on the 20th or the 21st with about 3,000 men. The Emperor said that he intended to await the detachments at Laon, to reorganize the army and to merge Grouchy's corps with it.

'I will stay here until the rest of the army is re-formed,' he said. 'I have given orders that all stragglers be sent to Laon and Reims. The gendarmes and national guard are to scour the countryside and bring in the stragglers; the good soldiers will come in of their own accord. In twenty-four hours we shall have a nucleus of from 10,000 to 12,000 men.

'With this little army I will be able to give Grouchy time to arrive and the nation time to pull itself together . . . '

Around him objections crackled and sparked. Bertrand, especially, evoked the rout of the army. What could be done with only 12,000 men? Where to find arms? All citizens must take up arms . . . His presence was necessary to 'restrain the enemy', to inflame the loyalty of patriots . . . If he were not to be seen, it would be thought 'that he had been killed or taken prisoner'; the federals and national guards would lose heart . . . La Bédoyère, blinded by patriotism, repeated that everyone at Paris would follow the Emperor in the defence of the country. Flahaut, more intelligent and knowing men better, said that His Majesty was only safe in the midst of his soldiers. To go to Paris would mean to abandon them, would show that he could no longer halt the enemy, would mean to submit himself to the deliberations of the Chamber, to the leaders who controlled it, to Fouché who led the leaders . . .

In that inn courtyard, covered with straw that he trampled at every step, the Emperor listened to those surrounding him. He wavered . . . condemned, then approved, the various opinions, began discussions; precious time slipped away. What was to be done? He vacillated, but to the argument that there was no longer an army he reacted violently. 'What about Grouchy's corps?'

Grouchy? 'If he has managed to cross the Dyle,' objected Bertrand, 'he will have fallen into the hands of Blücher or Wellington. If he tries to retreat on Namur, the Prussians are bound to reach Gembloux or Temploux before him and cut him off . . .'

'No!' The Emperor was right.

During the day Grouchy had crossed the Sambre and the Meuse to Namur and his corps was marching towards Givet. That same morning, just at Gembloux, with a division of the 4th Corps, he had warded off the Prussians of Pirch 1st, awakened from their torpor, while the 3rd Corps halted Thiel-mann's men near Falize.

'Don't worry,' he told the wounded, who were going through a calvary because of the forced march, the heat and the impossi-bility of getting medical care, 'we swear that we will not aban-don you; be sure that we shall save you.' Then, having sent on the rest of the 4th Corps and the convoy to Namur under the protection of Teste's division, he summoned the cavalry and, moving swiftly between his two army corps to Rhisnes, drove out the Uhlans who had infiltrated into it. About four o'clock in the afternoon the French entered Namur where they were welcomed; pretty girls offered them bread and refreshments while, on the Salzine heights, Teste's five battalions were ordered to hold fast at all costs until six o'clock. By that time Grouchy's corps would have had time to cross the bridges and the rear-guard would withdraw as best it could.

Teste, formerly a National Guard from Gard, promoted brigade commander after Marengo, a general in Italy, seriously wounded at the Moskva, was a tough soldier and a born leader. Three battalions of the 8th Light, the 65th and 75th of the Line defended the terrain foot by foot, whilst two others consolidated the breaches of the Sambre bastion, occupied the Porte de Fer, concealed two guns loaded to the throat in the undergrowth, pierced loopholes in the walls of the nearby houses, brought timber and pitch to the Dinant Gate and barricaded the bridges. About five-thirty the Prussians prepared to storm the Brussels Gate, but were halted by fierce fire. Colonels von Zastrow and von Bismarck were killed, as well as forty-four officers, and 1,300 men put out of action.

Then the retreat began without the knowledge of the enemy. Sergeant-major Baptiste of the 75th of the Line closed the bars of the Brussels Gate and took the key away with him. It is now in the Lorraine History Museum at Nancy. Teste's infantrymen crossed the barricaded bridges on the parapets. About eight o'clock the last detachment of the 75th set the bonfire alight at the Porte de France and vanished in the direction of Profonde-ville and Dinant. Teste's division, which had carried out its task as rearguard magnificently, lost only sixty men, thirteen of whom were killed and who, from 1857, rest beneath a monu-ment in the Namur cemetery.

Next day, the 21st, Grouchy and his men (28,000 men and a hundred guns) and their prisoners were to reach Charlemont, Givet and the camp of Mont d'Or. One regiment was put in barracks, another in cantonments; the remainder bivouacked. The men rested. The wounded were at last cared for; there was bread, meat, brandy and munitions. In the disaster, when all seemed lost, the Marshal had preserved, and communicated to his troops, an energy that did him great honour. Marshal Soult and General Demonceau were told of his arrival. More than 40,000 fighting men had crossed the Sambre; 15,000 arrived at Laon.

But the Emperor was no longer there. He had rushed to Paris. The nearer he got to the capital, the more his companions wanted to enter it. Without him, they said, the civil war which they had known in the times of the Revolution threatened to break out again and make the squares run with blood. But Napoleon was no longer the man he had been then.

Twenty years before he had been quickened by a tremendous faith in his own destiny; he had believed in it implicitly even when no one shared his belief. The year before he had believed in it implicitly when no one believed any longer. The faith in his good luck, the belief in his star which had upheld him when he was preparing his departure from Elba and which had sustained him during 'the flight of the eagle' seemed to have abandoned him soon after he reached Paris. He felt that he was no longer backed by the ardent and devoted loyalty to which he had become accustomed. He believed that his wife and son had abandoned him, that all Europe was against him and against France, ill prepared to repulse the assault. He was hamstrung by the constitutional trammels which he had allowed to be imposed on him, had to take heed of a hostile parliament, rabid royalists, Jacobins dreaming of 1793, scoffing liberals. Before leaving for the campaign, he had had gloomy presentiments . . . On entering his study and seeing him drowsing, the Minister of the Marine, Decrès, was waiting for him to wake when, with a start, the Emperor stood up and, thinking that he was alone, said: 'And then, it will go as best it can . . . ' Shortly afterwards he had left Paris, leaving Fouché there.

Fouché?

Some days before his departure for the army, the Prefect of

Police had come to tell the Emperor that one of Fouché's cronies, a former senior police official, was about to leave for Switzerland with a passport signed by the minister. By order of the Emperor a telegram was at once sent to the authorities at Huningue telling them to arrest the emissary, but he had already crossed the frontier. A War Council, presided over by General Darricau, was already constituted. However, once again, at the moment of giving the order for arrest, Napoleon hesitated . . . The Chamber was about to meet; its hostility was already evident . . . 'I will leave for the army,' he said. 'If I lose, what good is the blood of this man? His execution is pointless. If I win, the courier who will bring the news will bring an order for his trial. The town criers, when they announce in the streets the triumph of our armies will also make known the condemnation and execution of Fouché as a traitor to France.'

The War Council remained in existence.

On the evening of June 20th, in a room of the Hotel des Postes at Laon, the Emperor had made an inventory of the material lost and the resources by which it could easily be replaced. If the Chambers supported him, he would reassemble the army around the fortress and would hold the enemy. In a room nearby, putting his things in order, was the valet Marchand, who heard snatches of the conversation:

'If I go to Paris and stain my hands with blood, I shall have to plunge my arms into it up to the elbows . . .'

After a silence 'Fouché's name was mentioned and the man seemed doomed to vengeance', noted Marchand in his memoirs. Then after completing and showing the text of the last bulletin of the Grande Armée to those around him, the Emperor sent it to his brother Joseph at his mansion in the Faubourg Saint-Honoré. Plagued by his thoughts, by the dream that always haunted him, the fear of being no longer loved, he felt his will faltering. He 'dared not' decide. 'For,' he used to say, 'not to dare means to do nothing when the time is ripe; one never dares without being convinced of one's good luck . . .'

Drawn to Paris by fear of Fouché's intrigues and those of his underlings, kept at Laon by his wish not to abandon his soldiers and not betray those loyal to him, he wanted to continue the struggle. He was to go to the capital, stay there a couple of days to feel the pulse of public opinion and overcome the opposition by his prestige and then return to his soldiers. Soult would rally them. It was a half-measure, a bad business!

'Very well,' he said suddenly, 'since you think it is necessary, I will go to Paris; but I am convinced that you are making me do something foolish. My real place is here. From here I could control all that is happening in Paris and my brothers would do the rest.'

Meanwhile a courier was leaving Paris bearing a letter. Lucien, in close touch with the Chambers and the political world, 'implored him to postpone his return to the capital'. Too late!

The Emperor ordered Marchand to take a post-chaise and go to the Elysée where he himself would be on the following day. A letter warned Joseph. On his arrival he would preside over a Council of Ministers, who must hold themselves in readiness. Then he appointed Colonel de Bussy, his aide-de-camp and former colleague at the La Fère Artillery School, as adjutant to the Prefect of the Aisne. He came from the district (Beaurieux) and would help him in collecting supplies for the army in the fortress.

General Neigre, commanding the artillery park, left for La Fère to organize his batteries. Dejean left for Guise where he was to have the fortifications repaired and stocked with food and munitions. Flahaut was sent to Avesnes to collect information about the enemy. Radet remained at Laon to rally the stragglers and fugitives. The Emperor would not wait for Soult, who was now furnished with all the orders he needed to take over command of the army. Since the berline that he had commandeered at Philippeville was in a bad state, he took his seat in a carriage placed at his disposal by the prefect; the Marshal of the Household sat beside him, Ali mounted the box, the postilions spurred their horses, and Napoleon, greeted by a few shouts of 'Long live the Emperor!', set off for Paris and his destiny. It was June 20, 1815, at ten o'clock in the evening.

That same day, Blücher, bold and impetuous, ordered his troops to cross the frontier and march on Maubeuge, Landrecies and Avesnes and urged Wellington to thrust forward next day an advance guard from Binche to Malplaquet.

Chapter II

THE EMPEROR AT PARIS

THE ELYSÉE

Paris was cheerless. The people who had first looked on the return from Elba as the presage of furious and bitter war had become reassured. 'There is nothing more gullible than the Paris mob,' wrote a contemporary. 'It swallows the most arrant nonsense, falls for the most childish incidents; a few unimportant police notices, a few words whispered abroad, a well-placed newspaper article, are enough to set the trend of opinion and keep the people on edge; and Fouché is an expert in controlling public opinion.'

On the boulevards, from the Porte Montmartre to the 'Chinese Baths', the newspaper sellers openly displayed their placards; in the evenings the crowds, eager for news, milled around a candle-end stuck on a table to read the papers and broadsheets, and to hear the news.

After the Emperor's departure, anxiety replaced the rejoicings of the Champ de Mai; the people were gloomy, for different reasons. The French were divided. In the salons, they expressed discreet hopes for the downfall of 'the Usurper'. The Marquise de Montcalm whose window boxes had been filled with lilies during the Hundred Days, wrote in her diary for June 15th: 'If he has reverses the Chambers will try to come to terms with the Powers and will propose recognition of the Duke of Orleans, or anyone else . . . But, should he be victorious, he will have much pleasure in paying them out for their spirit of independence . . . Opinions are divided,' she went on, 'whether it is wiser to leave Paris or remain there.' Indeed, the shopkeepers of the wealthier districts closed and re-opened their shops several times a day when the bands of federal workmen, which Carnot and Fouché had not dared to arm for fear of revolutionary enthusiasm, paraded the streets, banners flying, shouting for arms and singing the 'Marseillaise'.

In the suburbs groups collected at the factory gates. They discussed the chances of the army. They had faith in the valour of the soldiers and the genius of the Emperor, but they dreaded the weight of the forces on the Coalition side, the hate of the royalists, the 'treason' of the bad citizens who, in the private rooms at Tortoni's, drank champagne toasts to 'the death of the tyrant' and the defeat of his troops. At the Bourse, the shouting and the mad fluctuations of the state bonds caused fortunes to be won and lost overnight as in the times of the Directoire.

Fever rose among the patriots after reading the proclamation of June 14th, launched from Avesnes by the Emperor: 'Soldiers! It is the anniversary of Marengo and Friedland . . . With victory, honour and well-being will be restored . . . The moment has come for all good Frenchmen to be victorious or perish . . .'

Suddenly the entry into Brussels was announced for the following day! Next would come the conquest of Holland! The defeat of the Allies! Peace! Sceptics were manhandled, pessimists belaboured.

On the 18th a despatch sent by Soult announced a great victory over the Prussians at Ligny. It was delirium! 'There was,' wrote Thibaudeau, 'a moment of intoxication.' The representatives, courageous in words, but not reckless, renounced all opposition. 'Today,' wrote State Councillor Berlier, 'the Chamber has shown, almost unanimously, its will to do everything demanded by the needs of the state.'

A savage adversary of Napoleon, but in dread of his anger, the President, Lanjuinais, addressed fulsome compliments to him in the name of his colleagues and assured him that in the legislative body he had 'only enthusiastic admirers (!) and intrepid friends (!) whose devotion will not be shaken even by the most serious reverses' (!).

On June 19th, nothing.

'Two days without news!' Thibaudeau, Fouché's police minister, told the Chamber of Peers on the morning of June 20th. '. . . can it be that he has been defeated! I am afraid that Soult has been playing fast and loose with us.'

'I don't know why,' went on Thibaudeau, 'but I have the impression that Fouché knows something.'

He knew everything. About four o'clock in the morning a note scribbled by 'a royalist lady of his acquaintance' had reached him from Brussels: 'Bonaparte has been beaten about four leagues from Brussels; he is in flight. He is lost.' Without a word, Fouché had put the note in his pocket.

He had foreseen it. He had told Pasquier: 'The Emperor will win one or two battles; he will lose the third. Then our task will begin.'

His plan was ready. Thiers, who knew all the actors in the drama, and, after him, Madelin had studied it minutely. The aim to be achieved: to save his own neck. There was only one way: to seize power.

There were great obstacles. If the Allied armies, marching on Paris, were to impose Louis XVIII, then, despite the services he had rendered to Metternich and to the King by betraying the Emperor, Fouché, 'servant of the Usurper' and regicide, would, at the best, be exiled. If Napoleon, supported by Carnot, Minister of the Interior, Davout, the army, the Bonapartists, the people, approved by the Council of Ministers and perhaps even by the Chambers—cowards all in face of the mob and flabby when faced with the energy of their master—arose in a ferocious resistance, proclaimed 'the country in danger' and called the peasants to arms, then the war would begin again, the Assemblies would be dissolved and Fouché would be lost.

If the Chamber managed to overthrow the Emperor, the dictatorship of the Palais-Bourbon with La Fayette would be even more intransigent than that of the Elysée with Napoleon; the Bourbon cause would be compromised, if not lost, and Fouché doomed.

It must be so arranged that the Chamber could not be dissolved but also that, though eliminating Napoleon, it should not be allowed to play a leading role . . . that the Emperor should abdicate of his own free will in favour of his son, the King of Rome, as Fouché had advised him last April, and then, broadly speaking, there would be neither victors nor vanquished; the royalists would be for a time appeased by the accession of Napoleon II, and the Chambers, satisfied, would allow themselves to be guided. Fouché could get approval for the creation of a provisional government and would himself suggest the appointment of its members. He himself would take over the premier-

ship and would thus feel himself empowered to enter into negotiations with Wellington and Blücher . . . the Allies. The restoration of Louis XVIII could be assured by the good offices of
Fouché, who would thus have prepared his return to the throne
of his fathers.

And France? There was no thought of France in this bold and
Machiavellian programme, worthy of the master of intrigue,
perspicacious, subtle, cynical, implacable, saying this and that
since the beginning of the Hundred Days:

'This man (Napoleon) has come back even madder than when
he went away. He creates a great uproar but will not last three
months. That is as clear as daylight. It is a calculation of moral
arithmetic.'

'With good Chambers, good ministers, a good army, it will be
the very devil if one cannot break down a short-arsed king,
cretinous princes and a bunch of decaying and imbecile emigrés.'

'One must get rid of anyone who is in the way, and then we
shall see . . .'

'Assemblies are never dangerous, because their political
opinions, as well as their resolutions, depend on a dozen or so
chatterboxes whom one must have the gift of winning over or
dominating.'

He 'dominated' far more than a dozen in this 'Chamber of
Representatives', incapable of struggling against the present
dangers, who in no way represented France and who displayed
'a spectacle of anarchy, weakness and spinelessness'.

Thirty-three thousand voters out of 69,000 registered electors
(the royalists had abstained) had elected 629 deputies, of whom
about forty had been members of the National Convention, to
whose success Fouché had been no stranger: Cambon the
financier, Drouet who had arrested Louis XVI, Barère, Le
Pelletier, etc.; eighty Bonapartists and generals: Lucien Bonaparte, Regnault, Bory de Saint-Vincent, Sébastiani, Rapp, Beker,
Sorbier, Teste, etc.; 500 liberals.

These masters of the ballot-box, which they had organized
with Fouché's help, were bourgeois; many lawyers, doctors,
notaries, magistrates, bankers, merchants, industrialists, landowners, partisans of order, justice and 'the preservation of the
golden mean'. Rich, important, garrulous, scoffers, egotists, turn-
coats, they had rallied to the Bourbons in 1814. Loyal to Louis

XVIII when he bestowed the Charter on them, alienated from him when he had prorogued the Chambers, they had reverted to the Bourbons after the Emperor's return. Hostile to Napoleon through fear of the man of war, of revolution, of popular unrest and of danger, they were ready to do anything to save their wealth, their profits and their interests; they called themselves patriots without caring a fig about France. Partisans of liberty for themselves, they dreaded it for others, cheered the military parades, but avoided taking their places in the ranks and revolted against the National Guard because they were expected to serve in it. They had inspired the new Constitution set up by one of their own members, Benjamin Constant, and called euphemistically 'Additional Instrument', and had created 'Liberalism', that 'fad of the moment', a mere pretext to remain inactive and calculate the chances of 'slackening off' in order to 'avoid the consequences'. They manufactured 'The Liberal Empire', rallied to La Fayette and the tired old former Jacobins; even Béranger who, addressing Lise who represented Napoleon, wrote:

> Lise, *deviens bonne princesse,*
> Et *respecte nos libertés . . .*

They converted prefects and generals to their views — even Savary! — and paralyzed the 'right arm of the Emperor'.

This liberal mass considered itself patriotic and national, believed in its 'integrity', its 'knowledge', its 'experience', scorned the generals whom it feared, mistrusted Napoleon, dreaded 'an awakening of his despotism', discussed his 'abdication'. La Fayette already envisaged a 'parliamentary *coup d'état*'. A great landowner, vain, cold, ambitious, vindictive, he affected a superiority, a wisdom, a self-confidence, a certainty of being able to give lessons to everyone, even to Europe, after Napoleon had gone. Fouché influenced his thoughts and decisions by flattery, regarded him as a 'simpleton', an 'old imbecile whom one can use like a stepping-stone or a ladder which one throws down after one has used it'.

Fouché inspired and controlled the majority, made it move and act like a sullen opposition: Lanjuinais, 'the Jansenist of constitutional law', was appointed president of the Chamber in preference to Lucien Bonaparte, Boulay, Dupont de l'Eure, Merlin, etc.

The principal newcomers were summoned to his house on the Quai Voltaire in the early hours of June 20th : Manuel, a lawyer of the extreme left, a former officer wounded while on service with the army of Italy and then attached to the Court of Appeal at Aix, deputy for the Basses-Alpes; a young man who was to make his way, André Dupin, representative of Château-Chinon, a lawyer at seventeen, of great talent, the future defender of Ney, of Caulaincourt and of Savary, minister under Louis-Philippe, senator under Napoleon III, academician; Roy, deputy for Paris, adversary of the Emperor who had forced him to give up the estate of Navarre to the Empress Josephine; Jay, representative of Bordeaux, tutor to Fouché's three sons, a man of letters, refined, gentle, timid, a great traveller in America (Thiers had known him), etc. 'Poor political dupes,' wrote a contemporary.

There was desultory talk about 'the situation', of the dangers 'which might arise if, by some chance, the Emperor's armies should be beaten' . . . with the free and easy tone which came so easily to him, without ending his proposals or even finishing his sentences. 'We must,' said Fouché, 'back up the Emperor but, naturally, not let our share in the government be taken away by him. In a word, we must not allow ourselves to be dissolved . . . '

Of course, everyone agreed. Moreover, La Fayette, prophetically, replied : 'There is nothing else for the Chamber but to declare itself in permanent session and to demand the abdication of the Emperor'; in case of refusal, to decree his deposition.

To frighten the liberals who knew of his connections with Europe, he repeated that the Allies were waging war on Napoleon rather than on France. Once the Emperor was eliminated, everything could be arranged. Then he sent his compliments and encouragements to the royalists for their bold action and worked on his colleagues of 'the Peers', created by Napoleon to balance the resolutions of the elective assembly and made up for the most part of his faithful supporters like Clary, Champagny, Canclaux, etc., or of opportunists such as Roger Ducos, loyal to all régimes. 'You know,' he said to the Bonapartists, 'that there is great unrest among certain deputies against the Emperor and we have no other way to save him than to show our teeth and make them realize the full extent of the Emperor's power and how easy it would be for him to dissolve the Chambers.'

And when the intimates of the Emperor agreed with this suggestion, he reported to the liberals: 'You can see for yourselves
that his best friends are in agreement with this. In an hour or
two, if he is not forestalled, there will be no more Chambers. The
danger is imminent . . .'

More so as the army was rallying. Given time, it would consider its honour to be at stake, would keep the Emperor on his
throne by force and . . . would send Fouché to Grenelle.

That evening, seated at a gaming table, Carnot shuffled his
cards feverishly without settling down to play. The friends he
had invited to his house pressed him with questions, watched his
contorted face. Gérando, his partner, maintained a provocative
silence . . .

'Very well then, yes,' said Carnot, throwing his cards on the
table . . . 'The battle is lost!'

That afternoon Prince Joseph had read to the Council of
Ministers the letter sent by the Emperor from Philippeville to
announce the defeat. Caulaincourt, Combacérès and Decrès were
appalled, dejected; Carnot declared himself a partisan of a
struggle to the death, with all powers conferred on the Emperor,
behind whom all France must rally; Davout, a great soldier and
familiar with political crises, hoped that Napoleon would prorogue the Chambers. Poker-faced, finger to lips, Fouché kept
silent, sent notes to certain representatives, his friends, to inform
them and guide their actions. Then he began working with great
skill on his colleague, Regnault de Saint-Jean-d'Angély, Minister
of State. A dedicated Bonapartist, entrusted with keeping in
touch with the deputies, whose ill-will he became more aware of
every day, he lent an ear to Fouché's proposals. A devoted servant of the Emperor, Count Regnault would probably save, with
the King of Rome, the dynasty and the imperial régime if he
advised Napoleon to make 'a voluntary abdication'. After having
been his adversary, Regnault, without subtlety or finesse, did not
hide his feelings of admiration for Fouché.

In Paris the news spread quickly. At the home of Queen
Hortense in the Rue Cerutti, on the afternoon of the 20th, while
Benjamin Constant was reading 'his little novel *Adolphe*', Savary
said: 'There is news of an unfortunate battle.' In the evening
Mme Savary, the Duchess of Rovigo, remarked: 'Everything is
lost. We no longer have an army.' The day before, La Vallette

had announced the Emperor's probable entry into Brussels. Everyone remained silent.

In the cafés on the boulevards and in the Palais-Royal, anxiety brooded when, during the night, Sauvo, editor of the *Moniteur*, received by special messenger an account of the battle. In a few hours the excitement became intense. The Emperor was coming! His household had been warned and the Council of Ministers had been convoked. In the Chamber, Fouché's friends hawked the news and his advice. There was furious discussion, talk of dictatorship, of abdication. Wild ideas circulated.

There were countless visits, to Joseph, to Lanjuinais, to the ministers . . . furtive interviews, sketched-out intrigues . . . lightning proposals . . . general panic . . .

Unruffled, Fouché summoned no one. However, he received everyone. They came to ask for his advice, but he did not give it. By insinuation 'off the record' he made suggestions about the play, allotted the parts, but he himself remained in the wings.

'During the night of June 20-21st,' wrote Joseph, 'a great number of members of the Chamber of Deputies met in the house of M. de La Fayette, where there was no question of concerting means to save the Emperor and the nation but rather of dropping the Emperor to save the nation. It recalled the days of the Revolution. M. de La Fayette was represented as a saviour whom France could recognize, whom Paris knew, whom the Allies would receive as the mouthpiece of the Chamber which became, in their eyes, the real representative of the nation. The Allies would halt at his voice; Napoleon II would be recognized, with the Constitution which would be imposed on him. A regency would guarantee to Europe the peaceful intentions of France. The nation would be assured of peace, the friends of liberty would have a more liberal government, more in keeping with the English or American government.

'Heads were overheated . . .

'M. de La Fayette allowed himself to be persuaded that he could do anything he liked and that he could be certain of a majority in the Chamber.'

Dawn broke on June 21st.

* * *

The old road from Laon to Soissons passed through Mons-en-

Laonnois, Montbavin, Merlieux, Chavignon; the posting station was at Vaurain, at the crossroads to Craonne. Thence a branch led to Paris by way of Vertefeuille, Villers-Cotteret, Levigneu, Nanteuil, Dammartin, Le Mesnil-Amelot and Le Bourget. There were rather more than sixteen posts, that is thirty-three French leagues to the *barrière*.

Having arrived at the La Villette post at daybreak, the Emperor, not wanting to cross the entire city, turned right to follow the outer fortifications to the Barrière du Roule; then his carriage went down the Rue du Faubourg (Saint-Honoré), where the shops were for the most part still closed, and entered the Elysée about six o'clock in the morning.

A solitary figure was walking in the courtyard; Caulaincourt, the Duke of Vicenza. He ran quickly to the steps, welcomed the breathless Emperor, hat in hand, and heard the rapid jerked-out phrases: 'The army did wonders . . . there was panic; all was lost. Ney behaved like a madman; he got all my cavalry massacred. I am dead-beat . . . I need a couple of hours rest before getting down to my affairs.' Putting his hand to his chest, he said: 'I am choking.' Then, preceded by his minister, silent, sad and exhausted, he disappeared into his apartments, followed by Drouot and the Marshal of the Household.

He had occupied them since May 17th. Without the Empress and the King of Rome, the brilliant court, the daily receptions, the salons of the Tuileries, too huge and solemn 'in melancholy grandeur', recalled those at Fontainebleau the year before . . . and residence there had become unbearable to him. Crossing the antechamber, two salons, the state apartments, he reached his study, slumped into his green leather armchair, demanded a hot bath and some soup, summoned La Vallette and Savary, convoked the Council of Ministers, all the while jerking out a monologue to the horror-stricken generals: 'What bad luck! I no longer have an army! . . . I have only fugitives! . . . There must be a dictatorship . . . ' But he would not seize it; he hoped that the Chambers would have the patriotism to confer it on him . . . He was the only man who could save the country! . . .

He grew angry and over-excited and fell back in dejection.

'As soon as he noticed me,' wrote La Vallette in his *Memoirs*, 'he came up to me with a terrible epileptic laugh. "Ah, mon Dieu!" he cried out, raising his eyes to heaven . . .

walked once or twice around the room and then recovered his composure.'

The bath was made ready in the small suite that he usually occupied. Undressed by Marchand, he plunged into the water. 'Three times,' he said to Caulaincourt, 'I have seen the sure triumph of France slip through my fingers. Had it not been for the defection of a traitor I would have destroyed the enemy at the outset of the campaign! However, all is not lost . . .It is my intention to unite the two Chambers in imperial session. I will paint for them the misfortunes of the army and will ask them for the means to save the country . . . Then I will leave . . . '

'The news of your ill fortune has leaked out,' broke in Caulaincourt in despair. 'There is great anxiety. The attitude of the deputies seems more hostile than ever. I am sorry to see you here in Paris . . . It would have been better if you had not left the army.'

'The army! The army! It is horrible . . . ! My troops crushed after such heroic efforts . . . My wonderful Guard destroyed, betrayed, and I, I could not die with them!'

'I could find neither tears nor words; it was too much!' wrote Caulaincourt.

'I had thought out a bold manoeuvre,' the Emperor went on, 'which should have prevented the two enemy armies from meeting. I launched all my cavalry united in a single corps of twenty thousand men at the centre of the Prussian cantonments. This bold attack, carried out at lightning speed, could have sealed the fate of the whole campaign. Instead of attacking on the spur of the moment, I should have begun a pitched battle . . . '

Was he sincere?

'The desertion of that wretch Bourmont forced me to change all my plans . . . to go over to the enemy on the eve of a battle! The scoundrel! May his brothers' blood weigh on him! Everyone was despondent. Treason paralyzed every effort. Ney lost his head, carried away by foolhardiness. He acted like a soldier, looking neither before him nor behind him. The troops under him were cut to pieces, there was no need . . . It was atrocious! What I suffered, Caulaincourt, was worse than the tortures of Fontainebleau. I am a dead man; the blow that I received at Mont-Saint-Jean was mortal!'

He stopped, exhausted.

Then, once more the invincible optimist: 'I hope that the deputies will back me up. Caulaincourt, you have misjudged the mood of the deputies. Most of them are good Frenchmen. My presence among them will restrain my adversaries.'

With 25,000 men of the Army of the Rhine, 40,000 from Grouchy, the remnants left after Waterloo, the new levies that the patriotism of the Chambers would rouse, he could once more create a situation worthy of the nation! Raising his arms in the air, he let them fall back into the water, soaking Davout who had just come in.

'Well, Davout, what do you say?' he cried out. 'What will happen next?'

'Nothing is lost if Your Majesty takes strong measures at once. The most urgent is to prorogue the Chambers, for the Chamber of Representatives, with its passionate hostility, paralyzes all loyalty.'

Then to his treasurer: 'Peyrousse, I have lost all that you have given me. Have you anything more? What is there new?'

'Everything can be put right, Sire.'

'Certainly . . . panic . . . A general cheer along the whole line.'

Marchand announced Cambacérès, gloomy and despondent; then Fouché. In the morning Fouché had received La Fayette who had given him the details of the conspiracy concocted during the night and he now presented himself distressed, compassionate, smooth-tongued, 'as if he came to a sick-bed'.

'All is quiet,' he said. 'The Emperor has only to speak to be obeyed . . . '

It was too much.

'Citizen Fouché,' Napoleon interrupted in a terrible voice, 'why not show your joy? You have always desired my downfall and now you have got what you wanted. You think you have triumphed. You are wrong!'

Then, before leaving the room to meet the Princes Lucien and Joseph: 'I bequeath my vengeance to the King!'

'What do you think of what you have just heard?' said Fouché icily to the indifferent Cambacérès. 'Is this man in his right mind? It is inconceivable, the way he has treated me.'

'Perhaps he is right to bear you a grudge,' replied Cambacérès. 'Have you always been loyal to him?'

Furious and losing control of himself, Fouché retorted: 'You talk as he does. To whom is one loyal? Have you ever been loyal, even to your mistress? As for your King, who was also mine, he has had good proof of our common loyalty!'

And while the regicides hurled abuse and charges of treason at one another, in the next salon Napoleon, Lucien and Joseph embraced affectionately.

'My brother! My brother! What can we do for you?' said the first without glossing over the hostile attitude of the Chamber.

'Go back to your army and leave us to fight with them,' advised the second.

The Emperor insisted that he was doing the right thing. He believed that he could save the country by mobilizing its resources, but he must have the co-operation of the representatives. 'It is not I who must be saved, it is France,' he said. 'I cannot do it without the deputies . . . '

He was almost forty-six, his face pale, 'his complexion greenish', his hair ashy brown, sparse over the temples, thin on top, his expression often lack-lustre, his mouth drawn. He knitted his brows, frowned, to see more clearly. His chest and his stomach pained him. His cystitis, which had tortured him during the campaign, still made him suffer; none the less, he was sometimes overcome by a certain drowsiness, which he struggled against by drinking coffee. When he coughed he sucked pastilles. However, he seemed vigorous, continued to rise early to dictate while pacing about, humming songs, looking at his watch. He still went out of his way to be pleasant and he smiled readily. But he felt that 'his fairweather friends were wavering' and distrusted men more and more, their cowardice and treason. He was more circumspect, though still irascible; Benjamin Constant had noted in him a certain carelessness about his own future, a detachment from his own interests . . .

Napoleon had changed.

*   *   *

France had changed too. 'She is no longer as she was when I left her,' he said.

In fact, glory no longer interested the French. Eager for peace, they dreamed of freedom, of discussions, of literature, of art. The Emperor's former colleagues, grown old, were now routine-keepers and lazy, and had adapted themselves to the placid régime of the Bourbons. As always in time of crisis, the senior officials were timid, inert, careful not to become compromised. A pleiad of young men was needed, thinking as he did, eager for new institutions, able to adapt themselves to new habits and aspirations. Emperor of the army ('Up to captain,' as he said, 'the others only fear me.'), of the people, of the peasants and workers, detested by the royalists and abandoned by the middle classes, could he provoke revolution to let the new team rise to the surface, ready to take the place of the old gang?

The Council of Ministers met; the Princes Lucien and Joseph were there, the Duke of Bassano, State Secretary, the eight ministers with portfolio, the four Ministers of State, members of the Chamber of Representatives: Defermon, Regnault, Boulay, Merlin, and the Secretary of the Council, Berlier.

The Emperor said that the debates could begin without him. Did he feel that his collaborators would not support him? Had he already 'foreseen everything, accepted everything' as Thiers wrote? He was awaited with deference, but with impatience and anxiety. Finally, after fresh urging by Davout, he came.

THE CHAMBERS

In respectful silence Maret read the last *Bulletin de la Grande Armée*[1] and His Majesty opened the session.

'The misfortunes are great,' he said. 'I have come to rectify them, to urge on the nation a great and noble resurgence. If the people rise, the enemy will be crushed; if, instead of levies and measures of urgency, there are discussions, then all is lost . . . The enemy will enter France. To save the country I must be invested with great power. I could seize it for myself, but it would be better were it given me by the Chambers.

'These powers are those of the Committee of Public Safety. The dangers are those of a time of invasion . . . The country will not be saved by half-measures.'

Was this once more the Emperor of the battles? The free, spontaneous Emperor, taking counsel only of his own inspiration? On his return from Elba it was thought that he would seize the dictatorship; some had hoped, others had dreaded, but would it again be Napoleon, the 'armed representative' of the

[1] See Appendix.

people, proclaiming the principle of his authority, hurling himself to the frontiers to call a halt to Europe? To each his destiny. That of the eagle is to have wings and talons.

But he was no longer recognizable. He had listened to the blabber-mouths, constitution-makers, lawyers, jurists, politicians, adventurers, rabble-rousers. Had it been misfortune, exile and age that had changed him? He had begun to talk like them. 'The throne is only the support of the state', 'Rulers exist only for their peoples' . . . The ill-timed humbleness of a head of government who has grown weak, at the head of a country that has lost its courage.

Attentive to the parties, tolerating their supervision, the Emperor of Austerlitz seemed to consider the episodes of the epic as those of an age that had passed. Instead of *Malbrouk's s'en va-t-en guerre* one heard him humming, as in the times of the Consulate: 'There is a time for folly; there is a time too for reason . . .'

As a result of concessions made to political theorists, of renunciations conceded to liberal scoffers, Napoleon had seen his authority weakened and his prestige diminished; the bold and fiery man of March 20th had lost his energy, his boldness, his assurance. He liked to talk, sometimes for hours, with La Vallette and others, to allow discussion, to let himself be contradicted. He consulted those around him, still loyal to him but uneasy for him and for themselves; his ministers were plunged in inert expectancy when they were not hostile.

He was no longer the master gifted with complete self-confidence. He wavered, he hesitated. Instead of acting, of bounding into the Chamber in full uniform like an eruption, of saving the country and the throne by muzzling these unleashed brawlers, he asked his gloomy and dejected ministers what they thought of the situation and, when they did not reply, interrogated them. Carnot was the first. He said that the Emperor personified the Revolution, that he must proclaim 'the country is in danger', act as a great captain and put his plan of defence into operation, summon the armies of the Midi and the Vendée, mobilize the national guards and the federal workers and amalgamate them with Grouchy's troops. In the event of a check before Paris, he must continue the struggle on the Loire . . .

A straightforward and honest man without malice, Carnot

suggested demanding dictatorship for the Emperor from the Chamber. Only by his accord with the Chambers could the country be saved, interposed Cambacérès, broken and grown old, chicken-hearted, lugubrious, a bird of ill-omen, Maret, loyal but without illusions, and Caulaincourt, in despair.

'There must be a single head,' thundered Davout, who had known the Convention, the Five Hundred, and who distrusted assemblies. 'The Emperor must call France to arms after having, as is his right, prorogued the Chambers.'

'If the Chambers do not support the Emperor,' shouted Lucien at an unmoved Fouché and a hesitant Regnault, 'then the Emperor will go his own way . . . The safety of the country comes first.'

'The people have elected them to support me,' stressed Napoleon.

Fear gripped these men, embarrassed, apprehensive, weighed down by their responsibilities, trying to evade them and trying to find what was later to be called, after the event, 'a compromise'.

Two hundred yards away the mob, eager for news, beat against the Palace gates. Within, the courtyard, the salons, the galleries, were crammed with people of importance, some official, some not, deputies and military men. The appearance of the aides-de-camp, who had not changed their clothes since the battle, made a great impression. Their faces, covered with dust, lit up. They said nothing about the casualties. The army no longer existed. The enemy was coming. Surrender was inevitable. Here too, there was talk of the abdication of the Emperor.

At the Palais-Bourbon the fever of excitement grew. The leaders commented on the news, true or false, brought from the Elysée by messengers, and asserted their prestige, which was rarely due to their intelligence or the services they had rendered. In the corridors there was endless discussion in an atmosphere of agitation, confusion and passion. Paris was threatened. The Emperor could not stop the invasion, nor treat with the Allies. The ministers were still in session.

*   *   *

Fouché was fighting for his life.

'Deeply afflicted by His Majesty's misfortunes', he pointed out to the Council that it should let the Chambers know that it did not wish to by-pass it, but to remain in close touch with it . . . to ask it for the resources needed to resist the Allies . . . 'Furthermore,' he added, 'public opinion is calm and . . .'

'Ah! Ah! According to him everything is calm,' interrupted the Emperor sarcastically.

Fouché felt things were going badly. Rapidly he sent a few notes from the Elysée to his friends in the Chamber announcing that Napoleon, supported by Carnot, Davout and Lucien Bonaparte, was preparing for a dictatorship, that danger threatened the representatives. Regnault de Saint-Jean-d'Angély, outwitted by him, emphatically protested his loyalty to the Emperor. 'The Chamber believes that the Allies are waging war more against him than against France,' he affirmed. 'If His Majesty would withdraw voluntarily, he would save the King of Rome; under the regency of the Empress, the imperial dynasty . . .'

'Explain yourself! Speak! Don't hide anything!' shouted the Emperor, awakened from his torpor. 'It is not a question of my person, which I am willing to sacrifice and of which, only three days ago, I made every effort to rid you . . . but it is a question of France and her salvation . . . Who can save her? Does she know the individuals who compose the Chamber? She knows only me . . . If I throw all the speechifiers out of the window, as at Saint-Cloud, the army will applaud and France will say nothing . . .'

But to pose the question was no way to solve it.

Continuing his monologue, Napoleon threatened, treating the question of the King of Rome as a silly fairy-tale. 'I know what is going on in Vienna,' he shouted, fixing his eyes on Regnault. 'They will never accept my wife.' Then he spoke of the Bourbons 'who were perhaps better than any other alternative'. Anyway, he 'no longer had any interest in all that and his role was over . . .'

However, once more, he clung to his dream, enumerated his forces, developed his plan, appealed to the patriotism of the members. 'I am linked to France,' he said. 'I represent her before Europe . . . To sacrifice me is to offer her hands to the fetters . . .' He became intoxicated by words which, despite a brutal and pessimistic intervention by Decrès, shook the flabbiness of the Council, which decided:

English map showing the situation of the French and English troops at Waterloo
on the afternoon of June 18, 1815

'The parliament is transferred to Tours. Davout is appointed to the command of Paris, Clausel to be Minister of War. The Federals will be incorporated in the National Guard; Maret is to prepare the decrees. The speech which His Majesty will make to the Chamber will be transcribed . . . Should he appear in parade dress or in his uniform soiled by the dust of battle? . . . '

It was such things that they debated.

Meanwhile, in the Chamber, there was action. Fouché's friends brought news and commented on it: Jay, Manuel, d'Argenson, member for Belfort, former aide-de-camp to La Fayette and Prefect of the Empire, Flaugergues, emigré, sub-prefect dismissed by the Emperor and his most savage opponent . . . It was a question only of Fouché's hints, of those reticences of his which spoke volumes . . . of the 'bloody dictatorship', of the 'threadbare ghost' madder than before. The leaders influenced the gullible crew of deputies by their prestige, their energetic statements, their precise plans, their vague generalities. Hatred, rage and above all fear breathed over these bewildered men. Everything was exaggerated, magnified, distorted, multiplied.

* * *

Midday. Fearing lest the Emperor dissolve the Chamber, M. de La Fayette, vice-president, made a demand to the president that the day's session be opened earlier than was usual. The Duke of Choiseul wittily called this ambitious and very rich aristocrat, envious and discontented, haughty and arrogant, whom Bonaparte had freed from an Austrian prison, Gilles the Great or Caesar-Gilles. Moreover, he had thanked him and later had congratulated him on the Brumaire *coup d'état*. After which, loaded with honours by the grateful Americans, impatient to play a leading role in the state, jealous of the Emperor, he had rejected as unworthy a place as senator and the ribbon of the Grand Aigle and had withdrawn to his estates where he had lived embittered and forgotten. M. le Marquis de La Fayette, royalist, had held in his hands the fate of the old monarchy, had signed the warrant for the arrest of Louis XVI, and had then deserted and demanded the overthrow of Napoleon during the ceremonies on the Champ de Mai.

Let us look at the *Moniteur* for June 22, 1815:

65

CHAMBER OF REPRESENTATIVES

Under the Chairmanship of M. le Comte Lanjuinais

'The session opened at 12.15.

'The minutes of the previous session were read and adopted.

'The President announced that M. de la Fayette and M. Lacoste had proposals to put before the Chamber.

'M. *de La Fayette*: Gentlemen, when for the first time for many years I raise a voice that the old friends of liberty will still recognize, I feel myself called upon to speak to you of the danger to our country which you alone, at this moment, have the power to avert.

'Sinister rumours have been bruited abroad; they have unfortunately proved to be true. This is the time for all of us to rally around our ancient standard, the tricolour, the flag and symbol of '89, of Liberty, Equality and Public Order; it is that alone which we shall have to defend against pretensions from without and upheavals from within. Gentlemen, allow a veteran of this sacred cause to submit to you certain preliminary proposals, whose necessity you will, I hope, appreciate:

'Article 1. The Chamber of Representatives declares that the independence of the country is threatened.

'Article 2. The Chamber declares itself in permanent session. Any attempt to dissolve it is high treason; whoever may be guilty of such an attempt is a traitor to the country and may summarily be judged as such.

'Article 3. The army of the line and the National Guard who have fought and who are still fighting to defend the liberty, the independence and the territory of France have deserved well of the country.

'Article 4. The Minister of the Interior is requested to summon the General Staff and the commanders and senior officers of the National Guard in order to consult above giving them arms and encouraging to the full this citizen guard whose patriotism and zeal, proved over the past twenty-six years, provides a sure guarantee of the liberty, the property, the peace of the capital and the inviolability of the representatives of the nation.

'Article 5. The Ministers of War, of External Affairs, of the Police and of the Interior are requested to present themselves to the Assembly immediately.'

'Tumultuous applause.'

The Emperor's name was not mentioned. The French were not asked to rally to him but around the flag of '89.

'The Emperor and the nation have been sacrificed to vain imaginings,' wrote Joseph. 'The foreigners want to separate them and it is the deputies, in the main men of good will, who are serving the allied kings better than their millions of soldiers. La Fayette thinks himself at the tennis-court; he declares, like Mirabeau, that he is there 'by the will of the people'. All the schemes that he proposes are welcomed by a majority which has no other opinion than that of the deputies who were scheming that night at his house. The National Guard has been called to the aid of the national representatives . . . that no one may threaten them! The Emperor has been accused!'

Were the Bonapartist members in agreement?

Not one of the representatives pointed out the irregularity of these measures.

Jay shouted: 'Public liberty will never be established in France under a military régime!'

The proposals were adopted unanimously and transmitted, in the form of a message, to the 'elective authorities', that is to say the House of Peers and the Emperor.

'It is a *coup d'état* against the national sovereignty,' wrote Frédéric Masson, 'a revolt against lawful authority, an outrage on the country, the most foolish and dastardly aggression against the only man who can still save the nation, the work of a man who, in the annals of his wretched life, has registered three memorable dates: October 5, 1789, when he betrayed his king, August 20, 1792, when he deserted to the enemy, and June 21, 1815, when he overthrew the Emperor.'

Physically and morally harassed, Napoleon had wasted three hours in futile discussion and had let himself be outpaced by Fouché. Faced with the news, brought at one o'clock by Regnault, he flushed, protested, strode up and down, made threats of expelling 'those wretches who will ruin France'. Looking to the Council for an energy that it no longer possessed, he found only contrite expressions masking relief. Even Davout considered that the time for action was long past.

'To make another 18th Brumaire? I refuse to be the instrument,' he said.

Lucien alone burst out: 'Let there be no hesitation. By wasting time, we let the Assembly grow bolder. Better make use of the constitutional powers of the crown to dissolve it . . . '

Napoleon hesitated. He sent Regnault to the Representatives and Carnot to the Peers; they were to read a statement describing the battle, the panic, then the rallying of the army, the return of the Emperor to take counsel with his ministers, with the Chambers, in order to take measures of public safety. A middle course, peurile, which left the deputies indifferent, even hostile. Moreover, the 'Peers' accepted La Fayette's proposals.

The Peers! Marshals, generals, men of the Consulate, Lacépède, Roederer, State Councillors, ghosts, Sièyes, Roger Ducos, old faithfuls like La Vallette and Savary, even Drouot, had not thought it their duty to protest when the Upper Chamber too declared itself in permanent session.

His pride outraged, Napoleon reacted: 'If they push me too far, I will throw them in the Seine . . . ' Simple, violent words which masked his weakness and were mere trifles. A trifle too the prohibition to the ministers to obey the summons of the deputies since it was rescinded soon afterwards in the form of a concession, an enormous concession which allowed ministers chosen by the Emperor to be called to the bar of the Assembly, now surrounded by a guard, whose audacity, force and intransigence increased from minute to minute.

'They are madmen,' he said to Joseph, 'and La Fayette and his friends are political simpletons; they desire my abdication and tremble in case I do not give it to them. Well, I will give it to them and make them responsible for all the ills which will fall upon France. They want me to abdicate in favour of my son; it is a mockery when our enemies are at the gates of Paris with the Bourbons behind them. United, we could save everything; divided, we are without resources.'

At the Elysée there were a few more paroxysms, but if the right had passed to those who violated the law it seemed that the resolution of the representatives, illegal as it was, had become an accomplished fact. Had the Empire received its death-blow?

'I see that Regnault was right when he tried to get me to abdicate,' said the Emperor. Then, after a silence: 'Very well, so be it. If it must be; I shall abdicate. It is not a question of me, but of France . . . I do not resist for myself, but for her . . . If she no longer needs me, then I shall abdicate . . . '

The meeting of the Council was adjourned. It breathed freely. Three ministers were grieved, five or six relieved.

'That devil of a man made me afraid; I almost believed he would begin everything again!' Fouché was to say.

The people cheered the Emperor noisily.

Half-past five. The people crammed the Avenue Marigny. A threatening crowd beat against the walls of the Elysée and shouted loudly for the Emperor. Here he was: having summoned Benjamin Constant, he was walking in the gardens with Lucien. After that scorching, exhausting day he breathed for a moment under the limes and the chestnuts, calmed his nerves among the shrubberies and green arbours, on the banks of the lake and by the stream, in the grotto. He admitted, without stressing it, that he had cheapened himself by this persistent inertia, so foreign to his character.

Street urchins, climbing up the trees in the Avenue, saw him and shouted: 'Long live the Emperor!' and the crowd backed them up with loud cheers. Unemployed, former soldiers, the labourers of the Halles known as the 'Grey Musketeers', the colliers, known as the 'Black Musketeers', and the workers from the suburbs were there. One thought alone moved them: treason hovered over Paris, the treason of the deputies, of the royalists. They wanted to hand France over to the foreigners who would bring back the Bourbons. Let Napoleon put himself at their head and, with the army, they would drive back their enemies and would stop the royalists. The boldest amongst them, perched on the wall, demanded guns and yelled: 'Long live Napoleon! Long live liberty!' The Emperor waved to them.

They were called the 'Federals'.

When he had come back in March, the workers, by contrast to the trembling bourgeoisie unfavourable to the Emperor and fearful of war, were wholeheartedly for him and were ready to fight. Their condition was distressing; work was uncertain and he had come to their aid; works carried out at the Tuileries and the Louvre, at the Montmartre redoubts, at the Champ de Mars, the manufacture of uniforms, arms and equipment. The suburban muse had lampooned Napoleon:

'Emperor of the Faubourg Saint-Marceau;
King of the Faubourg Saint-Antoine;
Protector of the Courtille;
Mediator of Les Porcherons;
Husband without a wife;
Father without children;
King without money;
Crown without diamonds.'

In May, at the threat of the foreigners, enthusiasm mounted; the workers of the Faubourgs Saint-Antoine and Saint-Marceau 'federalized' and demanded arms to defend Paris, 'to strike the traitors with terror'; a pact was drawn up and everyone swore 'boundless obedience to the Emperor' ,with rallying cries of 'Long live the Nation!', 'Long live Liberty!', 'Long live the Emperor!' There were three thousand signatures. On May 14th there was a great patriotic workers' demonstration; there were 12,000 Federals of Saint-Antoine and Saint-Marceau in working clothes, joined by ex-soldiers and officers of the National Guard. Led by bands, they paraded along the boulevards and the Rue de Rivoli and entered the courtyard of the Tuileries where waiting for them—was the Emperor.

The spokesman read an address to 'the man of the nation who will know how to satisfy the rights of the people who demand arms'.

'You will be the advance-guards of the National Guard,' replied Napoleon. The next day he signed a decree. 'Twenty-four battalions of Federals of the good city of Paris' were formed. The uniform would be a blue coat with a yellow collar.

'This stinks of the Republic,' wrote Thibaudeau.

Napoleon had neither time nor opportunity to make use of the Federals. He had not enough guns to arm them all, but he placed them under the strict control of General Darricau, veteran of Toulon, of Italy, of Egypt, etc.

*　　　　*　　　　*

In the Elysée gardens, the conversation between the Emperor and Lucien became more animated. Did he hear the shouts of the people asking for arms? They wanted him to lead the forces of the people. His prestige was immense with these workers with blackened hands, these artisans struggling for their daily bread.

It was so throughout the Empire. Was he going to abandon France to the factions?

'Am I more than a man?' retorted Napoleon, in answer to the shouts of the crowd. 'Am I more than a man to bring about that union of 500 misguided deputies which alone might save France? Am I a wretched party leader to light the torch of civil war? No, never!'

If Lucien, thanks to his gift of oratory and his knowledge of the Assemblies, could, despite the memories of Saint-Cloud, restore the confidence of the representatives, then he would ask nothing better. 'I can do anything with the support of the Assemblies,' the Emperor went on. 'I could do much in my own interest, even without them, but perhaps I would not be able to save the country.' Then, taking leave of his brother Lucien, who accompanied by the ministers who had been summoned by the Chambers was making his way to the Palais-Bourbon, he said:

'Read them this message, but above all do not harangue the mob. I forbid you. I am ready to try anything for France, but I do not want to try anything for myself alone . . .'

'Message to the Chamber of Representatives
'Elysée Palace, 21st June 1815

'Monsieur le Président,

'After the battles of Ligny and Mont-Saint-Jean and after having prepared for the victualling of the army at Avesnes and Philippeville and for the defence of the frontier fortresses and of the cities of Laon and Soissons, I went to Paris to consult with my ministers on measures of national defence and to come to an agreement with the Chambers on all matters touching the salvation of the country.

'I have formed a committee, made up of the Minister of Foreign Affairs, of Count Carnot and the Duke of Otranto, to renew and follow up the negotiations with the Allied foreign powers in order to ascertain their real intentions and put an end to the war, should that be compatible with the independence and honour of the nation. But the closest union is necessary and I count on the co-operation and patriotism of the Chambers and on their devotion to my person.

'I have sent to the Chambers as my commissioners Prince Lucien and the Ministers of Foreign Affairs, of War, of the

Interior and of the Police to bear this message and to provide any news or information that the Chambers may require.

'NAPOLEON'

'I considered for a long time,' he was to say later to his companions in captivity on April 3, 1816, 'weighed the pros and cons and, since I foresaw immediately . . . I concluded that I could not resist the coalition from without, the royalists from within and the crowd of seditious factions that any violation of the legislative body would have created and finally that moral condemnation which imputes to one, when one has met with misfortunes, all the ills that crowd upon one . . . Abdication meant the loss of everything despite all my efforts. I saw it, I said it, but I had no other choice. History will judge.'

Cries of 'Arms!', 'Death to the traitors!' broke out when Benjamin Constant, anxious and uneasy, appeared. The previous day, at Queen Hortense's, General Sébastiani had come to announce the disaster. That morning he had received men from every party, intriguers of every colour, who had expected to find the 'imperial councillor . . . royalist' in a state of open revolt against Napoleon. But the author of the Constitution had not encouraged the imprudent in any way, judging wisely that in these difficult times the abdication of the Emperor might be dangerous.

As the hours passed, faced with the parliamentary folly, the popular demonstrations and the panic fear of the rich who were beginning to flee Paris, he did not know what to think. Summoned by the Emperor, just as he had been three months earlier when he had given the *Débats* a violent and abusive article against him, he expected to find him raging and ready to hold his own with the deputies by unleashing 'wild demagogy'. Napoleon could become 'the French Marius'; France 'would become the tomb of the nobles and perhaps that of the foreigners . . . '

Then, breaking the silence: 'You see them,' said the Emperor, his eyes fixed on the crowd. 'It is not they whom I have laden with honours and gorged with money. What do they owe me? None the less, the instinct of necessity enlightens them . . . If I wanted, in an hour the rebel Chamber would no longer exist . . .

But the life of one man is not worth such a price. I did not come back from Elba to make Paris a bloodbath!'

'In a crowd an individual is no longer conscious of his acts,' wrote Gustave Le Bon, who added: 'Decisions of general interest taken by a group of men who are distinguished but are of varying backgrounds are not noticeably superior to the decisions which would be taken by an assembly of imbeciles.'

The Assembly of the Representatives was unleashed; it was awaiting the ministers who had been summoned but who did not come. The Elysée scoffed at the elect of the people. Two battalions of Federals were rumoured to be marching on the Chamber. Cries, shouts, threats, filled corridors and bays; amongst others could be heard: 'Deposition! Arrest! Down with . . . '

A deafening tumult. Then, suddenly, complete silence. Lucien Bonaparte, commissioner of the government, was announced. A date, a memory was recalled: the 19th Brumaire, the drums of the grenadiers, the voice of Murat, their predecessors leaping from the windows of Saint-Cloud.

It was evening. The hall grew dark; two torches framed the rostrum with dim light. A funereal scene. The Chamber decided to meet in secret session. Smiling to reassure himself, less self-confident than usual, Lucien, in a voice which in the semi-darkness was scarcely audible to his almost invisible listeners, read the Emperor's message.

Coldly received, he concluded by proposing the appointment, by each of the two Chambers, of five commissioners charged with coming to an agreement with the ministers on the measures of public safety to be taken and on ways of making peace.

The members breathed again. There was to be no show of force, no dictatorship to be feared. Was the Emperor resigned? This was the moment to strike him down. Courageously, Jay, deputy for the Gironde, took up the task. Fouché's accomplice, he asked the ministers to say if they thought France could resist 'the combined armies of Europe and if the presence of Napoleon were not an insuperable obstacle to peace'.

Returning the ball, Fouché declared that he had nothing to add to his report on the state of France: 'Troubles in the provinces, growing opposition, etc.' Upon which Jay continued his task:

'You, Prince, who have shown such nobility of character both in victory and defeat,' he said to Lucien, 'remember that you are a Frenchman and that everything must take second place to love of country. Go back to your brother. Tell him that the Assembly awaits from him a resolution that will bring him more honour in the future than all his victories. Tell him that by abdicating power he can save France.'

Then, ending with a threat: 'Tell him that his destiny presses upon him; in a day, perhaps an hour, it will be too late.' He asked that 'a commission be appointed to place before Napoleon the urgency of his abdication and to tell him that, in case of refusal, the Assembly would decree his deposition'.

'Supported! Supported!' cried the hotheads of the majority, who applauded the orator and his conclusions.

After recovering his poise, his stress, his resounding phrases, his colourful images, with no other arguments than affirmations, sometimes bold and sometimes even borrowed from his antagonist, Lucien returned to his audience:

'I beseech you, citizens, in the sacred name of the country, to rally round the leader that the nation has replaced so solemnly at its head. Know that our salvation depends upon our union and that you cannot cast off the Emperor and abandon him to his enemies without losing the state, without betraying your oaths, without for ever staining the national honour . . . '

It was upon this abstraction that La Fayette, robed in his prestige, sprang to the rostrum and evoked 'the sands of Africa, the banks of the Guadalquivir, the deserts of Muscovy, where sleep the bones of our children and our brothers, the three million Frenchmen who have perished for a man who, even today, wants to fight the whole of Europe . . . We have done enough for him! Now it is our duty to save the country!'

In the utmost excitement, the blind and enthusiastic crowd of opponents, driven on by hatred, the devoted friends of Fouché and the irreconcilable and 'unconditional' sectaries declared to the minister that if Napoleon did not abdicate he would be deposed on the morrow at first light.

It was five o'clock in the evening. At the Palais-Bourbon, Lanjuinais declared the session closed.

THE ABDICATION

At the Elysée the Emperor dined alone with Queen Hortense,

Duchess of Saint-Leu by the grace of Louis XVIII since May 30, 1814. After his return to France, forgetting that they had not thought it necessary to advise him on Elba of the death of their mother, the Empress Josephine, he had forgiven his adopted daughter and her brother Eugene their ingratitude and lack of feeling, even as he had overlooked so many disloyalties.

In his solitude he 'liked to see people' and took an interest in the children. Hortense held her salon at the Elysée. Fouché had noticed her sadness in the midst of all the enthusiasm at the Champ de Mai.

'And after all that, war . . . The very idea is horrible,' she had said.

'What would you? The Emperor has missed a good chance . . . I advised him to abdicate today; had he done so, his son would have reigned and there would be no more war.'

On Sunday, June 12th, at a family dinner, she had found the Emperor less cheerful than he had tried to appear, 'talking literature, chattering more than usual'. That evening she had brought the children to say goodnight to him. 'If only we do not regret Elba,' he said on saying goodbye.

When she had learnt of the defeat, she had come on the morning of the 21st to the Elysée, but the Emperor was shut up with his brothers and she had not seen him. General Bertrand had told her the details and she had concluded: 'Our cause is lost. He deludes himself if he thinks he will ever again find the enthusiasm that brought him back to Paris; the French are so wayward! If he had been lucky, he would have found everyone for him; unlucky, he will find no one . . .'

That evening, seeing her eyes filled with tears: 'What were you told?' he asked her.

'That you have been unlucky, Sire.'

Seated at his desk, weighed down by tiredness and his thoughts, he abstractedly opened a batch of letters and looked at them without reading them. Then they came to say that dinner was served.

At table he was preoccupied and spoke little; one moment he questioned himself, the next he wanted to end everything and abdicate. Uneasy at his indecision, so foreign to his character, she felt him to be threatened and wished he would go to America immediately ... that he should take guarantees, should refer to the Austrian Emperor, to the Tsar ...

'I will never write to my father-in-law,' the Emperor replied curtly. 'I already owe him enough for having deprived me of my wife and my son! It is too cruel! Alexander is only a man ... if I am forced to that point, I would prefer to turn to a people, to England.'

Hortense had once told him that 'women are not for you, because you do not take enough trouble to be nice to them' and had added, 'none the less, they have a greater influence over men than you suspect'. That morning, discussing the Emperor's future with the wife of General Bertrand, Madame Bertrand had told her that 'the free and enlightened English are the only people worthy of welcoming him and capable of understanding him'. General Bertrand saw only through his wife's eyes ... and he was the intimate confidant of the Emperor.[1]

'Save me from Madame Bertrand,' the Emperor had told Hortense.

*   *   *

'They wouldn't dare,' he replied without much conviction to Lucien who came, about nine o'clock that evening, to tell him of the stormy session of the Chamber and the threat of deposition.

There was no hope of winning its support. In twenty-four hours he must make his choice; abdication or dissolution of the Chambers by force. Lucien insisted on the second solution; Caulaincourt and the Duke of Bassano, present at the meeting, urged the opposite course.

Napoleon withdrew. Did he sleep?

Eleven o'clock at night. At the Tuileries, in the hall of the State Council, Joseph and Lucien were hoping for the regency; the ministers were weary of shilly-shallying, compromises, re-drafted proposals, amended solutions, made and rejected over the past fifteen hours. The delegates of the Assemblies, admitting or desiring abdication, sitting under the chairmanship of Camba-cérès, were at the end of their tether. Repetitions, stale figments about the salvation of the country, liberty and so forth and so

[1] The Countess Bertrand was the daughter of Brigadier-General Arthur Dillon, an exiled Irishman who had distinguished himself in the French service, and of the Comtesse de La Touche, a distant relative of the Empress Josephine.

on, proved that no one knew what to say. One representative proposed that negotiators be sent to the enemy headquarters 'in the name of the Chamber'.

A last blush of shame made the ministers, except Fouché, reject the motion—which was, however, finally adopted thanks to a patent compromise: the plenipotentiaries of the Chambers should be appointed with the approval of the Emperor. After interminable bickerings, the dawn of June 22nd broke behind Notre Dame as Cambacérès refused to put to the vote a proposal of La Fayette that 'the commission will attend the Emperor to point out to him that his abdication is necessary'.

Was it for that day?

*　　　　　*　　　　　*

That night he dreamed; he was marshalling his troops at Paris.

TROOPS AVAILABLE AT PARIS

Imperial Guard — General Dériot

Old Guard

Regimental depots of Chasseurs and Grenadiers, both mounted and infantrymen	2,500 men

Young Guard

5th, 6th and 7th Voltiguers	3,000 men
5th, 6th and 7th Tirailleurs	
	5,500 men

Regiments of the Line

Depots of the 1st, 2nd and 4th Light	
Depots of the 1st, 2nd, 11th, 23rd, 69th and 76th of the Line	5,500 men

Versailles Cavalry Depot

Lancers and Hussars	650 men

Artillery Reserve — General Valée

Eight companies of the 2nd and 4th Artillery	
Twelve companies of the naval artillery: about	1,000 men

Gendarmes	700 men
	7,850 men

That is to say about 13,000 men, to whom should be added:
    Eight companies of veterans
    Two battalions of pensioners
    Seventeen thousand Federals, of whom 3,500 have arms
        and uniforms.
Let us say about 20,000 men.

It was no dream! Coming from the front, Captain Vatry of Jérôme's staff reported: Five thousand men of the Guard, assembled at Avesnes. On the march, 20,000 men of the Line, guns, limbers, wagons, cartloads of rifles found by the Guards officers. Dejean reports 1,700 cavalrymen of Roussel, Jacquinot and Piré rallied at Guise.

On June 20th Soult wrote from Rocroy that he was in touch with Grouchy, whose 30,000 men were on the march without being pursued by the enemy. At Philippeville 'yesterday in the evening' there were 1,200 men of the Old Guard, 500 to 600 of the Line and 800 cavalrymen. More than 10,000 men had already passed through, some on their way to Mézières, some to Rocroy and Laon; an even larger number, amongst them 1,200 Old Guard veterans, should have left for Beaumont. De Beauvau, aide-de-camp to General Gérard, had preceded his chief; the Major-General was on his way to Laon. He had met no other general officers and few senior officers. There were therefore 60,000 men on the northern frontier. Ten thousand could be sent . . . every national guard who abandoned his colours would be branded as a traitor to his country. The enemy could be halted, the invasion checked. Order to the Minister of War to rush to the Chamber and give this important news which should raise the courage of the representatives.

The defence of the country did not greatly interest the representatives. Some of them claimed that the information about the state of the army brought by Davout was false. General Solignac, deputy for Aveyron, proposed to send urgently to Wellington and Blücher the plenipotentiaries whose names must be approved by the Emperor.

'Useless to send them to the outposts,' protested a deputy from the Isère, son of the former president of the Tribunal and related through his mother to the 'Casimir Périer' of Grenoble, Antoine Duchesne. Ranting against the Empire, he roused the Chamber;

relying on the text of a letter from Metternich to Fouché, which the Minister of Police had shown secretly to everyone, he stated that the Allies would never come to terms as long as Napoleon was on the throne.

What was he waiting for? The Assembly was wasting valuable time. His unbridled oratory unleashed rebellion. 'Abdication! Deposition!' were outstripped. 'Arrest him! Outlaw him! Death!' were to be heard. Lanjuinais tried to pacify these madmen, advised them to await the Emperor's message. General Solignac insisted that a commission of five members go to the Elysée to explain to Napoleon the 'urgency of his decision'.

He was warned by Regnault, the Ministers of State and Lucien, whose ambition was revealed in a proposal made to his brother to hand over to him the sword of France after he had taken over dictatorship by going to the Palais-Bourbon. An imperative 'Stay where you are' nailed him to the spot.

In the midst of this terrible confusion, of which Fouché realized the danger, Solignac was announced. Was he accompanied by Durbach (of the Moselle), by Flaugergues and 'certain others', as Pasquier says? Or was he alone, as he claims? Was he trying to make a semi-official step to spare Napoleon a formal summons?

The Emperor knew him. Hothead, Jacobin, he had at one time thrashed a representative, had served a prison term at La Force, had served in Vendemiaire in the 'Police Legion', in Brumaire at Saint-Cloud; Chief of Staff under Masséna in Italy, he had been twice dismissed for misappropriation of funds and despite countless demands and emphatic protestations of loyalty and fidelity had not been employed again until 1814.

Surrounded by his ministers, by Savary and La Vallette, Napoleon listened irritably to the evocation of the fears of the newly rich, of those speculators who, formerly unleashed against the privileged, had become, once they had made their fortunes, the defenders of peace at any price, ready, as they had been the year before, to welcome the foreign armies.

'He should have denounced them to the people!'

He strode up and down, stopped, muttering words that could scarcely be heard . . . 'Tell them to wait!'

Fouché remained stark and impassive. Regnault, Caulaincourt and Savary urged him to yield, while Lucien still advised a sudden blow, to which Carnot, Bassano and even Cambacérès half agreed. The Emperor had made up his mind the day before. Once more calm and smiling, even ironic, he said to Fouché: 'Write to these fine fellows to rest easy. They will be satisfied.'

And while the mob beat at the gates of the Elysée shouting 'Long live the Emperor!' he dictated to Lucien in a solemn voice:

Declaration to the French People

'Frenchmen, in beginning the war to preserve the independence of the nation I counted on the union of all efforts, of all wills and on the assistance of all the national authorities; I felt justified in hoping for success and defied all the declarations of the powers against me.

'The circumstances now appear to have changed.

'I offer myself as a sacrifice to the hatred of the enemies of France. If only they are sincere in their declarations and only desire my person! All of you must unite for the public good to remain an independent people . . .'

Nothing for the Chamber which he despised.

What point in naming a successor? He knew very well that the Allies would not tolerate one of his family. Nevertheless, on the insistence of his friends and by the desire of his supporters, he added:

'I proclaim my son Emperor of the French under the title of Napoleon II. The Princes Joseph and Lucien and the present ministers will form, temporarily, the Government Council. My concern for my son binds me to ask the Chambers to organize the Regency, without delay, by law . . .'

Then, after an observation by Bassano, who feared lest the princes might not be acceptable, he struck out their two names. What did it matter?

The atmosphere in that overheated room was oppressive. There was a funereal silence. Fleury de Chaboulon's pen could be heard scratching on the paper on which he was making two copies of the last official document of the Empire. Silent witnesses of the sacrifice taking place before their eyes, the ministers and the companions of the Emperor saw their past collapsing:

Carnot, sixty-two years old, thought of his eventful life, wept for the liberty for which he had fought so often; like him, Caulaincourt, forty-two years old, dreaded the coming of the Bourbons; La Vallette, Bassano, Decrès, nephew by marriage of Joseph Bonaparte, Mollien, Gaudin . . . what mediocre or tragic fate was in store for them? The luckiest would be forgotten; all Davout's glory was behind him.

Deferred the year before, the story of the marshals came to an end that day. Darkness would cover their prowess, wavering and disputable in the anterooms and the assemblies, their jobs the modest ones of retired bourgeois, mayors of communes or chairmen of agricultural societies, because on June 22, 1815 the prodigious light in which for fifteen years an extraordinary man had bathed them was extinguished. Only Fouché triumphed . . . for the time being.

The copies were finished. Then, glancing through the document, the Emperor murmured 'It was their wish' and signed: 'Napoleon'. It was about one o'clock.

Carnot, Gaudin and Mollien left for the Luxembourg to hand over one copy to the Chamber of Peers and to read to it Davout's report on the military resources which France could still muster.

'Duke of Otranto (Fouché),' said the Emperor, not without humour, 'you will take the other copy to the Representatives.'

*   *   *

They were not yet at the end of their troubles! At first welcomed 'without approval or disapproval' according to the rules, the abdication was finally greeted with cheers and applause.

But the Emperor gone, who was to replace him? There was much talk and discussion. When an Assembly does not know what to decide, it appoints commissions. Several were suggested: one to draw up the Constitution, one to negotiate with the Allies, one to convey thanks to the Emperor, one to take his place. Noisy interventions, motions, proposals, declarations, twined and intertwined. There was a speech by Regnault to try, without compromising himself, to defend Napoleon II; then a counter-attack by Dupin who considered as null and void the paragraph of the abdication concerning the succession. He proposed that the Assembly should declare itself Constituent.

Fearing anarchy, Fouché wanted nothing to be precipitate. He wanted to preserve, to 'reorganize', according to a process familiar to parliamentarians . . . The tumult increased, while at the Elysée the committee of the Chamber received an icy welcome.

'I thank you,' said the Emperor, standing alone and without ceremony. 'I want my abdication to bring happiness to France, but I have little hope of that. It leaves the state without a head . . . The time lost in overthrowing me would have been better employed in making France ready to crush the enemy. Strengthen the armies immediately. Do not place this great nation at the mercy of foreigners. Take care not to be deceived in your hopes. There lies the danger. In whatever situation I may be, I will always be content if France is happy.

'I recommend my son to France. I hope that she will not forget that I have abdicated only for him.'

Did La Fayette, Flaugergues and the others feel any emotion? In any case, not daring to reveal to the French people the exact words of the Emperor, Lanjuinais paraphrased them thus for the *Moniteur* of June 23rd:

'His Majesty replied (to the delegation) and showed the most moving concern for the nation and the most lively desire to see its liberty, independence and well-being assured.'

Eight o'clock in the evening. Unanimous in the morning to overthrow the Emperor, the Assembly foundered, like a ship without a rudder, and became noisy and tumultuous concerning Napoleon II. Bonapartists, royalists, Orleanists, republicans, liberals, etc., openly insulted one another. But, having by his intrigues eliminated Lanjuinais, La Fayette, Flaugergues, MacDonald, etc., Fouché was elected a member of the Commission of Government, together with General Grenier, the compatriot of Ney, deputy for Meurthe-et-Moselle, a good soldier who had done brilliant service in Italy, vice-president of the Assembly. Carnot led the list with 324 votes. Fouché was eager to know the names of the peers appointed by the Upper Chamber if the proposals of the Representatives were accepted.

They were. The Upper House was merely a satellite of the other. A group of peers composed of compromised nobles, moribund senators, ageing generals and disappointed republicans, it could not be expected to resist the incessant domination of the representatives' oratory. Bonaparte's peerage, without dash, without aristocracy and without tradition, awaited the messages and decisions of the Chamber only to adopt them. It listened in silence to the Act of Abdication, after which Carnot 'in a low and broken voice' read Davout's report.

Then, suddenly, with body tense, features set and distorted, with red hair dishevelled and face flushed, stabbing at the minister with outstretched finger, a tall, heavily built man interrupted the orator, shouting: 'All that is false! They are deceiving you!'

It was Marshal Ney, 'seized by a fit of madness' according to contemporaries. On March 14th last, by his proclamation 'The cause of the Bourbons is lost forever . . . ' he had betrayed the King to whom he should have brought 'the usurper in an iron cage'. Later, at the Tuileries, he had deceived the Emperor—who had asked nothing of him—by saying that his promise to Louis XVIII 'concealed a contrary plan . . . ' From that time, kept at a distance by Napoleon, the Bonapartists and the royalists, the 'bravest of the brave' had retired to his estate at Coudreaux near Châteaudun. Racked by remorse, torn by 'complexes', engulfed in fatal 'nervous depressions', he burst into fits of temper, spoke publicly against the Emperor, to such an extent that the Prefect of the Ardennes, his host on the road to Waterloo, 'doubted if he were in his right mind'.

Recalled for the campaign, he had behaved, at Quatre-Bras on June 16th and at Waterloo on the 18th, with his usual bravery but also, at moments, in the most inexplicable manner. The Emperor had reproached him for his unprepared attacks at La Haye Sainte, his abortive cavalry charges, his final offensive with the Guard. That day, in despair at the loss of the imperial cause, his outbursts of fury, his spite, his fears at seeing the Bourbons return, exploded in a fit of rage.

'They are cheating you!' he repeated. 'The enemy is the victor; I saw the rout . . . 60,000 men at the frontier? . . . It's a lie! Grouchy has scarcely managed to save seven or eight thousand!'

Then he gave his own account of the battle, justifying his conduct.

'What has been said of the position of the Duke of Dalmatia (Soult) is not true,' he yelled. 'Not one man of the Guard has rallied! The Allies will be at the gates of Paris in a week.

Resistance is futile. We must treat with the enemy.' All this was jerked out in a trembling voice, in gasps.

Carnot was thunderstruck. Neither Thibaudeau, nor Siéyès, nor Masséna, nor Lefebvre, nor Moncey, nor Mortier, all present, intervened to recall the unhappy marshal to reason and duty. Not only did he consider all resistance useless, but he had no intention of taking part in it should it be decided, for he had obtained from Fouché two passports, dated the 20th, one in his own name, the other in that of Michel Neubourg, merchant.

Flabbergasted, the Chamber, presided over by Lacépède, suspended its session. When it was resumed the Chamber heard General Drouot give in a sullen voice the correct account of the battle of June 18th. He stressed, in order to calm down the excitement, the French valour and the disorder of Wellington's troops at the moment of the Prussian attack, and concluded : 'If in this last crisis we had shown the necessary energy, then this final misfortune could only have increased our glory . . . '

Respected by all, Drouot was listened to in silence and warmly applauded. But the damage had been done, the impression on the country deplorable. 'Ney's outburst has done more harm than a battle; the young soldiers are deserting. He has taken even hope from us,' wrote General Lauberdière, deputy of Beaugé in Maine-et-Loire. 'The people accuse the hero of Krasnoye of treason.'

Awaiting the messages of the Representatives, the Peers did not resume their session till nightfall.

*   *   *

Nine o'clock. The delegation had returned from the Elysée where it had visited the Emperor to thank him for his magnanimity. A dusty welcome.

'I only abdicated for my son,' he had said. 'If the Chambers do not proclaim him then my abdication will be void . . . I shall return with all my rights . . . Do what you will, the Bourbons will be restored . . . You will weep tears of blood. You flatter yourselves that you may get the Duke of Orleans, but the English will not have him; in the eyes of kings by right divine he too will be a usurper!'

Lacépède, like Lanjuinais, had not the courage to report these prophetic words to his colleagues, but one of them took it on

himself. Revolted by the words of Pontécoulant and Boissy
d'Anglas who had just shown that the Chamber without protest
had made up its mind 'to accept a sovereign from the hands of
foreigners', La Bédoyère leapt to the rostrum.

'Napoleon has abdicated in favour of his son,' he said. 'His
abdication is void if Napoleon II is not immediately proclaimed
. . . And who opposes that resolution? Individuals steadfast in
adoring power and who know how to forsake a monarch with
as much facility as they show in flattering one. They stand aside
when he is in misfortune. They reject Napoleon too, because
they are eager to accept the ruling of the foreigners, to whom
already they give the title of allies, perhaps even of friends . . . '

Murmurs arose.

Pitilessly the young general spat out his scorn of the turn-
coats. Under his phrases, lashing them like whips, cries of anger
rose: 'Enough! Order! Order!'

But La Bédoyère dominated the tumult.

'The abdication is indivisible,' he cried, hammering out his
phrases. 'If we refuse to proclaim the Prince Imperial, Napoleon
must draw the sword . . . ' Then, pointing out some notorious
opportunists: 'Shame to the vile generals who have forsaken
him and who, perhaps at this very moment, are considering fresh
betrayals.'

Finally, evoking the Champ de Mai: 'Only a few days ago,
in the face of Europe, before all France, you swore to defend
him . . . Where are those oaths now? . . . that frenzy? . . . '

Under the protests that crackled from all sides, he fixed his
eyes on Marshal Ney: 'Napoleon will find them if, as I ask of
him, he declare that every Frenchman who deserts his colours
will be judged, his name made infamous, his house seized, his
family proscribed. Let there be no more of these traitors, no more
of these manoeuvres which have caused the recent catastrophes
and of which, perhaps, some of the authors are seated here . . . '

Under a tempest of cries and threats, the president put on his
hat. The fiery orator was torn from the rostrum, but had time
to say: 'Has it then been decided, Great God, that only words
of perjury may be heard here!'

'Young man, you forget yourself,' shouted a marshal.

Irony. In the town halls of the capital and in the headquarters
of the National Guard a notice read: 'While the Chambers are

debating the salvation of the country (?), their deliberations must proceed undisturbed . . . ' It was a fragment from the Order of the Day issued by General Durosnel, aide-de-camp to the Emperor, second-in-command of the National Guard.

From Vienna, Metternich wrote to his daughter: 'We have got Napoleon's hat. Now, it is to be hoped, we shall get all of him.'

At the Luxembourg all was calm once more. Despite La Bédoyère's lashings the Peers suspended their debate on Napoleon II. 'Is this the moment to worry about individuals when the country is in danger?' said Duke Decrès, Napoleon's Minister of Marine since 1801, to Flahaut.

It was after midnight when Caulincourt, friend of the Tsar, and the regicide Quinette, well known for his indecision, were appointed members of the Commission of Government.

*   *   *

Davout had already taken the Emperor's place at the head of the armies and, on June 22nd at eight o'clock in the evening, sent this strange letter to Marshal Grouchy:

'I have just learnt from a letter from General Bonnemain (commanding a brigade of dragoons of Exelmans' corps) to General Dumonceau that you are at Dinant and Namur with your cavalry and the 3rd and 4th Corps of General Gérard and General Vandamme. It is an event of very great importance to our country. For after the unfortunate happenings to the 1st, 2nd and 6th Corps and to the Guard near Jemappes (?) we were in a state of great anxiety; the assurance that your corps is intact is of incalculable advantage in the present circumstances . . . I do not know what orders the Duke of Dalmatia may have given you, but these that I give you now are those that you must follow. You must move towards Laon by way of Mézières . . . You must send me frequent despatches . . . Take every measure to ensure the discipline of your troops. You will keep them informed of the latest events in Paris: the Emperor has just abdicated, wishing to remove any pretext for the foreign powers to continue the war against us since, according to all their declarations, they have said that they were waging war against him only. The Chambers have appointed a provisional government; commissioners will be sent to you to announce this event which should remove all pretext for war. If the Allied powers, as one must hope, have been of good faith in their declarations, then in a few days the world will be again at peace.

'You realize, Marshal, that should this declaration be no more than a decoy, then it is essential, for the service of the country, to take all measures to prevent any attempts to create disorganization and desertion among the troops.'

Then the tone of the letter changes:

'You can, and indeed you must, send reports of these events to the Allied generals in your vicinity, asking them to suspend all hostilities until they have received the orders of their sovereigns. Write to all the prefects to acquaint them of these matters . . . '

And the Minister of War ends his letter by inviting the Marshal to 'conjure the generals' in the name of the country, to take all measures to maintain all their troops and to remind them of all the duties of the French soldier.

'France relies on you. The arrival of your corps has made a sensation in Paris.'

Davout had already by-passed Marshal Soult, the Chief of Staff, and gives political orders to Grouchy. The curtain falls on the second act.

In 1814 Napoleon, unconquered, was deposed by Europe with the connivance of a traitor: Talleyrand. In 1815, led by another traitor, Fouché, it was the two French Chambers that, trembling with fear and hoping to ward off the anger of Europe, tore him down from his power and his sword because, as La Fayette said, 'the salvation of the country lies only in his abdication'.

'The country? Where is it to be found during an invasion?' wrote Achille de Vaulabelle. 'Is it on the soil occupied by the invaders or with the cowards and traitors who rush to surrender?'

In the face of the enemy the country is where one fights, under the leader who wants to save it, and not in the assemblies of chatterers where in destroying the one, the other is sacrificed. La Fayette violates the Constitution, so that it may no longer be threatened. Forcing the Emperor to withdraw in fear of a dictatorship, a thousand or so average Frenchmen hand it back, the same day, to five irresponsibles, hand over the fortunes and honour of their land to a corrupt policeman, after having withdrawn it from the foremost warrior of all time and 'the brilliant manifestation of the national glory'. But it is the character of peoples and not of governments that determines their destiny. Abandoning him who, fifteen years before, had saved France from the abyss and made her the first nation in the world, the French of 1815, indifferent, let this be done.

Chapter III
'THE FIVE EMPERORS'

CONFUSION

June 23rd. The tricolour replaced the Emperor's standard on the Tuileries. The city was quiet. But when the news of the abdication reached the Palais-Royal, the boulevards and the suburbs, officers, soldiers, workmen, shopkeepers and artisans met, argued, grew angry.

At the Café Montansier (the present Palais-Royal theatre), the Bonapartists sang:

> *Croyez-vous qu'un Bourbon*
> *Puisse être*
> *Roi d'une grande nation?*
> *Non ! Non, non, non ! Non, non, non !*
>
> . . . .
>
> *Chantons donc à perdre haleine*
> *Vive le Grand Napoléon !*
> *Bon ! Bon, bon, bon ! Bon, bon, bon !* [1]

Then the tension rose:

> *Je me f . . . du roi,*
> *Du comte d'Artois*
> *Et du duc d'Angoulême*
> *Et du duc de Berry*
> *Et de la duchesse aussi*
> *Et de ceux qui les aiment.* [2]

In the Place Vendôme, soldiers, workmen and women knelt before the Column, called on Napoleon and shouted: 'Long live

---

[1] Do you think a Bourbon could be a king of a great nation? No! No, no, no! No, no, no! Then let us sing at the top of our voices: Long live the Great Napoleon! Good! Good, good, good! Good, good, good!

[2] A fig for the king, for the Count d'Artois and the Duke d'Angoulême; for the Duke of Berry and his Duchess as well, and all those who love them.

89

the Emperor!' Revolutionaries distributed pamphlets forecasting massacres as in 1793. To the annoyance of the angry Bonapartists, gamblers on the Exchanges were buying state bonds as fast as they could. They rose in a few hours to 4·50 francs.

The bourgeois bolted themselves into their houses and the traders shut their shops when they heard the drumbeats of the Federals. Preceded by banners, the procession coming from Saint-Marcel joined the workers of the Faubourg Saint-Antoine, bearing green branches as on July 14, 1789; to the strains of the *Marseillaise* and the *Chant du Départ* they paraded up and down the boulevards, drew to their ranks the crowds eagerly discussing the news and marched towards the Elysée chanting: 'The Emperor or death! Treason! Treason!'

A yelling mob gathered in the Faubourg Saint Honoré around the palace gardens, and in the Champs-Elysées, before the gates; on the breast-high enclosing wall eager partisans continually threatened the 'traitors', called for the Emperor, crying 'Do not abandon us!'

Madame Mère and Queen Hortense, who were strolling under the lindens, were appalled.

'Would you believe, Madame,' murmured the Prefect of Police, Réal, who was walking with them, 'that I have been scattering money right and left by order of the provisional government just to restrain this popular frenzy. These fine fellows pocket the money, which is always handy . . . wherever it comes from, and shout "Long live Napoleon!" a little louder than before.'

*　　　*　　　*

He could hear them from his study. Perhaps nothing was irrevocable! Perhaps one could hope for an upsurge of patriotism? Would the deputies realize in time that the Allies were going to have their revenge on France? Time was pressing. Would they understand that he was the one man who could save her? If not, what could he do with the enemy at the gates? . . . Alone, in the midst of cowards, traitors, poltroons, babblers, hate-filled royalists, unleashed partisans, all creating a hullabaloo which increased hourly?

'My good and noble friend,' he said to La Bédoyère, who had come to tell him about the session of the Upper Chamber, 'I am deeply grateful for what you have done for me. But, are you really astonished at the conduct of your colleagues? It would have surprised me even more had they acted otherwise. Those whom I have laden with good things want to keep them; they will sacrifice me, France, everything, just to increase their fortunes. The stock market is their sovereign, their honour, their God . . . The worship of the Golden Calf is the mania of the century . . .'

So it was in 1815!

If he resisted the people, if he still resisted them, it was because 'it is no longer the unanimous voice of the nation . . . I want five hundred million men for my friends', this ambitious sentimentalist said one day to Roederer.

On the other hand, he listened to Marchand. In Paris they did not understand his abdication; they were astonished that His Majesty did not seize the dictatorship in so critical a moment. 'All those with whom I have talked today,' said the faithful valet, 'say that it means to hand them over, bound hand and foot.'

If he withdrew his abdication, signed in weariness to satisfy those around him, uneasy about their future, he would reply to all these appeals that tortured him; he would put fresh heart into his soldiers, now forsaken and without hope . . . He had, moreover, advised Drouot to accept the command of the Imperial Guard and Caulaincourt to take a place in the Provisional Government. But would that not mean a useless shedding of French blood?

'I was a conqueror,' he said to Caulaincourt. 'I could still be one but I lost the throw at Waterloo. I do not want to demean myself by playing the tyrant.'

What part was he to play? Remain at the Elysée? At Malmaison? He talked about it, but it was impossible. Go abroad? If they wouldn't let him stay in France, where did they want him to go? To England? His stay there would be ridiculous and alarming!

He had many visitors: his mother, his brothers. They held a family council. Lucien would go to London, to try to get passports for America, and vigorously protested when Napoleon rejected his advice. 'The smoke of Mont-Saint-Jean has obscured his brain,' he said. Those loyal to him declared that they were ready to accompany him wherever he might go: Savary,

Méneval, his two chamberlains, Montholon and Las Cases, who had returned to the Elysée on the 20th, Bertrand, Gourgaud, the officers of his suite, Planat de la Faye, Saint-Yon, Chiappe, Résigny; then, too, Flahaut and La Bédoyère . . .

'The French are no longer worthy of your care, since they have forsaken you,' repeated Queen Hortense making her way into his study. 'Do not lose a moment, save yourself . . . The English? It would be giving them too much glory. They would imprison you in the Tower of London . . . If it is to be Austria, then state your conditions immediately. If it is to be America, make haste and get to a port before the English become aware of your intentions . . . The Emperor of Russia was your friend; he is loyal and generous. The Duke of Vicenza inclines to this solution . . . '

Later, after the Congress of Aix-la-Chapelle, Alexander, when visiting M. Ludvig's spinning mill, saw on a wall a picture of his interview with Napoleon on the bridge over the Niemen. 'Why didn't he do the same in 1815?' he said. 'He could have done it, and, if he had done it perhaps he would still be Emperor of the French.'

'But, Sire,' said the industrialist, 'there were the Bourbons.'

'True,' replied the Tsar. 'But why didn't he do it in 1814? The Bourbons were not in the war.'

Did the queen know that on June 22nd, that is to say a few hours after the abdication, Napoleon had asked Decrès for the frigates *Méduse* and *Saale*, at that time in the roads at Roche-fort, to take him to America with his suite? On the morning of the 23rd he sent Bertrand to repeat his request. The Minister of Marine replied that he would give the necessary orders as soon as he received the authorization of the Commission of Government.

Who could have given the Emperor this advice? In any case, the Minister of Marine was not unaware that Rear-Admiral Sir Harry Hotham, with his flag in the *Superb*, a seventy-four-gun ship, was operating with his squadron off the coast of Vendée and was in touch with the insurgents in the west. He knew that from the beginning of the month the *Bellerophon* and the *Eridanus* were off Rochefort to keep an eye on the French war-ships there, the *Méduse*, the *Saale*, the *Bayadère* and the *Epervier*, that the narrows were being watched, that the port, situated at the head of the Gulf of Gascony, was a 'mousetrap' and that at Brest (Captain Constantin was sure of it) there were two frigates available which could 'more easily assure the departure of the Emperor'.

*   *   *

That night Fouché received notice of a meeting from Carnot. Appointed first of the members of the Commission of Government, with thirty-one votes more than Fouché, the former 'Organizer of Victory' notified his colleagues that he had assumed the Presidency and summoned them, at eleven o'clock on the 23rd, to the Ministry of the Interior, Rue Grenelle.

Fouché leapt for his pen. Feigning to know nothing, he asked the members of the Commission to come to the Tuileries at eight o'clock 'to incorporate themselves'. Carnot waited in his office in vain and went to the Tuileries at the urgent appeal of his colleagues. To do what?

'To incorporate ourselves,' said Fouché, 'to elect the president, appoint the secretary, nominate . . . '

Carnot was outwitted. They voted. A good gambler, he gave his vote for Fouché who, harvesting Quinette's votes, added his own and took the president's chair and the succession to Napoleon.

It was a difficult task. The royalists mistrusted him. The previous evening he had brought M. de Vitrolles out of the Abbaye prison, who had been imprisoned there through his own good offices the previous April. He summoned him early in the morning to his house in the Rue Cerutti. He advised him to get in touch with the King at Ghent to tell him that he, Fouché, was working in his interests, when Vitrolles insinuated that he would perhaps be more useful to the royal cause by remaining in Paris. 'I could also make His Majesty aware of the frankness of your intentions . . . ' Ironic proposals from one intriguer to another.

Fouché had raised no objections to this protection nor this supervision, without paying much heed either to the one or the other. But a little later, coming from the Elysée, Regnault told him that Napoleon, exasperated and offended by the way in which the Chambers had eluded the recognition of his son, had reproached, in extremely lively terms, his equivocal behaviour and that of the Bonapartists: Defermon, Boulay de la Meurthe, etc.

'I have not abdicated in favour of a Directory,' he had said. 'If they do not proclaim my son, then my abdication is void. The Chambers know very well that the people, the army and public opinion want him, long for him, but the foreigners hold them back. It is not by appearing before the Allies with their tails between their legs and their knees to the ground that they will force them to acknowledge our national independence. If the Assemblies had any feeling for their situation, they would have proclaimed Napoleon II spontaneously. The foreigners would have seen that you had a will, an aim, a rallying point. National unanimity would have more effect on them than your obsequiousness and shameful poltrooneries!'

Napoleon was quite capable of annulling the abdication and of seizing power again with the support of the army which was approaching, of the whole turbulent population of Paris, of the Federals, more and more irritated, and of the garrison troops, some of whose officers said that 'they would go and demand the Emperor from the Chambers and if they did not get him they would burn the capital to the ground'.

It was urgent to take some measures to handle Napoleon, Caulaincourt, the army; for example the Chamber could recognize Napoleon II without getting too involved, above all without forming a Council of Regency which would suppress the Commission of Government and would take its place.

* * *

In actual fact the Commission of Government was holding its first meeting. Fouché wanted to consolidate his position not only as President but above all as the holder of power in such a way as to become indispensable. First, military measures: Davout, Minister of War, was entrusted with the defence of Paris and became officially Commander-in-Chief; General Andréossy was put at the head of the 1st military division; Hulin commanded the fortress. Despite the promise he had made to La Fayette, and to so many others, to put him at the head of the National Guard, Fouché appointed the Prince of Essling (Masséna) in his place. His military record, his equivocal attitude at the time of the Emperor's disembarkation, placed the appointment of the Marshal, who was moreover a very tired man, above all criticism; finally, Drouot, wise, honest and universally respected, was placed in command of the Imperial Guard because he alone could restore it to obedience.

The putting of Paris into a state of defence was interrupted. Irregularly paid (1·75 francs a day), the workers abandoned their tasks. In the government, Caulaincourt did no more than complain; Quinette and Grenier had never believed in defence and Carnot no longer believed in it. Fouché did not want it at any price.

The Chamber was also asked to vote the estimates, to despatch commissions to the army, to call up the 1815 class, a process which, already ordered by the Emperor on June 11th, was in full swing; also the suspension of individual liberty, which Napoleon had never dared to do, and the proclamation of a state of siege, already in force! It would, however, remain a dead letter, since Fouché had forbidden the arrest of royalists. The Commission let him do as he liked, the Chamber did not even protest! So-called liberal, adversary both of king and of dictatorship, democratic as are all meetings of at least five hundred men, it accepted the last proposal by 359 votes to sixty!

Carnot, an honest man without guile, whom Fouché openly called a 'fanatical idiot', said nothing, but preserved an icy decorum. Caulaincourt, indifferent, very uneasy about his own future, was only there to see that the person of the Emperor was respected and to suggest the possibility of a treaty with the Allies in the manner of that of Châtillon. Grenier represented the military, revolutionary past, but was of no more importance than Quinette, insignificant and inoffensive, a tool in Fouché's hands.

A few clerks were rapidly elected to replace those ministers who had been chosen as commissioners or who had resigned. To console Carnot, his brother was appointed Minister of the Interior; Bignon, without credit among the Allies because of his behaviour in Germany, became Minister of Foreign Affairs. A simple department chief, Pelet de la Lozère, was at the head of the police where, naturally enough, he did not replace Fouché. Boulay de la Meurthe, a Bonapartist whose support was needed, became Minister of Justice and did what he was told. The other ministers, Davout, Decrès, Gaudin, Mollien, remained in their posts. Count Otto was sent to London to make overtures for peace.

In the morning there was a meeting at the Police Ministry with Manuel and the more influential of the deputies in order to draw up the agenda which must be adopted by the Assembly at the close of the session.

The session was opened at eleven-thirty by Lanjuinais. A grandiloquent intervention by Regnault on a question of procedure provoked a few ripples, when Félix Lepeletier de Saint-Fargeau, deputy for Dieppe, former member of 'The Mountain', supporter of Baboeuf and a savage adversary of Napoleon, protested against the journalists who assumed the right of 'calumniating the Chamber'. Then Bérenger returned to the measures taken the day before:

'You have replaced the imperial power by a provisional government,' he said. 'The government was made up of an inviolable prince and a responsible ministry. Is the provisional government inviolable?'

Dupin asked that it take an oath of obedience to the laws and of loyalty to the nation.

Defermon: 'In whose name will it act? What will be the superscription of its documents? Have we, or have we not, an Emperor?'

'We have Napoleon II.'

A large number of deputies rose and shouted 'Long live Napoleon II!'

Boulay de la Meurthe, stressing Defermon's argument, showed that Napoleon's abdication 'was indivisible' and went on: 'I keep my eyes open outside this Assembly ... We are surrounded by intriguers and sedition-mongers who want to declare the throne vacant in order to put there the Bourbons of one ...'

'No! No! Never! Never!'

'... or the other branch. It maintains connections with the patriots, but it is purely royalist.'

There were protestations, for a large number of the representatives (there were not more than about half a dozen royalists) wanted a constitutional monarchy with the Duke of Orleans. Fouché, moreover, recruited the party; the generals rallied to it. Soult wrote from Laon to the Emperor (June 22nd): 'The name of Orleans is on everybody's lips.'

The debate languished. Dupin proposed a republic. Regnault

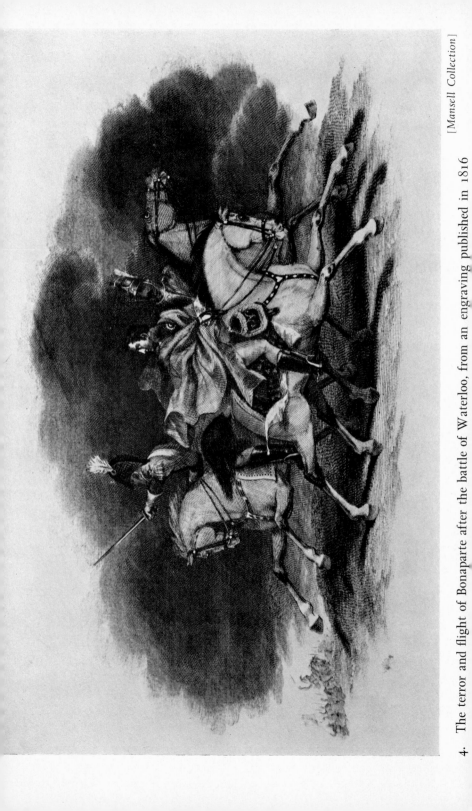

4. The terror and flight of Bonaparte after the battle of Waterloo, from an engraving published in 1816

5. The attack on Napoleon's carriage

insisted on an immediate vote. Manuel, after a most eloquent speech, submitted the agenda ... artfully and cunningly drawn up that morning by Fouché.

'The Chamber of Representatives, deliberating on the various proposals made during the meeting and referred to in its minutes, passes to the current agenda, as follows:
'First: that Napoleon II has become Emperor of the French as a result of the abdication of Napoleon I and according to the Constitution of the Empire.
'Second: that the two Chambers wish, by the decree dated yesterday concerning the appointment of a Commission of provisional government, to assure the nation of the guarantees that it desires, in the present unusual circumstances, for its liberty and peace through an administration which has the full confidence of the people.'

At first, general satisfaction, both for the Bonapartists and the military since 'Napoleon II has become Emperor'. He has only become so, it is true, after his father's abdication, 'according to the Constitution of the Empire' ... ! There has been no word of any Council of Regency. As this ascension gives no pledge for the future, since the Constitution of the Empire will cease to exist, royalists and liberals, etc., will not be offended. On the other hand, since the King of Rome is a prisoner, a Commission of Government, moreover a 'provisional one', is indispensable and must be set up without delay to assure the conduct of current affairs in the circumstances in which France is placed. Finally, it must have the confidence of the people since it has been appointed by their representatives ...
This masterpiece of astuteness and political and parliamentary fraud was voted unanimously. The Bonapartists shouted 'Long live the Emperor!' as if their cause were won. The Assembly thought that all was saved. But the Emperor did not share those illusions.
'What's happening?' he asked Regnault, who arrived straight from the Chamber.
'The mood is very good,' replied the chamberlain, who had perhaps understood nothing. 'Napoleon II has been proclaimed with much enthusiasm.'

D

Having read the agenda, Napoleon perhaps thought that at least honour had been saved. 'What are they doing now?' he said abruptly.

'Discussing the articles of the Constitution.'

'Still the *Bas-Empire*! Poor fellows! With the enemy at the gates!'

It was three in the morning when Lacépède closed the session of the Chamber of Peers which had accepted responsibility for Fouché's agenda.

That night, in Fouché's rooms, all the intriguers, plotters, schemers and hangers-on crowded pell-mell. 'Well, that's all to the good,' Fouché commented mockingly, rubbing his hands. 'They have confronted the *Ancien Régime* with the Constitution of the Empire . . . I hope that both plaintiffs will soon be non-suited and that something more suitable to the needs and reason of the century will emerge . . . '

He had only one programme: to paralyze the last energies of the Chambers and to confuse them utterly by making them vote laws which he could never put into force, affirming 'that the Commission makes use of the patriotism and devotion of the citizens for the defence of French independence without ceasing to take measures to support the negotiations by the development of all the forces of the nation . . . ', which meant nothing at all.

'Do you know?' he said to Vitrolles, 'that the Chamber has proclaimed Napoleon II?'

'What? Napoleon II!'

'Certainly. It's a necessary step.'

'But surely they cannot be serious?'

'It's not common sense, but you'd be surprised how many people swear by that name. Many of my colleagues, especially Carnot, are convinced that with Napoleon II all is saved.'

'How long is this foolery to go on?'

'Long enough to get rid of Napoleon I.'

'But if M. Carnot is so set on it?'

'Bah! You don't know Carnot. To make him change his opinion it will be quite enough to proclaim "The French people!" . . . The French people! I ask you!'

Both burst into laughter.

'But after Napoleon II and "The French people", I hope you will spare a thought for the Bourbons.'

'Undoubtedly, but then it will be the turn of the Duke of Orleans.'

'The Duke of Orleans! Do you think that the King will accept a crown that has been so bandied about?'

'His party is more important than you think . . . And after . . .'

That was what Fouché called 'passing through Napoleon II, then passing through the Duke of Orleans, to reach at last Louis XVIII . . .'

FOUCHÉ

Albert Sorel has summed up the man:

'False by nature, perfidious by temperament, deprived even of those scruples of private friendship that mitigated the public treasons of his like; impudent in lies, shameless in desertions . . . superficial in his judgment of affairs, profound in intrigue, light and sparkling in suggestion . . . using his skill to play on the passions, the vices and especially the stupidity of men; maintaining an outward composure even when frightened, bolder in conception than in execution, with wits sharpened in crisis and enthusiastic as soon as he scented a conspiracy, on the other hand lackadaisical, depressed and almost inert in regular government, he always needed the atmosphere of revolution to bring him to life. It was his life-blood.'

To Carnot, a regicide like himself, to Quinette and Grenier he posed as an enemy of the King; to Caulaincourt he longed for Napoleon II without daring to hope, stressed his wish to treat the Emperor in the manner most worthy of his greatness and his glory.

'But how to tear Napoleon II from the grip of the Allies?' he said to the peers entrusted with maintaining liaison with the Chamber. 'The Empress seems to care very little about seeing her son reign over France . . . If this solution seems impossible . . . then perhaps the Duke of Orleans, a Bourbon but devoted to the cause of the Revolution . . .'

The agitation, the uncertainty, grew. Fouché called on Vitrolles to moderate the zeal of the three marshals, Macdonald, Gouvion-Saint-Cyr and Oudinot, neophytes of the royalist party, ready to step into the lists and commit the irreparable. He told the Bonapartists and the revolutionaries, now intermingled, not to give themselves up to the follies of despair. To calm the 'patriots' of the Chamber, so incensed against the House of France that they 'would prefer to accept the Prussians or the English, a Prince of Brunswick, Hanover or Saxony, than recognize Louis XVIII or an Imperial dictatorship', Fouché announced the imminent departure of plenipotentiaries entrusted with discussing peace with the Allies.

He proposed to the Commission of Government, which at once accepted, the nomination of La Fayette, who would thus be kept away from Paris and politics; of Pontécoulant, Lucien's adversary, a peer of Louis XVIII and of Napoleon; of Sébastiani, a general and a diplomat; of the Marquis d'Argenson, former aide-de-camp of La Fayette and liberal prefect of Deux Nethes (Anvers); of Laforest, a skilled diplomat sent to Spain by Napoleon after Tilsit and former Foreign Minister to the King; and, as secretary, of Benjamin Constant.

They would go via Laon to the sovereigns' headquarters . . . At Mannheim, perhaps at Hagenau, they would ask for passports from the Duke of Wellington and would try to obtain an armistice. Bignon drew up their official instructions : integrity of territory, national independence, no victimization of persons, recognition of Napoleon II.

Fouché had no anxieties on this score. Enemies of the father and charged with defending the interests of the son, the plenipotentiaries would present their case badly and would never be able to obtain from the sovereigns the recognition of Napoleon II —nor of anything else. La Fayette's mission was only conceived to get these trouble-makers out of the way, to give satisfaction to the liberals in the Chamber, to lull the suspicions of the members of the government and to allow Fouché to conduct the negotiations in his own manner, particularly with Wellington, whom he knew well and with whom he was in correspondence. Having duped Napoleon, the Bonapartists, the royalists, the liberals and the Chambers, it now only remained to dupe the nation.

From his rickety throne Fouché launched a shameless proclamation to the French people, drawn up by Berlier and revised by him :

'Napoleon has abdicated the imperial power; his son has been proclaimed.

'Your new Constitution, which till now contained only good principles, will be developed and even those principles will be refined and extended. There are no longer powers jealous of one another; the field is open to the enlightened patriotism of your representatives, and the peers think and vote in the same way as do your mandatories.

'The plenipotentiaries are leaving to treat with the powers of Europe in the name of the nation and to negotiate that peace which they have promised on one condition which has now been fulfilled.'

The rest of it, in his own handwriting, deserves study:

'Their reply will show whether justice and promises mean anything in this world.

'Frenchmen, be united. All must stand together in these critical moments. Whatever may have been his party or his political creed, any man born on the soil of France cannot fail to rally to the country's flag to defend the independence of his land!

'An intrepid people that fights for justice and liberty is not destroyed; above all, it does not surrender.

'By his abdication the Emperor has offered himself as a sacrifice.

'The members of the government have dedicated themselves by accepting, from your representatives, the reins of state.

'(Signed): The Duke of Otranto (Fouché), President.'

When they read this document in the *Moniteur* of Sunday, June 25th, did the French people know that the King, forewarned by Wellington of 'the destruction of the French army', had come from Ghent at his invitation and had reached the British headquarters at Cateau-Cambrésis the previous day? Or that Metternich had written that same day to the Duke: 'I consider the victory of the 18th as one of those thunderbolts that only the elect of heaven may wield . . . '? That the traitor Dumouriez had told 'his dear hero' that he was 'drunk with joy'? That Talleyrand, regarding himself as a patriot, offered him 'his compliments on his great and wonderful victories . . . '?

All this recalls Voltaire congratulating Frederick II on his victory over the French at Rosbach.

When the Count of Caraman, Envoy Extraordinary at Berlin, invited his colleagues of the diplomatic corps to present his congratulations to Madame Blücher, wife of the Marshal, one would have thought that the nadir of abasement had been reached, if one had not learnt from the *Journal Universel de Gand* of June 21st that, on the previous day, the King had said to Marshal Victor at dinner: 'I never drank to the success of the Allies before the Restoration; their cause was just, but I did not know their intentions concerning France. Today, now that they are the Allies of my crown, that they are fighting not the French but the Bonapartists, that they have nobly dedicated themselves to the deliverance of my people, we can salute their victory without ceasing to be Frenchmen.'

Oh! the poor dead at Waterloo!

*　　　　　　*　　　　　　*

After so many intrigues, ignominies, treasons and crimes, here is a pure note sounded by the Military Academy and sent to the provisional government: 'We demand to follow the national cause and to be the first to march to meet the enemy in order to avenge our brothers or die like them under the standard of independence . . . ' Two hundred and twenty-five pupils signed.

It was an encouragement for the government, for the war was still going on amid all the political discussions and the wranglings in the High Command. Had Davout written a private letter to Marshal Soult to tell him of the Emperor's abdication? In any case, the letter had not reached him; Davout wrote direct to Grouchy, appointed Commander-in-Chief of the Northern Army, while Soult, Chief of Staff, continued to give him orders!

That day, the 23rd, Soult had detained the minister's aide-de-camp taking despatches to Marshal Grouchy, had broken the seals and had thus learnt all that was going on in Paris. Furious, he sent to Davout an account, in impersonal style, of the situation:

'Today, the 23rd, the troops rallied around Soissons, together with Grouchy's men, amount to fifty thousand men and a hundred and twenty guns. It would be possible to bring the army up to one hundred thousand infantry, twenty thousand cavalry and three hundred guns if an effort is made and some of the men in barracks are made available. The 2nd Corps is at Soissons. The 1st Corps is at Anizy and will be at Soissons by tomorrow. The infantry of the Guard and two batteries (General Morand) took up their position this evening in front of the wood at Mally, guarding the bridge at Etouvelles. The cavalry of the Guard (Lefebvre-Desnoëttes) is on the march from Mons-en-Laonnois to Lizy by a roundabout way from Laon to Soissons. Three divisions of light cavalry hold the line from Crépy to Corbény.

'There is a shortage of camp equipment. The soldiers have not been paid . . . We haven't a sou.

'It should be noted that since the abdication of the Emperor, the duties of Chief of Staff carried out by the Duke of Dalmatia have ceased. The minister is requested to consider his mission as completed and that he should cease giving orders after having sent the orders concerning the Emperor's abdication; that he should command the army until the arrival of Marshal Grouchy; and that he is no longer able to carry out his duties for reasons of health.'

After which the former minister of Louis XVIII and the future marshal of Louis-Philippe, deeply vexed at the way in which he had been treated, sent on to Grouchy, about five o'clock that evening, the despatches intended for him: 'The aide-de-camp of His Excellency whom I met on the road stated that the Emperor has abdicated, but he brought no letter for me . . . That seemed to me so extraordinary that I opened your despatches and took copies of them in order to advise the generals of their contents.'

He added that he should go to Soissons, where the headquarters were to be, that the enemy was at Vervins sending out scouts towards Laon, and that it was of the greatest importance that Grouchy—then at Rethel, Montcornet and Rumigny—should go to Soissons by way of Reims.

At Laon the troops amongst whom, as Colonel de Briqueville commanding the 20th Dragoons wrote, 'the sacred flame of patriotism still burns' were assembling on the parade grounds in the bivouacs deserted by the Guard.

June 24th. Having recovered their morale and driving the stragglers before them, 6,000 of Morand's, Roguet's and Petit's chasseurs and grenadiers and 2,500 of Lefebvre-Desnoëttes' and Colbert's lancers, chasseurs and mounted grenadiers broke back towards Soissons. They were marching at a good pace when they were ordered to halt on leaving Etouvelles and told to draw up on the heath at each side of the road; the guns took up their position on the paved road. The 1st Chasseurs remained north of the village.

What was happening? They had been scarcely two hours on their way and there was not a sign of the enemy.

Here was the Chief of Staff, who had by now resigned, in a most remarkable get-up: Soult was wearing a civilian coat with the Star of the Grand Aigle and no other military attributes save his white-plumed hat! Having dismounted, he walked fussily to and fro, about a hundred paces from the grenadiers, his hands behind his back in the manner of the Emperor. An hour later he took from his pocket a paper which the officers of his suite had been copying. It was then read to the companies:

'Frenchmen! When commencing the war to maintain the independence of the nation I had every reason to hope for success . . . I offer myself as a sacrifice . . . I proclaim my son . . . Napoleon II, Emperor of the French . . . Be united . . .

'NAPOLEON.'

'June 22, 1815.'

The last words were drowned in an uproar of protest. Crying 'Treason!' the men broke ranks, yelled, blasphemed, threatened. It was a fake! Another abdication. They would believe it when they had seen and heard the Emperor! Till then — nothing doing! No grenadiers for cowards and traitors. It was another trick of the marshals, just as the year before! He had been warned not to trust them! The officers were jeered at, the generals booed: 'If you say that again, you die!' cried a grenadier, aiming his gun at a general who threatened to 'have him shot'. Some smashed their arms and tore their uniforms; others jostled officers and N.C.O.s and took the road for Soissons and Paris.

Others were indifferent and passive. Seated on the heather, they played cards on their drums, blissfully watching their angry comrades.

Very quickly General Petit exhorted the grenadiers to follow him to Étouvelles, where his regiment was to relieve the 1st Chasseurs in the rearguard. But it was time wasted.

'Very well,' he said. 'Since the grenadiers want to dishonour themselves in the presence of the enemy, it will never be said that their colonel failed in his duty. Bring me the eagle. I will put it in the extreme rearguard and will myself remain on sentry-go beside it.'

Loubers, the battalion chief, accused Petit of wanting to hand the eagle over to the enemy! After a lively altercation Loubers fell on the grass, fuming and foaming at the mouth. Little by little calm was restored. Three-quarters of the regiment followed the colonel. A few men took to the woods, in fear 'of being taken prisoner by treason'. A thousand infantrymen of the Guard, some with arms, some without, took the road for Paris. They wanted to see the Emperor, to hear him. But they no sooner reached Soissons when the gendarme officers stopped them. General Mouton-Duvernet, sent by Davout 'to study the morale of the troops', induced them to return to their posts.

'Who is there to fight for, if there is no longer an Emperor?' Roguet took command of the infantry of the Guard and restored order and discipline.

Meanwhile, knowing nothing of these events, the undefeated troops of Grouchy applauded the magnificent proclamation launched by the Marshal on June 22nd.

'Soldiers!

'Victors at Fleurus, at Wavre, at Namur, you have beaten the enemy everywhere you have encountered them. Your valour has seized their military trophies from them, and they cannot boast of having ravished a single one of yours. Strengthened by reinforcements and once more under the leadership of the chief of the Empire, you will soon take the offensive as you desire. Defenders of our beloved country, you will preserve its sacred soil and all France will proclaim your right to gratitude and love.

'I am happy to have been your leader wherever you have won your glory in these great events and I wish to pay to your valour the meed of praise due to it. In your name I give your pledge to our country that, faithful to your oath, you will perish rather than see it humiliated and enslaved.

'Long live the Emperor!
    'Marshal commanding the right wing of the army,
                                        'GROUCHY.'

The morning of that same day, at Aubigny on the Rethel road, the Marshal read Davout's letter with satisfaction: 'You have rendered France a service which will be recognized by everyone . . . ' If only it had been true!

*   *   *

Had it been true? Marshal Grouchy, the man who had saved the army and who was also to save the remnants of the French army on June 29th, despite the pursuit of the 'Allies of H.M. the King of France', as they were called in Wellington's Order of the Day on June 20th, should have seen his old age crowned with true glory . . . But national vanity must be appeased and, as always in times of reverses, a scapegoat found to bear the shame of defeat in place and lieu of the nation.

It was only in the evening at Rethel that he learnt, from the despatches which Soult had delayed, of the abdication of Napoleon. His army was made up of 22,000 infantry, 5,000 cavalry and 104 guns, perfectly equipped, serviced and in battle order. 'Contact with the fugitives has somewhat weakened the morale of my soldiers,' he wrote to Davout, 'and has led to several desertions. I hope that the infection will not spread.' He was to reach Reims on the 25th, then Fismes and finally Soissons on the 26th. His liaison with the Army of the North, reorganized and stationed at Laon, Soissons, Craonne and Jonchery, was practically certain.

General d'Erlon commanded the 1st Corps, with 4,000 men; Reille the 2nd and 6th with 11,000; Kellermann, Milhaud, Jacquinot, Domon and Subervie commanded cavalry units amounting to roughly 4,000 sabres; the Guard mustered 9,000 men. In three days the arsenal at La Fère had sent five batteries. The artillery of the Guard had 1,000 gunners. There was no lack of supplies. Munitions and rifles were provided by the stores at Laon and Soissons. The stragglers and the wounded were sent to regimental depots.

Marshal Grouchy had 60,000 men who, according to his reports and those of Mouton-Duvernet, had regained their morale, but had again become angry and dispirited by the news of the abdication.

'The Emperor has just abdicated,' wrote Grouchy in his proclamation. 'He has thought fit to make this sacrifice in the interests of France . . . The Chambers have recognized his son as Emperor under the name of Napoleon II.

'What is now your duty? To be loyal to the new chief of the Empire as you have been to his august father; to rally around your eagles and to act in a heroic manner which will force the foreigners to respect your independence.'

'The foreigners'—150,000 English and Prussians—advanced slowly. Blücher's march, somewhat haphazard, for the mustering of his troops had been long and difficult because of the state of the roads, was by way of Noyales-sur-Sambre, near Guise. A brigade had taken Avesnes from a few National Guards and veterans after a score of cannon shots. Detachments of the 4th Corps (Bülow) advanced towards Maubeuge, Landrecies and Guise.

Wellington's army reached Le Cateau on June 22nd. The two commanders-in-chief met at Catillon on the 23rd. The Englishman, cold, methodical, trained in the Tory school, now preferred to play a political rather than a military role, to exercise on the French government an influence analogous to that wielded, in the previous year, by the Tsar. According to Castlereagh's instructions, the role of France must be reduced to that of an auxiliary of Great Britain in the future conflicts which seemed inevitable. Fouché was the man of his choice to facilitate the entry into Paris of Louis XVIII, whom he had brought with him in his train. On the contrary, Blücher, quick-tempered and vindictive, like the generals of the old German school, paid little heed to politics. Overbearing in words, imperious in action, he had kept the habits of the banks of the Elbe, loved quarrels, got drunk, often appeared in his shirtsleeves, and lost huge sums gambling.

The two men, so different in character, education and tastes, ended by agreeing. They decided to ignore the 'French debris', now certainly irrelevant, which were mustering at Laon. The main movement down the right bank of the Oise, aiming at Paris, would be masked by a light Prussian detachment, heavily laced with cavalry.

The itineraries: the Prussians via Saint-Quentin - Chauny - Noyon - Compiègne; the English via Le Cateau - Vermand (west of Saint-Quentin) - Péronne - Nesle - Creil. Crossing of the Oise at Compiègne, Pont Sainte-Maxence.

In this way the left flank of the French would be turned. Their retreat must be cut off and Paris must be reached before them. It would be a rapid march across unfamiliar country; no battles were to be fought.

'We have dealt Napoleon his death-blow,' wrote Wellington to Uxbridge on June 23rd. 'From all I learn, his army is totally destroyed; he can no longer stand up to us . . . He can only hang himself.'

Guise surrendered to von Jagow on June 24th. The English Colville division took Cambrai on the 24th and 25th, while the Prussians invested La Fère. The morale of the Allies was high, since Wellington and Blücher had just learnt that the French themselves had torn from Napoleon not only his crown but also his sword. What had they to fear?

On the northern and eastern frontiers the Austrian armies, till then immobile, had begun to advance.

On June 23rd the 4th Bavarian Corps (Field Marshal de Wrede — 60,000 men) crossed the Sarre at Sarrebrück and Sarreguemines; and the 3rd Corps (the Prince of Württemberg) crossed the Queich and marched on Wissembourg. But General Rapp, commanding the little army on the Moselle, having given up an offensive against Germersheim on hearing the news from Waterloo, took up his position on the Lauter with 20,000 first-class troops and resisted for thirty-six hours the threats of the first and the violent attacks of the second. Then, instead of with-drawing to Paris by way of Saverne and Nancy according to the Emperor's orders which he had not received, he retreated slowly along the Rhine from June 25th onward in order to get closer to Strasbourg. A battle for honour was to take place on the 28th in front of the city, before a withdrawal covered by the guns of the fortress.

The rest of Schwartzenberg's corps, concentrated on June 25th around Basle, on the 27th invested Huningue, which was defended by General Barbanègre, and clashed with the little corps (13,000 men) of General Abbé, hero of the armies of Italy and Spain. His command was taken over by Lecourbe on June

30th. Day after day, these stout fellows were to hold out, out-numbered two or three to one, in fierce combats at Dannemarie, Chavannes and Montbéliard, before entering Belfort where they were to receive news of the armistice on July 14th. Davout was to propose Lecourbe as a Marshal of France.

*   *   *

The 4th Russian Corps (Rajewski) protected the headquarters of the Allied sovereigns at Mannheim; it was to cross the Rhine on June 27th, marching on Haguenau, where the plenipotentiaries of the Provisional Government were due to arrive on the 30th.

On the Alpine frontier Suchet, with 17,000 men, began to march on June 14th from Chambéry towards Savoy. The Piemon-tese were driven out of Montmélian and the Desaix division was marching on Geneva, when an Austrian army coming from Italy appeared in two columns, one by the Simplon Pass (General Frimont) and the other by the Mont-Cenis Pass (General von Bubna). Trained in mountain warfare, Suchet's units resisted at Evian, in the Maurienne and the Tarentaise. But Suchet, the Duke of Albufera, asked for an armistice which was concluded on June 28th. However, Colonel Bugeaud at the head of his famous 14th Regiment of the Line, refusing to retire to Mont-mélian, stormed and captured the bridge at Conflans, taking 750 prisoners.

In the rear, the Russian armies in reserve remained in depth along forty leagues from the Rhine to the Main.

In the two camps, operations proceeded very slowly; the Allies were always in fear of an 'unexpected blow' from Napoleon. Soult considered that after the abdication a tacit armistice should be observed.

On June 24th Davout sent a proposal to the Prussian advance posts which was, however, rejected on the following day. Since neither he nor Soult had even dreamed of occupying Compiègne, Grouchy, arriving at Soissons on June 26th to take command of the Army of the North, learnt that the Prussians had been there since the morning! The withdrawal on Senlis, ordered by the Minister of War, was impossible; the enemy was in occupation. Kellermann had just escaped being caught with his cuirassiers. D'Erlon had slipped away to Dammartin-Gonesse. The rest of the army, Reille, Vandamme and the Guard, had skirmished on

Grouchy's orders with the Prussians at Villers-Cotterets and then set out for Claye . . . and Paris.

The Chambers, the Commission of Government and the royalists trembled before the rumblings of revolt and the approach of the Allies. Fouché was nearly abducted by a handful of Federals. The unrest reached the provinces, where the parties were more or less at one another's throats. In the north, prefects and generals reported riots and desertions. Some of the King's bodyguard roused the National Guards of Cambrai. White flags (that is to say royalist flags) floated here and there in the 16th military division (centred on Lille), and the command was entrusted by the King to the deserter Bourmont on June 21st! In Normandy they wanted Louis XVIII and peace. In the towns of Brittany, the Bonapartists set up altars with a bust of Napoleon among the flowers. In Vendée, on June 24th, the leaders of the revolt accepted the proposals of General Lamarque, commanding the Army of the Loire, an able negotiator and a passionate opponent of any sort of conflict between Frenchmen. In Alsace, Lorraine and Champagne, the patriots had the upper hand; after the news of the abdication, soldiers and National Guards took to the forests. Royalists were manhandled at Dijon, Moulins and Limoges. At Bordeaux, on June 25th, General Clausel, a strict martinet, maintained discipline among his troops . . . but the 66th of the Line swore hatred to the Bourbons before its colonel. At Lyons, posters announcing the defeat at Mont-Saint-Jean were torn down; the Federals paraded a bust of the Emperor through the streets, calling on *les purs* to 'September massacres' in the manner of St Bartholomew's Day. In the Midi there were bloody riots; at Montpellier murders of royalists. At Marseilles it was the other way round; fugitive mamelukes and the men from the regimental depot of the Guard were hideously massacred.

Fouché staked on all the tables. The same day he sent his friend Gaillard to Wellington to find out what he thought of the Duke of Orleans . . . of the conditions for peace; he was to ask for a passport which would allow him to appear before Louis XVIII to assure him of his loyalty. But he spoke of the King in coarse terms to La Fayette at the time of his departure for the headquarters of the Allied sovereigns.

Meanwhile the Emperor was talking at the Elysée with Benjamin Constant, who had come to take leave of him. Napoleon had not yet decided where he would go. 'Flight revolts me,' he said. 'I will go to Malmaison . . . And then? . . . To England? At the first sight of a green coat disembarking from the long-boat, some would fly and others cry "Outlaw!" By saying "He is coming" they will tempt me to come! . . . America would be better . . . But what have I to fear by staying in France?'

Outside the palace, 10,000 men and women were shouting for him.

UNDESIRABLE

Fouché knew the truth. Wellington had not concealed it from Gaillard. 'Neither peace nor truce until Bonaparte is handed over to Europe.' He had been branded by a Decree of Proscription at the Congress of Vienna; the warrant must be served. Place of exile: the island of Saint Helena.

That was why Fouché broadcast in Paris, to the army and the people: 'The one obstacle to peace is Bonaparte . . . He must be handed over to save the country and the integrity of the national territory . . .'

'We shall have a generous and honourable peace when we have rid ourselves of that powerful and popular man . . .' Manuel, Mourgue and Lanjuinais said in the Chamber.

Fouché wanted first of all to get the Emperor out of Paris, where there was a danger of riots. At the same time, in order to confuse both his colleagues and the Bonapartists, he would ask the Allies for passports allowing Napoleon to leave France, knowing very well that they would never be granted, but he forbade him to be provided with official means of leaving the country lest the Allies claim him and make his committal a con-dition of peace. Not daring to appear again before the man he had betrayed, Fouché sent Marshal Davout to pledge Napoleon to leave the capital.

*   *   *

June 24th, in the afternoon. The Prince of Eckmühl (Davout) entered the courtyard of the Elysée, bullied the officers whom he found there, reproaching them for being lazy and keeping out of danger. Then, having been announced, he went in to the Emperor. Icily he explained his mission.

Filled with scorn for this marshal who, laden with so many

111

honours, had so easily deserted him, Napoleon reacted violently, thundered against renegades, peers, deputies, ministers . . . against 'the five emperors' of the Provisional Government.

'Had I wanted to place myself at the head of the people, which realizes the real needs of the country, I would soon have finished with all these braggarts who only have courage to face me when they see me defenceless . . . Now they want me to go!'

Davout remained impassive and Napoleon turned away. The victor of Jéna and the victor of Auerstädt left one another without a handshake, without a sign of emotion, never again to see one another.

What had happened to Davout? Involved in 1814 in the plots against the Bourbons whom he detested, he had, after the return of the Emperor, advised the prorogation of the Chambers and condemned the intervention of La Fayette who, he wrote, 'had consummated the suicide of the country'. Did he suddenly believe in the authority of the national representation?

'Is Malmaison yours?' the Emperor asked Hortense just before dinner.

'No, Sire . . . After my mother's death it fell to my brother Eugène . . . But it's just as if it were mine.'

He expressed his wish to go there and asked her to stay with him. He would leave on June 25th and did not want to occupy the Empress' apartments.

And later? Had he made up his mind?

That evening the Marshal of the Household, always afraid of running short, drew up a request to Baron Desmazis, administrator of the Crown property, 'that sufficient to furnish a town house, a country house and a few rooms for the suite be put at the disposition of His Majesty'. Scrupulously Bertrand stated the number of rooms: 'Two salons, eight rooms for personal use in the town, two apartments for personal use and several for his suite in the country . . . '

There followed an impressive list of furniture: 'Eight iron or mahogany bedsteads with taffeta coverings and bed-linen; ten complete suites for rooms and salons, with fittings and loose covers; four screens, ten carpets, material for wall hangings and curtains; six chests in bronze, elm and mahogany, two writing desks, couches; big chandeliers, clocks, bibelots, china . . . The furniture necessary for two personal apartments and several for the suite . . . The objects, stored in a repository, will not be sent to Malmaison without further advice.'

On this strange demand, sent to the Commission of Government, Fouché wrote 'Hold'!

At her house in the Rue Cerutti, Queen Hortense replied to the musings of her reader, Mlle. Cochelet, who pointed out to her the danger she was running . . . It was one more reason to prove to her father-in-law her affection and devotion. She at once sent her children to Madame Tessier, a stocking merchant, who agreed to take them under the supervision of Mlle. Bure, the 'pretty wet-nurse' of the youngest, and left for Malmaison, where the windows had not been opened since early spring.

Meanwhile, at the Elysée, the Emperor looked through his personal correspondence with the European sovereigns, ordered his aides-de-camp to burn the letters received since March 20th, read one or two of them, threw some on the fire and gave several which might be of value to him later to Fleury de Chaboulon.

Documents about those dramatic days are very few. Here, however, is one, quite unpublished. Jean-Baptiste Esdouhard, mayor of Beaune (Côte d'Or), Count of the Empire, deputy during the Hundred Days of the Chamber of Representatives, after having been at the Convention during the Revolution, writes in his *Journal-Mémorial*:

'Paris, June 25, 1815.

'Yesterday I returned exhausted from the meeting of the Chamber. To relax a bit, I walked back through the boulevards. Everything was quiet; even the night was a fine one.

'The day before, my wife and I had paid our respects to Queen Hortense; from her we had learnt of the Emperor's intention to withdraw, from today, to Malmaison and to wait there for the safe-conducts that he needs. After telling this to my colleagues, General Vaux and the Attorney-General, Chantrier (both of them deputies of the Côte d'Or), we all three decided to try to see the Emperor at the Elysée before his departure. Queen Hortense had given me a letter to Marchand (the Emperor's personal valet) so that he could admit us to his master without having to wait too long. We were there that morning, about eight o'clock.

'As we entered we passed Carnot who was just coming out. He told us that the Emperor was calm, that he had made up his mind to do what he believed to be his duty and that, after chatting amicably with him, the Emperor had assured him that he would leave that very day for Malmaison ... Carnot added that he had dissuaded him from his proposal to surrender to the English, amongst whom he had too many irreconcilable enemies, and had advised him to try and get to America instead. There, he said, his presence might even be useful to our country in case of need. For, Carnot went on, I insisted in my opinion that, at the present moment, Napoleon, by his origins, represented the country itself, and that he might become its Palladium against royalist reaction. We replied that that was our viewpoint too and asked him if it were Fouché's also. He alone can tell you, he muttered as he went away.

'I could see that he had no trust in Fouché's patriotism, nor, for that matter, in Talleyrand's. The one in Paris, the other in Vienna, were playing a role which, I fear, could only be hurtful for the future of those liberties for which we had struggled so hard for twenty years. Carnot's uprightness and patriotism always makes him believe that others feel the same. For my part I do not share any of the illusions that he has about Fouché who, at the present moment, must be thinking only how to safeguard his own interests. Berlier (secretary of the Provisional Government and a friend of Esdouhard) told me that he was at that very moment preparing to marry a Castellane, an avowed royalist, in order to win the favour of Louis XVIII in case we should have the misfortune of seeing him restored by the foreigners and reddened by the blood of Frenchmen.

'When we reached the antechamber I went up to Marchand who was standing at the door of the Emperor's study and handed him the letter from Queen Hortense. The room was already full of people and I was afraid that we might have to wait a long time for our turn. But almost at once that amiable young man admitted us to the Emperor, who told us that he thought we must be in a hurry to go to the Chamber and thanked us for our vote in favour of his son, as Queen Hortense had told him in her letter to Marchand. We reminded him of our visit together, all three of us, to Chalon, where he had passed the night last March and assured him that, since we were still prompted by the same sentiments, we would continue to defend, in the person of his son, the cause that was in the true interests of the nation and that our Burgundians were in complete accord with their representatives.

'Just then loud cries of "Long live the Emperor!" sounded from without.

' "Listen to them," he exclaimed. "They are calling for me, and yet I must go since it is expected of me and I have promised . . . "

'Our emotion was deep-felt. I was anxious to tell him that for the twenty-one years since I had had the honour of meeting him for the first time at the Empress Josephine's, then Madame de Beauharnais, I had never forgotten the marks of good-will shown me both by him and by her and that my gratitude and my loyalty were undying. He gave me his hand saying: "I thank you for remembering those things and for reminding me of them today." My eyes filled with tears and I could only bow without replying, for the look that the Emperor gave me remains for me the most precious of all the favours that he could have granted me.'

Outside, the news spread quickly. The Emperor was leaving the Elysée. Perhaps too moved to face the enthusiasm of the people, or perhaps fearing to give way to it, Napoleon, on the plea of some of his servants influenced by Fouché, went on foot accompanied by Bertrand to the gate that led into the Champs-Elysées where the carriage of the Marshal of the Household was waiting. Both disappeared into it. Noverraz, footman in the imperial stables, shut the door and leapt on to the box; the berline, like so many others, passed unnoticed and vanished swiftly in the direction of the Barrière du Roule.

Meanwhile, in the Faubourg Saint-Honoré, held back by the Guards outside the gates of the palace, the crowd was shouting 'Long live the Emperor!' on seeing Napoleon's six-in-hand leave, surrounded by an escort, with his equerry, Baron de Montaran, riding at the door; other carriages followed bearing aides-de-camp. A picket brought up the rear. It was only on the far side of the barrière, after joining the official procession, that the Emperor got into his coach, while Bertrand, Montholon and Las Cases, M. de Beauveau, the orderly officers, Gourgaud, Planat de la Faye, Résigny, Chiappe, Saint-Yon, Saint-Jacques, Autric, and the young page Sainte-Catherine d'Audiffredi, nephew of the Empress Josephine, took their places in the other carriages. The staff had left earlier; 'the very numerous kitchen', 'the Household as at Paris'.

At half-past one the procession entered the courtyard of the Château. The Emperor was greeted by Queen Hortense. She was, she wrote, greatly moved 'to see him again in the depths of misfortune', whom she had known, in this very place, 'at the height of his glory and happiness'. An officer and twenty-five chasseurs and grenadiers from the Rueil depot, and a picket of the dragoons of the Guard presented arms and assured the protection of the Emperor.

Hortense had set the whole south wing of the château aside for him and kept the apartments on the north for those who accompanied him. The 'little gallery' (the present music-room) was converted into a dining-room. The Emperor went into the audience hall. No one! Once they had jostled one another to see him. 'It is always the same,' said Gourgaud. 'Many people whom we see in days of prosperity abandon us in adversity.'

Crossing the former billiard-room, the dining-room and the hall of counsel, he went into the library which he had always used as a study. Nothing was changed; the pedestal table in the middle of the room, the busts of Josephine and himself between the columns. Jacob's bookcases were still filled with books bearing the Empress' cypher (P. B. La Pagerie Bonaparte); on the huge desk a book of history was marked at the page where, at one time, he had broken off his reading. There were the same pens on the mahogany writing desk; in front of the window the same globe he had so often turned carelessly . . . some 'relics' as the Empress Josephine had called those familiar objects that she had dusted in person.

Filled with memories, he stopped before each piece of furniture; then he went back to his desk, perhaps dreaming of the countless notes and orders he had sent out from it, and dictated his farewell:

'TO THE ARMY

'Malmaison, June 25, 1815.

"Soldiers! When I bow to the necessity that forces me to go

far from the gallant French army I take with me the happy assurance that it will justify, by the outstanding services that our country expects, the praises that even our enemies have been unable to withhold.

'Soldiers! Although absent, I will follow you step by step. I know all the corps and not one of them shall win any conspicuous advantage over the enemy without my rendering justice to the courage that it will have displayed. You and I, we have been slandered. Men unworthy of appreciating your deeds have seen, in the marks of devotion you have given me, a zeal of which I was the sole object. Let your future exploits teach them that it was our country above all that you served by obeying me and that, if I have any part in your affection, I owe it to my burning love for our common mother, France.

'Soldiers! A few more efforts and the Coalition will fall to pieces. Napoleon will recognize you by the blows that you will give.

'Save the honour and the independence of the French; remain to the end such as I have known you for twenty years and you will be invincible.'

Since he had renounced power, he signed himself: Napoleon I.

Sent to the government to be published in the *Moniteur* and to be read by the troops, this last proclamation of the Emperor to his soldiers was to remain unknown. It rests today among the War Archives.

Fouché had thrown it into a drawer.

At Rochefort, the port-admiral received a letter from the minister Decrès, dated June 23rd, announcing the abdication of the Emperor:

'Great events have taken place which have led to a great sacrifice by Napoleon. You will see in the *Moniteur* that the trust of the nation now rests upon the two Chambers . . . They have appointed a Commission of Government to carry on the executive powers . . . I know your feelings too well to believe that I have any admonishments to give you. Do all in your power to curb the enemy from without, should it exist . . . There will be some who will not accept with alacrity the will of the

French people as shown in the organ of government appointed by the Chambers. Men pass; France is immortal.

'Let us therefore redouble our zeal and our courage; let us make ready for struggles to obtain a peace worthy of a nation determined to preserve its independence, cost what it may, a peace whose postponement cannot long be delayed if it be true, as one must believe after their formal declarations, that the foreigners fought only against Napoleon.

'DUKE DECRÈS.'

Captain Bonnefoux, port-admiral of Rochefort, made the most of these exhortations and sent a copy of the letter to the units under his command: 'Captains in command in the port and at the island of Aix; Captain Philibert commanding the port division of the island of Aix; the frigates *Saale* and *Méduse*, the brig *Epervier*, gunboat No. 135, patrol-boats Nos. 24 and 2, the *Dédaigneuse*; Captain Coudein, commanding the 14th Seaborne Marines, formed at Rochefort from the 27th and 28th ships' companies by Imperial decree of April 26th last.'

Chapter IV

THE FIRST STAGE

MALMAISON

Having learnt of Napoleon's inconspicuous arrival at Malmaison from his colleagues in the Commission of Government Fouché revealed his uneasiness to them. What if he escaped? Rueil is so near Paris! Generals and partisans could reach the château through the forests, neutralize or win over the soldiers of the guard, carry off Napoleon and put him at the head of the army which was clamouring for him, and thus continue the struggle. During the session the Commission decided to send General Beker, representative of Puy-de-Dôme, to Malmaison 'to ensure the Emperor's safety'.

Queen Hortense and the officers in the great salon at Malmaison were also uneasy; what if Fouché's clique carried off the Emperor in order to hand him over to the enemy? He must be roused from his indecision, demand frigates and passports, reach America as soon as possible. La Bédoyère would organize the defence of the château; officers would come from Paris every evening to mount guard.

Now more self-assured, Napoleon received visitors in his study; Joseph, Jérôme, etc. Lucien had just left (on the morning of the 25th) his splendid residence at the Palais-Royal, armed with several passports in different names issued by Fouché. He had galloped to Boulogne and there chartered a ship; but, having met Otto on his way to London and far from optimistic, he feared he might be held by the English and retraced his steps without telling anyone. He reached Turin, where he was lodged in the citadel under surveillance, by order of the King of Sardinia.

Here was Savary. The shilly-shallying and ambiguous replies by Fouché to the demands for passports and frigates boded ill. In any case, he had agreed to follow the Emperor into exile.

Then came La Vallette.

'And you?' asked the Emperor. 'Drouot remains in France;

the minister wants to keep him in the country . . . It is a great loss to me . . . the best brain and the most faithful heart I have met . . . That man is born to be a minister . . . '

But La Vallette felt forced to refuse; he had a girl of thirteen; his wife was four months pregnant . . . 'Give me a little time and I will come to join you wherever you are. I have been loyal to Your Majesty in better times; Your Majesty may count on me. In any case, if my wife did not need every care, I would do better to leave, for I have gloomy presentiments about my fate . . .'

The Emperor did not reply.

'I went to see Monge,' wrote d'Esdouhard in his *Notebook*. 'His sadness is as deep as ours . . . his admiration for Napoleon's magnanimity was, if possible, still greater. Like myself, he envied those who could follow him and serve him in his misfortune.'

Would Bassano, who had just been received by the Emperor, be among them?

An officer announced General Beker, representing the government. Hortense burst into tears; was he going to arrest the Emperor? Ushered at once into the library, he said with a bow: 'Sire! Here is an order (from the Minister of War) which entrusts me, in the name of the Provisional Government, with the command of your guard to assure the safety of your person.'

'Paris, June 25, 1815. Four o'clock in the afternoon.
'To General Beker.

'I have the honour to inform you that the Commission of Government has appointed you to command the guard of the Emperor Napoleon at Malmaison.

'The honour of France requires you to watch over the safety of his person and the respect that is due to him. The interests of the country demand that evil-disposed persons be prevented from making use of his name to stir up unrest.

'Sir, your character is a guarantee for the government and for France that you will carry out this twofold task. I ask you to go at once to Malmaison to make yourself known to the guard there and to take all measures to fulfil this duty.

'I am, dear General,

'Marshal and Minister of War,

'PRINCE OF ECKMÜHL.'

Napoleon protested. 'Monsieur, I should have been officially informed of an action which I regard as a matter of form and not as a measure of surveillance to which it is useless to subject me, seeing that I have no intention of breaking my word.'

'Sire,' Beker replied with emotion, 'it was with the sole object of protecting you and watching over your safety that I accepted this mission; if it does not obtain the consent and full approval of Your Majesty I will immediately withdraw.'

And, as his eyes filled with tears:

'Be assured, General,' the Emperor said to him with much tenderness and goodwill, 'I am very pleased to have you near me. If they had given me the choice of an officer, I would have named you for preference, since I have long been aware of your loyalty.'

Napoleon pretended to believe that he was not now a prisoner.

Who was Beker? An Alsatian from Obernai, forty-five years old and brother-in-law of Desaix, whose sister he had married. As dragoon, chasseur and hussar, he had participated in all the campaigns of the Revolution. Brigade commander in 1795, Chief of Staff of the Army of the Sambre-et-Meuse and that of Saint-Domingue, he had been promoted brigadier-general in 1801 and general of division in 1805. He had commanded with distinction the dragoon divisions of the Grande Armée and had fought at Zehdenick and Pultusk. Count of Mons (Puy-de-Dôme) in 1808, he became Chief of Staff of the 4th Corps (Masséna) at Essling. A little later, having violently criticized the Emperor's orders, he was sent back to France, placed on half-pay and finally retired in 1811. Recalled to service by the King on June 3, 1814, he had been elected representative of Puy-de-Dôme on May 8, 1815 and, on June 20th, 'by order of the Emperor, put at the disposition of General Grenier for the defence of Paris'.

Beker therefore had every reason to bear a grudge against Napoleon who had broken his career. It was for this reason that Fouché and Davout had chosen him. But, though stubborn and hard-headed, Beker was a good soldier and devoted to his duty. Very dissatisfied with the mission confided to him, he had in vain pleaded his rights as a representative and then, as he wrote, 'burdened with a heavy responsibility, I took the road for Malmaison, leaving to Paris the intrigues and cabals which were being plotted on all sides . . .'

Napoleon took him for a stroll in the gardens. Ill at ease with this man whom he had scarcely ever seen, this dreaded sovereign with nothing left to him save his enormous prestige, Beker did not know what to do. Was he, from then on, subject to him as to a gaoler? Overwhelmed with doubts, he stammered, made excuses, his eyes filled with tears.

'What are they saying in Paris? What are they doing?' the Emperor asked him.

The general replied that the parties were divided: 'They have differing views about the abdication and the proclamation of your son as heir . . . ' A section of high society was ready to receive the foreigners a second time, but the remnants of the army, now mustered under the walls of the capital, had remained loyal and were ready to put up a defence. A part of the people and of the bourgeoisie had also remained loyal. 'If a strong hand could rally all these elements and make a last effort to preserve the dynasty at the head of the nation, the situation would not be so desperate.'

Beker was mistaken, or pretended to be mistaken. Except for a million Frenchmen, the rest were indifferent. That evening, in Paris, they were taking the air in the Tuileries, the theatres were packed, the cafés turning away custom! The Town Council sent a delegation to Fouché to implore him not to defend the capital. Anyone who had a flat or a lodging or a shop regarded the struggle as a crime. Pamphlets circulated: 'For whom are we fighting?', 'What can we hope for?', 'Put an end to all this!' As Talleyrand said: 'Anything rather than the Emperor, even the Bourbons!'

All those who had denied the Revolution to rush to Saint-Cloud to applaud the Emperor in 1804, had acclaimed Louis XVIII the previous year, and had rushed to the Tuileries on March 20th, now once again turned their coats. Prices soared on the exchanges . . . 'Above all, let's get back to business.'

Napoleon was very well aware of it. 'Everything is upside down,' he said. 'No one cares any more.' Under a starry sky, the Emperor went back to the château.

'I have asked for two frigates and passports to go to the United States,' he told Beker on taking leave of him, 'but I must still be able to get to them without falling into the hands of my enemies . . . Those fellows would hand me over . . . I cannot

122

leave without ships and without passports; otherwise the first
village mayor would arrest me . . . It would be enough if someone were to tell him that I was taking valuables away with
me . . . ' He would write to Paris. The Provisional Government
would not reply. Things would take their course and everything
would end in disaster.

'If they agree to my demand, I will renounce any part in
public affairs; I will leave at once for Rochefort. If not, I will
apply to the Chambers. I will go amongst them and see what
happens and leave to them the job of handing me over to the
enemy.'

A visitor was waiting for him : M. Laffitte.

'I was sent for by the Emperor to be here at half-past eight, at
the request of the Marshal of the Household,' he said to M. de
Montholon, the chamberlain on duty. 'It is now nine o'clock. I
would not like my lateness to be construed as a lack of respect. Is
there no way of letting him know that I obeyed his orders
punctually . . . '

A minute later, through the double doors of the library, he
was welcomed by the Emperor, 'calm, self-assured, with nothing
changed of his fine presence'.

'Well, M. Laffitte, how goes it?' he said, smiling. 'Can you
find me a ship to get to America?'

'At these words a deathly chill ran through me,' wrote the
banker in his *Mémoires*. 'It was long before I could reply. The
victor of Jéna, of Austerlitz, of Marengo, the man who once
kept all the sovereigns of Europe waiting in his ante-chamber,
the master of almost the whole world . . . To see this
colossus, overthrown, trying to escape by ship and to flee to
America . . . '

'Yes, Sire, I will get you one, even if it costs me my life.'

The Emperor took a packet of banknotes from his desk :

'Here you are,' he said. 'Here are 800,000 francs. I will send
you tonight, in a wagon, three millions in gold. M. de la Vallette
and Prince Eugène will hand over to you 1,200,000 francs . . . I
will have my decorations placed in your carriage. That is all I
have left. You will look after them for me.'

Seating himself at the Emperor's desk, in his armchair (!),
Laffitte began to write.

'What are you doing?' the Emperor asked, catching hold of his arm.

'Giving you a receipt.'

'I don't need one.'

'I might die. I must keep the secret; since this sum will not be entered in my books, you must have some sort of title to it.'

'And if I should be arrested en route, it might compromise you.'

'When I do a service, I do not consider the danger.'

'No matter! I must consider it for you. I don't want one.'

'So large a sum handed over without title!' wrote Laffitte. 'The remnants of his fortune, the bread of his exile! I had never received so magnificent a proof of trust, nor anything that moved me so deeply.'

'You have never been a warm supporter of my system of government,' added the Emperor, 'but I know you; you are a man of honour . . .'

And after Laffitte had declared his political convictions:

'Bah! Bah! Your representative government! An English folly . . . To rule France one needs iron hands in velvet gloves.'

Louis-Philippe's future Prime Minister was to remember this phrase of the Emperor, his expression 'for a moment or two severe', and then the charm of a meeting in which for two hours they discussed his position and the world situation. For 'he talked of everything, covering the present, the past and the future, without repeating himself, without vanity, without false modesty, as one talks of history, impartially'.

Then the conversation turned to the United States, its trade, its customs and the way of life of its people, whose qualities Laffitte was far from appreciating.

'So it's a boring country to live in!' concluded Napoleon. 'Goodbye to all the charming conversations and cultivated society of Paris! Farewell to the arts, farewell to the sciences! I shall have no other sympathy with them than a common hatred of the English!'

'You would not be alone there for long, Sire,' went on Laffitte. 'But can you get there? . . . That is what worries me . . .'

'What do you mean?'

'Fouché is already in league with the Bourbons and the Holy

Alliance. Will you be able to get away from here? Aren't you already being watched?'

'Fouché will betray me, that I know,' replied the Emperor. 'He always has a finger in every pie.'

Fearing to have discouraged him, Laffitte recommended caution and affirmed his faith in the future. 'The blunders of the Bourbons will lead to your return,' he said.

'Don't deceive yourself,' Napoleon went on. 'The tricolour will always be dear to the hearts of the people, but the Bourbons will last longer than you think. Be prudent and discreet in your words. Be on your guard against them and against your gaolers. Europe is absurd; the peoples march and the governments do not budge!'

Sketching out a prophetic picture, he went on: 'Don't dream of anything sensational; my son can do nothing for you; his name will resound for another fifty years in Poland and in Italy; his grandfather will allow him to go on living, but that is all. This is not the time to concern yourself with systems and undertakings; the dice are too heavily stacked against you . . . Wait! Poor France! Above all, do not compromise her independence . . . perhaps better opportunities will come. Do not let them slip . . .'

The Emperor seemed to have recovered his poise. He held his listener by the charm of his clear, exact, picturesque turn of phrase, the profundity of his thinking. 'I felt as if I would never tire of listening to him and admiring him. He seemed to me the best man in the world,' wrote Laffitte. Perhaps, on the eve of losing his sovereign power, on leaving France and his people, he still thought that his career was not yet over; that the cabinets of old Europe and the efforts of the peoples to win their freedom, that the Spanish colonies, might have need of him to awaken them.

Laffitte smiled.

'Why are you amused?'

On his reply that it was only something silly, not worth considering, the Emperor insisted.

'You are going to America,' the banker replied. 'What if after being Emperor of the French you should become Emperor of Mexico!'

What couldn't he do in that rich country, semi-civilized and enslaved, with his supporters, the outlaws, the discontented, his glory and his genius?

'I do not know what is in store for me,' he replied, 'I am well, I sleep and wake up when I like. I can spend four hours on horseback and work ten hours a day. I am not very expensive to feed; a little game in the morning, at dinner a cut off the sirloin and a half-bottle of wine. With a louis I can live very well anywhere . . . We shall see.'

He had once more become the artillery lieutenant, the youthful owner of Malmaison, the magnificent dreamer, ready to begin life again.

It struck eleven. 'Heavens! It is very late and you have a long way to go,' he said, stifling his emotion.

'I went out with eyes filled with tears,' ended Laffitte. 'I took away in my carriage the 800,000 francs and his decorations. I received the wagon with the 3,000,000 in gold and, next day, sent him a letter of credit for 3,800,000 francs on my American correspondents.[1]

'He did not mention again the ship that I was to get for him.' Why?

By the little staircase which led into the shrubbery below the library, Napoleon went up to his room, which was exactly above. Marchand was waiting for him; he served dinner at once and said that during the afternoon he had been wandering about in the Elysée and had brought back with him 'a few small portable objects' which could be of use: some silver-gilt cassolettes, the large miniature of the King of Rome by Isabey, the portrait of the Empress, the fine tripod of swans' necks with the large bowl and the silver ewer which the Emperor used every day after shaving. He had visited Mesdames Pellapra and Walewska. 'The countess intends to come tomorrow with her son.' Madame Pellapra expressed 'her regrets at not daring to come to Malmaison without express orders . . . '

In the great salon there was a silent group, overcome by grief. Would there be an emergency on the morrow? . . . They

[1] On April 25, 1821, at Saint Helena, the Emperor wrote a letter to M. Laffitte ordering him to hand over after his death (May 5th) to the Count de Montholon his decorations and the money in trust for him, with interest at five per cent from July 1, 1815, after deducting all payments he had been told to make on his orders.

would keep vigil all night. Beker, invited to dinner by Queen Hortense, spoke of the Emperor's wish to go to America . . . but what preparations was he making? What means had he at his disposal? Passports were merely a farce . . .

Midnight. In Paris, Davout had received Grouchy's letter sent from Rethel on the 24th in which he had given a report of his march on Soissons. He replied to the Marshal immediately:

'June 25th, at midnight.

'I have just received your letter of the 24th and am hastening to communicate its contents to the Commission of Government which, without doubt, will speak in the name of all France in proclaiming that you, the generals under you and the troops have served the country well. The gratitude of the nation, I would like to believe, could not be better bestowed.

'You must base your movements on your left wing, occupying Compiègne, including Pontoise, and holding all the bridges over the Oise, setting up temporary defences and placing batteries behind them. There are stores available in Compiègne which can supply your army. Until your services are properly organized, draw your provisions from Reims.

'There is much disorder in the 1st, 2nd and 6th Corps. As I instructed you yesterday evening, take strong measures and have letters sent to all the communes telling them to arrest looters and bring them to your headquarters. It is my experience that a drastic example is enough to restore order.

'Send me a detailed report of your actions, so that all France may know them. Let me know the names of the officers and soldiers you think should be rewarded.

'There is a rather bad feeling among the inhabitants of Soissons and the country around. Warn your generals and officers. Put the gendarmes on watch at the posting-stations. Try to get in touch with the garrison at Laon to improve its morale. You will send cavalry detachments commanded by good officers to get into touch with La Fère and Ham, and to get definite news of the enemy columns which are there.

'Be assured of my respect and high consideration.'

Davout was now considering the proposals made him by Marshal Oudinot. Denounced by the Minister of Police as being a regular visitor at the secret meetings held at the house of

M. Vitrolles, the royalist centre in the Rue Saint-Florentin, Oudinot, summoned by Davout, had 'given his word' that he had never had any intention of leading a royalist coup . . . Then the two marshals had discussed the situation. Oudinot considered that 'all resistance is futile; the King must be accepted'. It would be even better to call on him to take the throne of France, stipulating certain conditions. Davout protested. Oudinot insisted. No one was in a better position than the minister to bring about the union of all Frenchmen. If he drew up proposals, Oudinot would submit them to Vitrolles 'who has full powers'.

The marshals were to meet again. Meanwhile, in the shadow of Saint-Germain-des-Prés, Rue de Tarane, General de Tromelin and his son were getting into their carriage to go to Wellington's headquarters to try to get passports for Napoleon. Royalist and loyal soldier, he had been the last to quit the field of Waterloo, the last to leave the army. He had reached Laon on June 23rd and Paris on the night of the 24th. A summons from Fouché awaited him. Tromelin has left an account of his interview, on the morning of the 25th, with Fouché, whose pupil he had been thirty-five years earlier at the Military School of Vendôme.

'What is the army doing?' Fouché asked him, after making enquiries about the military situation.

'It has regained its morale and puts its faith in Napoleon,' Tromelin replied.

The president of the government did not insist. He posed discreetly as the plaything of circumstances, without revealing that he himself had provoked them. He went on: 'The Emperor has taken refuge at Malmaison . . . the shadow of the King of Rome has been removed . . . so we come, inevitably, to Louis XVIII, now at Cambrai behind Wellington's lines. But what are the real intentions of the Allies with regard to Napoleon, who has himself asked to withdraw? It is important to let them know the real situation in Paris, where the influence of the Emperor is so great that it needs much effort to counteract it . . . Then too, there are many factors in favour of a regency; a movement of the Federals, the presence of the Bonaparte family in Paris, the support of a fraction of the Chambers, not to speak of the detachments coming from the regimental depots to reinforce the army . . . one and all, these are for him.

'The Commission of Government has therefore decided to send

an envoy to ask for passports for Napoleon to go to England (sic) . . . It is in the interest of the Emperor and of the government that he should be able to leave France as soon as possible.

'Nobody is better qualified than Tromelin, royalist in sentiments, liberal in views, a general of the Emperor, a diplomat, knowing the English well, with whom he formerly served, knowing their character and their language, to go to the Duke of Wellington.

'If he accepts, the order for his mission is ready and will be signed this evening, in his presence, by the members of the Council.'

'Not seeing in this mission anything dishonourable and which a general, with respect for his uniform, could not undertake.' wrote Tromelin, 'I bowed and prepared to withdraw.'

Fouché kept him for a moment longer. 'We must also know the views of the British government and its allies about the return of Louis XVIII, about the trust they may have in the Commission of Government and especially in its president being able to affirm the royal authority, the only way to reconcile all parties and bring the revolution to an end . . . Naturally, if the Duke of Wellington should agree to discuss such matters, the general will report 'only' to the President . . . '

The King would thus get to know the role played in favour of his restoration by the former regicide.

Had Tromelin's mission any other aim, as Thibaudeau, Boulay, Savary, La Vallette, etc., have written? To warn the English of Napoleon's projected departure, to give them the chance to prevent it by intensifying the blockade of the coast? It is possible. Bignon, Minister of Foreign Affairs, wrote the same day to Lord Castlereagh to ask him to grant passports. Both of them knew perfectly well that they would be refused. Dupe or not, Tromelin agreed and at ten o'clock that evening received, in the presence of the Commission, his orders for the mission accrediting him to the Duke of Wellington. It was a question (naturally) 'of obtaining passports for Napoleon as quickly as possible . . . '

On returning home very late the general found awaiting him 'a person who had come from Malmaison, on behalf of the Emperor, with a similar request'.

Who was he? Who had been able to warn the Emperor of the mission entrusted to Tromelin? We do not know. Could it have

E

been Savary, who wrote: 'The Emperor wants to go to America . . . or England, if there is not time . . . '

In a letter dated June 26th from Planat, the orderly officer, we read: 'The Emperor has asked the English government for passports to go to America.'

In any case, Tromelin was well on his way along the Soissons road, towards Grouchy's headquarters.

INTRIGUES

Midday, June 26th. Night had brought counsel at Malmaison.

'Very early in the morning' Beker wrote a letter to Davout which reached its destination about nine o'clock. It was a report of his conversation with the Emperor the previous evening. 'Let me have two frigates and I will leave at once for Rochefort . . . His Majesty realizes the claims that the enemy may make on his person; he is anxious to leave France in order to escape this catastrophe, the shame of which, he says, will fall upon the nation.'

Despite his hopes and the optimism buoyed up by the continual reports of the devotion of the army, Napoleon understood that he no longer had freedom of movement. The Allies were advancing from all sides, with no obstacles before them. If he went away, they would arrest him, thanks to Fouché's complicity. Siéyès had warned him that this might happen and the day before Savary had expressed his fears about it. As he told Beker, it would be better to leave for Rochefort as quickly as possible, wait there for the passports and, as soon as they arrived, leave France on board a frigate. Savary, sent early in the morning to Paris, would make the demand.

But Fouché, to whom Davout had sent Beker's letter about nine o'clock that morning, was so involved in his intrigues and his letters to Wellington that he would not even hear of Napoleon's departure.

'The Minister of Marine has written to me about some frigates,' he said innocently to Savary, 'but I don't quite understand what he wants. It is too late to see to that today, but you may rest assured that it will be settled tomorrow morning.'

'I will come back tomorrow for the frigates,' replied Savary, 'but about the passports, for which you alone are responsible, the Emperor, who is anxious to leave, has asked me to demand them from you.'

'That is different . . . Where does the Emperor want to go?'

'Where can he go, except to America?'

'That's the first I have heard of it. I do not want to take the responsibility of letting him go . . . I will ask for passports for him from My Lord Wellington. I want my reputation safe-guarded in the eyes of the nation.'

As many lies as empty phrases. Even worse.

Summoned by Davout, Beker returned to Malmaison in the evening with some extracts from a departmental order:

'Article 1. The Minister of Marine will give orders that the two frigates in the port of Rochefort will be made ready to transport Napoleon Bonaparte to the United States.

'Article 2. Up to the point of embarkation he will be provided with an escort under the command of General Beker, who is responsible for his safety.

. . . .

'Article 5. The frigates will not leave the roadstead before the safe-conducts have arrived.'

It was a question of getting the Emperor out of Paris where, canvassed from all sides, his presence was becoming more and more embarrassing, of keeping him prisoner at Rochefort and of driving him little by little towards the English who were keeping watch on his departure by sea and would certainly not let him slip through their hands.

That morning, walking in the gardens with Hortense in won-derful weather, he recalled memories of the Consulate. 'Poor Josephine,' he said. 'I cannot get used to living here without her! I always seem to see her coming along one of these walks and picking the flowers she loved so much. Poor Josephine . . . Any-way, she would be very unhappy just now. We only quarrelled about one thing . . . her debts, and I scolded her about them often enough! She had more charm than anyone I have ever known . . . the best heart!'

Then, after a pause: 'Have another portrait made of her; I would like it to be a medallion.'

On the Rueil road, the traffic increased; horsemen, carriages, moving in both directions. Flahaut and La Bédoyère, coming from Paris, said that everything was quiet there; 'only a few royalists walking about with their noses in the air . . . ' 'However, our young people,' wrote Queen Hortense, 'are once more beginning to prepare for an attack.'

Pistol shots . . . in the gardens! The patrols of dragoons search for the miscreants . . . no one. Government agents, who want to scare the Emperor! In the courtyard carriages were setting down visitors, who were received immediately. They were those who remained loyal to the Emperor, the men of the Tuileries, generals . . . Colonel Sencier, aide-de-camp to General Exelmans, commanding the Army of the North, 'implored the Emperor to cast away his fetters and rejoin his soldiers'.

Baron Peyrusse was announced. The Emperor had ordered him to sell a 5% Consolidated Bond for 15,150 francs in the name of 'Napoléon Buonaparte' but, as the faithful treasurer pointed out to him, a power of attorney was necessary. The Emperor snapped at him. 'Write,' he said curtly, 'M. le Baron Peyrusse. Sell my bond for 15,150 francs and remit the proceeds to me . . . On which, I pray God . . . ' and signed it 'N'.

'The Transfer Office requires a power of attorney,' Peyrusse explained.

'Refer to my lawyer.'

'I have foreseen Your Majesty's wishes,' Peyrusse replied. 'The lawyer is in the anteroom.'

Brought in at once, Maître Noël presented the document that he had drawn up.

After reading: 'Before us . . . His Majesty, Napoléon Buonaparte . . . ' the Emperor turned brusquely to him, looked at the two men one after the other, and, without saying a word, signed: 'Napoléon'.

Then, after a timid observation by Peyrusse that the bond bore the name 'Buonaparte' he scrawled his name and, looking away, handed him the paper bearing this signature of exceptional rarity: 'Napoléon Buonaparte'.

He was now only Monsieur Napoléon Buonaparte.

This is the text of the document:

'R No 116

'26th June 1815

'Before Maître André and Maître Claude Noël and his colleague, notaries of Paris, undersigned.

'Were present:

'His Majesty Napoléon Buonaparte, resident in the Château of Malmaison, parish of Rueil, district of Versailles.

'Who has, by these presents, made and appointed as his general and special representative M. le Baron Guillaume-Joseph Peyrusse, living in the Tuileries Palace. To whom His Majesty empowers to have sold at the current rate a bond, duly entered in the register, for fifteen thousand one hundred and fifty francs, belonging to him and numbered 20896, Volume 35, together with interest accrued until March 22nd last, the same to be returned to the Treasury, replaced or whatever circumstances determine.

'Made at the record office of Malmaison, parish of Rueil, district of Versailles, in the year one thousand eight hundred and fifteen on the twenty-sixth day of June, and signed by His Majesty and the above-mentioned lawyers after having been read.

Napoléon Buonaparte

Lara   Noël
'Registered at Paris on June 26th 1815, folio 157. Ref. Nos. 8 & 9. Received one franc ten centimes.

'Camusat'

That afternoon (June 26th) the Countess Walewska, who had already come several times to the Elysée with her son, brought him the comfort of her affection, shed many tears and offered to follow him into exile. While she awaited the consolations of the heart which would be much appreciated from the Emperor, Madame Pellapra told him, through Marchand, that 'Fouché is negotiating with M. de Vitrolles and the commissioners sent to the enemy camp have not been received . . . '

Despite so much cowardice and the countless follies of the men, the ladies of the Empire showed courage, energy and presence of mind and brought to their deposed sovereign their good wishes and the comfort of their smiles: Mesdames Caffarelli, Regnault-de-Saint-Jean-d'Angély, de Rovigo, de Turenne, de Beauveau, La Vallette, Duchâtel, the Duchess of Vicenza. Unknown women asked for audiences, amongst them that pretty woman who, at the church of Saint-Philippe du Roule, had asked Marchand for an audience to offer the Emperor 'the homage of her feelings'.

He had great need of them. Reading the text of the government order brought by Beker and handed him by Savary, he saw the snare set by Fouché. He had asked for French passports; what did these English 'safe-conducts' mean? Pacing up and down his study, he burst out . . . he would only leave if he were sure of being able to embark at Rochefort! Prison for prison, he preferred Malmaison. If there were danger, he would be under the guardianship of French honour! He would appeal to the army!

There, perhaps, lay salvation.

'I will not go to Rochefort unless I am sure of being able to leave immediately,' he said to Beker, who was at once summoned.

Then he calmed down and sent La Vallette to Paris in Savary's wake to demand the cancellation of Article 5.

June 26th. At the Tuileries the situation grew worse. Entangled in his lies and proposals and La Fayette's messages that 'the negotiations with Blücher's aides-de-camp were going well' (!) on condition that 'his (Napoleon's) escape does not compromise them', Fouché told the Council: 'The most urgent thing is to prevent Napoleon's departure.' Neither Caulaincourt, nor Davout, nor Carnot, nor Cambacérès, nor Thibaudeau, nor anyone else protested. Order to Beker: 'to keep watch on Malmaison so that he shall not be able to escape . . .'

Message to the minister 'to send all necessary troops and gendarmes . . . to keep these measures secret'. (!)

*   *   *

The government kept its eyes firmly fixed on the retreat of the vanquished man; agents and spies prowled in the gardens and around the château. The agents of Pasquier, former Chief of Police, noted the names of all persons received by the Emperor: deputies, men of science, artists, writers, officers. Napoleon welcomed them all and questioned them on the situation. Why had France abandoned him? He sent his aides-de-camp to Paris, to Versailles, to the villages, to question the people. On their return he looked eagerly for any sign of hope. Fleury de Chaboulon told him that the enemy was advancing, that Malmaison was threatened. The Emperor said that he would go to the United States or to Mexico. 'Why not the Russians?' insinuated Fleury.

'That would cost us both our lives! Bah!' he concluded, 'I will once more commit myself to the winds of chance.'

'What a dream!' he said to Maret. 'What a foolish chimaera to imagine that they will grant you a prince of your own choice, cut to the pattern of the Constituent Assembly, ready to accept a charter imposed upon him. Your future is clear; you will have the Bourbons. Alexander will do what the English want him to do; and the Austrian Emperor, as in 1814, will do what Alexander and the others want him to do.'

These forebodings, discussed in public places, together with the demands of the Allies and Fouché's intrigues threatening Napoleon's liberty, made men wary. The number of visitors diminished; only his devoted supporters and those who really loved him came; military men, members of his family, talked of the future; they had long discussions; they would meet again in the United States.

Then he received in his private garden a nine-year-old boy, big, strong and healthy . . . 'beautiful as an angel', said Hortense. It was 'little Léon', son of Eléonore Denuelle, Caroline's (Napoleon's youngest sister) reader, born on December 13, 1806.

'Look at this child,' the Emperor said to Hortense. 'Whom does he remind you of?'

'Your son, Sire. He is the image of the King of Rome.'

Napoleon was having him educated at a Paris boarding-school under the tutorship of the Baron de Mauvières, father-in-law of Méneval.

'When I am in America, I will send for him,' he said.

In the evening, patrols of dragoons and red lancers circulated, chasing away the bravoes sent by the royalists, who preached in their salons the duty of assassinating the 'sinister tyrant'.

Saint-Denis, sent to Versailles by Napoleon, brought back 'some shotguns, some horse pistols, a box of two pairs of fine pistols'. The way was open but the townspeople were uneasy at seeing the Emperor living calmly at Malmaison where enemy scouts could take him unawares.

*   *   *

The French troops had crossed the Oise. The enemy was ten leagues from Paris. Compiègne had not been occupied. 'This is a serious error,' wrote Davout to Grouchy on June 27th at three o'clock in the morning. 'I know this may seem strange to you, but the enemy must be prevented from getting between you and Paris. Move trustworthy troops to Senlis and Crépy. Reduce the convoys. Station gendarmes at Villers-Cotterets to stop desertions. Reach the capital by forced marches.

'You realize, Marshal, how necessary it is to muster the whole army in the Paris fortifications. At least this will give the Chambers and the government the means to negotiate and to obtain terms which may help to prevent the Allies from entering Paris . . . '

There was no longer any question of defence. Fouché and Davout were at one on that. 'I am as convinced as you are, Marshal,' wrote Fouché, 'that there is nothing better to be done than to treat at once for an armistice.'

Napoleon took certain precautions; Fleury de Chaboulon visited the bridges over the Seine. The minister had had the bridge at Bezons destroyed and ordered Beker to set fire to the bridge at Chatou. The bridge at Pecq remained intact by order of the mayor, a certain Martinville, the fiery editor of *The White Flag*, after having been secretary of the notorious Legendre of the Convention. 'I became an ultra,' he said. 'The job was worth 15,000 francs a year. If I had stayed in the opposite camp, I would have had only water to drink!'

The Emperor took his leave of Monge, who despite his seventy years had offered to accompany him, and then inspected the carriages put at his disposal; they were in a deplorable condition!

From time to time the sound of guns could be heard.

Bassano, La Vallette, Savary and Bertrand stayed continually with the Emperor; the Guard kept watch over the entire 'Household'. The Allies certainly knew of Napoleon's isolation; instead of passports, Fouché could easily have sent a Prussian patrol to kidnap him. Did Davout, who like him had secretly received Vitrolles and listened to the Allies' proposals, see the whole game clearly? Though in command of the army, he had no other will than that of Fouché. 'When honest men cannot understand and cannot carry out the designs of Providence, then dishonest men take over the task . . . ', Guizot was to say in 1830.

At Malmaison, courier after courier came from Paris.

Queen Hortense greeted Drouot, who was to take over command of the Guard, and Madame Girard, whose husband, the general, had just died. She was completely destitute.

Full of solicitude, the 'five emperors of the Commission' granted Napoleon, against 'suitable receipts', travelling equipment consisting of : a porcelain service, known as 'headquarters service', six services of twelve covers in official linen, twelve pairs of sheets of the highest quality, twelve pairs for everyday use, six dozen napkins, two coach-rugs, three saddles and harness 'of general's rank', four hundred volumes to be taken from the library at Rambouillet . . . some cards. Also a hundred thousand francs for travelling expenses.

Fouché, who had received 'his title and 20,000 francs of income', did things well!

But the Emperor showed no desire to leave and sent General de Flahaut to tell him of his intention (June 28th). He was received by Davout:

'Tell him if he won't leave, I will come and arrest him myself,' the marshal told him.

'Only he who sends such a message is able to deliver it. To obey you would be to dishonour my uniform,' the general replied, offering his resignation.

'Let him come!' the Emperor said to Flahaut a few hours later.

Then he went on reading Humboldt's book on America, *Travels to the Equinoctial Countries of the New Continent.* He called for everything written on the subject in order to study the history and geography of his future residence. He dreamed of 'magnetic storms, great scientific works, of Peru and of New Spain'. He was already in the United States when he greeted Méneval, Talma, La Bédoyère, General Lallemand and, later, several ladies preceding Joseph, Cardinal Fesch and Madame Mère . . . Also the Adjutant-Commander Delessert of the 3rd Legion of the National Guard, who arrived at full gallop : Prussian scouts were approaching Gonesse. Napoleon listened to his report and stuck some pins in a map spread out on the table : 'I have let myself be outflanked,' he said, laughing. Gourgaud and Montholon went out to reconnoitre.

The day came to an end, magnificent. The Emperor joined Hortense and Madame Bertrand in the gardens and all three rested for a few minutes on the river bank, under the trees.

'How lovely it is here at Malmaison,' the Emperor said. 'Wouldn't it be nice, Hortense, to stay here.'

The young woman repressed a sob, while the wife of the Marshal of the Household repeated that His Majesty would be well treated in England.

That too was Maret's advice, once more in the Council, a loyal servant without great pretensions but who had been bound up with the Emperor's life for many years: 'The Emperor should fly,' he said, 'hasten to the coast and, with a few loyal friends, seize a boat, land in England and appear before the nearest magistrate, declaring that he wishes to place himself under the protection of the British laws . . .'

The Emperor reflected and replied that he would prefer to go to America; but the idea of making an appeal to British honour would, thenceforth, 'stick in his mind'.

News and events crowded one upon another. Fouché became frightened. A report from Réal warned him that Grouchy's regiments wanted to continue the struggle under Napoleon's leadership. Exelmans' dragoons and Lefebvre-Desnoëttes' Red Lancers intended, in the great tumult, to seize Napoleon from Malmaison. The Chambers spied on him; his policy was severely criticized.

Davout saw Oudinot again. After listening to his suggestions, the marshal adopted them as his own, set them out as proposals and sent at once to Oudinot for M. de Vitrolles who, according to him, 'had full powers'. 'Entry of the King into Paris without foreign troops, maintenance of the Chambers and of the tricolour, no office-holders to lose their posts, amnesty, etc.'

Oudinot was the more certain that these conditions would be agreed since he had heard them expressed by M. de Vitrolles. On the other hand, Davout believed he could guarantee that the Commission and the Chambers would accept them.

A doubt catastrophe: Vitrolles had no real power and merely scrawled generalities in the margins of Davout's document. The day before, the Commission of Government had refused the proposal to recognize Louis XVIII, already put forward by the Minister of War, who was suspected of being little inclined towards defence.

Fouché recognized, in the conditions demanded by the Prince

of Eckmühl, those which he himself had addressed to Vitrolles!

The two marshals became entangled in the consequences of their decision. Davout sent General de Périgord to Cambrai, where the court was in residence, to let the King know what he was doing for the restoration of the royal family and, on Oudinot's demand, agreed to receive M. de Vitrolles. It was not yet known in Paris that, by agreement with him, the marshal had just renewed, in a letter to Fouché, the proposals which he had made to the Commission the day before.

Davout was 'the arm of the policy of which the Duke of Otranto (Fouché) was the head', but the two sponsors began to squabble. Fouché claimed to be the master, the only one to carry out his policy. The King must resume the throne only through him. The fate of Napoleon was to be reserved for his occult nego-tiations. On the night of June 27th to 28th, he appointed new plenipotentiaries to go to Wellington and put the proposals before him.

Outside, the Federals snarled, bawled patriotic songs in the cabarets. The National Guard kept order in the suburbs only with the greatest difficulty. Earth was being shifted on all sides and barricades set up. Twenty-five thousand peasants with their carts and beasts encumbered the squares and the carriageways.

A state of siege was proclaimed. The approaches to the capital would alone be defended. The troops of the line took up their positions outside the walls, beneath which the Army of the North was expected at any moment. Ex-soldiers and deserters rallied to their colours. The troops which were on the Loire would form a 'reserve' at Orleans.

Colonel Bory de Saint-Vincent, at the head of a group of representatives wearing tricolour scarves, harangued the regi-ments, who replied with 'Long live Napoleon II!' But neither the fortifications nor the army saved the city from anarchy that lowered and snarled. The Jacobins wanted to organize a revolu-tionary day against profiteers and property owners. The Opera had closed its doors the day before; the Théâtre-Français ceased its performances and the smaller theatres played to empty houses. Ragged and drunken men shouted threats against the bourgeois who wanted an armistice at any price. Paris was afraid, and prices rose!

'The enemy is coming by forced marches,' wrote Fouché,

scared and anxious, inducing the Chambers to send Valence, Andréossy, Boissy d'Anglas, Flaugergues and La Besnardière to the Allied Supreme Commanders to ask for a suspension of hostilities.

They were to say: You have stated that you are only waging war on the French because of Bonaparte. Very well, he will leave for Rochefort. He is no longer to be feared; we will hand him over to you. What reason have you to continue your march on Paris? Stop . . . Formal instructions to conclude an armistice with Blücher; better to sacrifice a few cities and fortresses than to sacrifice Paris.

These gentlemen were also to present 'an outline of policy' behind which could be discerned the shadow of the Duke of Orleans. Finally, Fouché gave them secret instructions:

'Offer to hand over Napoleon to England, or to Austria, if this will induce the Allies to conclude an armistice . . . ' The mission would be carried out, for Fouché was to pass on the offers of the French government 'in detail' to Lord Bathurst on July 3rd at Gonesse.

The plenipotentiaries were checked at every turn. They met with countless difficulties in passing the city barriers, manned by Federals who were dead-drunk, and long waits at the outposts. Finally, at half-past eleven on the night of June 29th, they received Wellington's reply: 'After consulting Marshal Prince Blücher, His Highness agrees with me that, in the present circumstances, as long as Bonaparte is at liberty and while operations are still going on, hostilities cannot be stopped.'

The Chamber was suspicious of these double-dealings; meeting the same night in secret session it formally accused Fouché of handing over Napoleon. He wrote personally to Wellington:

'You have increased the glory of your name by fresh victories over the French; it is therefore by you that the French will be known and valued. You will stand up for their rights among the European powers.'

After nauseating flatteries, Fouché went on: 'In all your conquests you have been just towards the rights of man and the voice of conscience has guided your policy. You will find the requests made by our plenipotentiaries in accord with the strictest justice.

'The French will never find a better king, a king more ready wishes that this monarch shall reign according to the rule of law . . .

'All eyes in France are fixed upon the British Constitution. We do not claim to be more free; but we will not consent to be less free. The representatives of the French people are working on 'their social pact' . . . The powers will be separated.

'As soon as the treaty has received the signature of the sovereign called upon to rule over France, he will receive the sceptre and the crown from the hands of the people.'

In a tone of entreaty Davout, too, asked Wellington and Blücher for an armistice. The rebuffs continued.

'We will follow up our victory,' the old 'Vorwärts' replied to Davout. 'God has given us the means and the will . . . You see what you have to do . . . Would you bring upon your head the curses of Paris as you have those of Hamburg? . . . We intend to enter Paris . . . It is only in Paris that an assured armistice can be drawn up.'

*   *   *

At the castle of Sorel (about a dozen miles north-west of Compiègne) General de Tromelin was received by the English Commander-in-Chief. The welcome was friendly, the discussion courteous but firm. His Excellency could not grant Napoleon a passport: he was authorized to receive him only as a prisoner-of-war. The general insisted in vain. The first part of his mission was over. There remained the more delicate part.

'It would certainly be easy, My Lord,' said Tromelin, who has recorded the conversation in his notes, 'for you to restore the Bourbons to Paris at the head of your armies; but it is more important, and what we expect from Your Excellency, to bring them to us in such a way that they will be able to remain there. For, without wanting to go into the reasons for the last revolution (he was speaking of the return from Elba) it is impossible that Your Excellency is so unaware of them as to believe that Napoleon could have reached Paris had not many persons, other than a few military men, rushed to his support and made his way easy for him . . . '

What did he mean? It is a mystery on which Tromelin, in his notes, throws no light.

'The French will never find a better king, a king more ready to set up a constitutional régime, since that seems to be the wish of the people,' replied Wellington.

'The one sure means of bringing the revolution to an end,' continued the general undismayed, 'is to reconcile all sections of opinion . . . If Your Excellency wishes to co-operate in this happy reconciliation there is no one who can give him better information about the state of public opinion than the Duke of Otranto.' Silence . . . Would Louis XVIII know next day that he would owe his crown to a regicide? Or to a Marshal of the Empire?

'I left the same evening, bearing His Excellency's reply to the president of the Provisional Government,' wrote Tromelin. 'I reached Pont-Sainte-Maxence at daybreak, where I met the deputation of the Chambers on its way to see Wellington. M. de la Besnardière, with whom I talked privately for a minute, told me that they were hoping for a reconciliation between Fouché and the King's ministers which should result in the setting-up of a national administration ready to reconcile all interests.

'I arrived, about five o'clock, at the Prussian headquarters at Senlis.

'Graf Gneisenau, Army Chief of Staff, received me haughtily and told me that, as the army was on the move, he could not allow me to return to Paris; I was only allowed to write to the Provisional Government, leaving the despatch open. I found the Prussians more concerned with reaping the benefit of their victory than in making the Bourbon cause triumph. They did not even take the trouble to conceal the lack of interest that it inspired in them. "We are here by right of conquest and it is as victors that we wish to enter Paris," he said to me . . . "It doesn't interest us whether you take back the Bourbons or restore the Republic, for we have not forgotten that three months after having restored Louis XVIII he threatened us about Saxony. We are waging war against Napoleon because no agreement with him is sacred and no firm peace may be expected from him . . . After having destroyed him, we no longer care. You may choose any government you like, except that of Bonaparte and his family . . . ".

'I followed the Prussian headquarters to Gonesse where I remained for the 29th and 30th June. On July 1st, after the Prussian army had completed its movement to Saint-Germain, seized the bridge at Pecq and rebuilt that at Chatou, Colonel Nostiz, aide-de-camp to Prince Blücher, told me that since the English were coming to occupy the Gonesse position I could go to the English headquarters at Louvres, whence it would be possible for me to return to Paris.

'In fact Lord Wellington assigned me an officer who escorted me to the outposts of La Villette, whence I re-entered the capital about two o'clock in the afternoon.'

At Rochefort, during a dinner in honour of General Butraud, Commander of the District, the port-admiral received a message from his ministry. It was an order to fit out the two frigates *Saale* and *Méduse* . . . Provisions for four and a half months. Absolute secrecy. But it was an open secret! The messenger had broadcast his news en route. How had he known?

'In twenty-four hours,' wrote Decrès, 'a French minister will arrive who is on his way to the United States. He will embark, with his suite, on the *Saale* and the *Méduse* (Captain Ponée) . . . Administration of Captain Philibert . . . High-class table . . . Great distinction . . . Secret . . . '

And in Decrès' handwriting: fifty hammocks and bedrolls.

At six o'clock in the evening a vessel appeared, running north-ward. At nine o'clock the *Bellerophon* hove to about six leagues outside the port.

PRECIPITOUS DEPARTURE

Meanwhile, at the Tuileries, before the Commission of Government meeting in night session, Fouché wavered. What were his feelings? Napoleon must not stay too near Paris. On the other hand he must not embark too soon! In any case, Fouché agreed to send the following note addressed to the Minister of the Marine:

'Since the present circumstances give rise to apprehension about the safety of Napoleon, we have decided to consider Article 5 of our ministerial order dated the 26th of this month as cancelled. In consequence the frigates are to be placed at Napoleon's disposal. There is now no hindrance to his departure. Both the interests of the state and his own interests require that he leave immediately after the notification which you will give him of our decision. Count Merlin will be attached to you for this mission . . . '

Perhaps this was to give evidence before the Commission and free Fouché from responsibility should the Emperor refuse.

Merlin however declined, so Decrès and Boulay left Paris at midnight and reached Malmaison about three o'clock in the morning, at the same time as Beker. Awakened by Marchand, Napoleon appeared in his dressing-gown. The Prussian cavalry was getting near; obviously he must leave that day. 'Greatly moved, the ministers withdrew. Passports would be brought for everyone who intended to share the Emperor's exile.'

Then there arrived, one after the other, Savary, Joseph, Flahaut, Résigny, who had been sent out in the early hours of the morning towards the Seine to reconnoitre. From the earliest hours La Vallette had been kept informed by runners.

Prussian advance-guards at Gonesse and Stains; the bulk of the army was advancing towards Senlis on the Soissons road. Not an Englishman in sight.

The Guard, the corps of Drouet d'Erlon, Reille and Lobau, entered Paris with Grouchy by way of Claye and Le Bourget; Vandamme, the 3rd and 4th Corps and most of the cavalry by way of Vincennes. In all, about sixty thousand men. The troops passing along the Saint-Germain road shouted 'Long live the Emperor!' and clamoured at the château railings.

Amongst them were not, as has often been said, 'the men of General Brayer, coming to Paris from Vendée . . . ' Brayer in fact commanded a division of the Army of the Loire, created by the Emperor on May 20th from the troops of the 12th, 13th and 22nd military divisions (Nantes, Rennes, Tours), that is to say about eight thousand men, entrusted to General Lamarque with the aim of pacifying the Vendée. Brayer and his two brigades, one of which belonged to the Young Guard, were at Cholet for the signature of peace with the royalists. The soldiers who acclaimed Napoleon at Malmaison belonged to the 2nd of the Line, commanded by Major Brayer, nephew of the general and his former aide-de-camp. Under the orders of General de Pully they were energetically to defend the bridge at Sèvres on July 2nd.

Moved by their cheers Napoleon, bending over his maps, noted that the Prussians were marching on Versailles, hoping to outflank Paris and cut communications with Orleans. In a flash he saw the manoeuvre which should be carried out immediately; launch an attack on the flank or on the rearguard with Grouchy's army and drive Blücher back towards the Loire.

A single blow would restore liberty to France and the traitor who was leading her to destruction, thanks to the apathy of the French, would be overthrown. Transfigured, the Emperor grew enthusiastic; his companions found him once more as he had once been. Beker was summoned. Order to leave for Paris . . . He maintained his abdication, but demanded command of the army as a general . . . there was time to destroy the Prussians. That task accomplished, he promised, on the word of a soldier, to leave for America. Beker hesitated, hazarded:

'Perhaps one of His Majesty's aides-de-camp could . . .'

Useless words which the Emperor did not even hear! Carnot, Caulaincourt, would help him to triumph over Fouché. His words became imperious, denunciatory, launched in the thrilling tones which no one had ever been able to resist. A soldier, accustomed to obey, Beker leapt into his carriage which left at a gallop and crossed the bridge at Neuilly with difficulty.

At Malmaison all was commotion. Horses were saddled, the grenadiers mustered. The Emperor was to leave to put himself at the head of the army. Peyrusse had come to bring him 180,333 francs, from the sale of his bond:

'Well, Peyrusse, are you coming with us?'

The task of handing over his affairs, the great responsibility that weighed on him, did not permit him to follow His Majesty just yet, but His Majesty was not going to the end of the world and could count on his loyalty.

At the Tuileries there was consternation. Beker has left an account of his last mission in his *Relation*: 'The Emperor has sent me to tell you that the situation of France and the wishes of the patriots and the soldiers call for his presence to save the country. It is not as Emperor that he asks for the command of the army but as a general. When he has driven back the enemy, he will leave for the United States.'

'Is he mocking us?' shouted Fouché in fury. 'We know how he keeps his promises. Tell the Emperor that his offer cannot be accepted. Let him leave for Rochefort, where he will be in greater safety than here.'

Caulaincourt, Quinette and Grenier kept silent. Carnot, much excited, jumped up and strode about the room, but said nothing. That morning he had received a letter: 'If you hand over Napoleon, if you force him to leave France, you will be dishonoured in the eyes of all men, both now and in the future.' But Carnot was a weakling.

Fouché dominated the Council and the ministers. He profited by the flabbiness of the French to lead the country in the way he wanted, to its downfall, without consulting anyone, like a dictator and a tyrant.

Demanding a written reply, Beker got a rude word scrawled by Fouché to the Duke of Bassano: 'I beg you, M. le Duc, to use that influence that you have always had on the mind of His Majesty to advise him to leave without delay, seeing that the Prussians are marching on Versailles . . . '

The Emperor knew and intended to beat them. In the courtyard, M. de Montaran, equerry on duty, was holding his horse's head, crop in hand. Clothed in his now legendary dress, sword at his side, the Emperor was ready to go. But here was Beker. Surprised to see troops in the courtyard and military preparations . . .

'Await fresh orders . . . ' he said to those pressing around him. Napoleon was alone in his study.

'Sire, by approaching Your Majesty in so dejected a manner, I show that I have not succeeded in my mission . . . ' and he told all the details of his conversation with Fouché. The Emperor made no comment. Did Fouché think he could hold him?

'I would only have to make a sign and the troops now guarding me would act as an escort for me to go wherever I liked . . . '

Disgust? Resignation? Weakness?

'These men will repent having refused my offer,' he said with a certain humour. 'Did you repeat my words and tell them of my oath?'

'Yes, Sire.'

'Very well, then. So I have no choice but to go. Give the orders. When they have been carried out, come and tell me.'

'They are still afraid of me,' he said to Hortense a few minutes later. 'I wanted to make a last effort to save France. They did not want it.'

Had he only known what General Exelmans was discussing with the commander of the fortress at Vincennes. His two dragoon divisions were with him: 2,000 horse! They could go to Malmaison, seize the Emperor and bring him, willy nilly, to lead the troops.

'Too late!' replied the brave Daumesnil, who had been kept badly informed by the Tuileries: 'The Emperor left for Rochefort at nine o'clock this morning.'

Five o'clock in the afternoon. The Marshal of the Household wanted everything in order and had got bogged down in detail. Carriages, wagons and limbers were lined up in the courtyard and formed several convoys of baggage and equipment. All were headed for Rochefort by different routes.

The Emperor, in blue trousers, chestnut coat, riding boots and cocked hat, waited in his study. During the day he had said goodbye to Joseph, to Hortense and to her children; he had put in a leather belt the diamond necklace given him by the Queen in exchange for a receipt for 200,000 francs.

'Go back home at once, daughter,' he said, 'and take Madame Bertrand away with you. I can do nothing with her husband when she is about.'

Then Talma came, in the uniform of a National Guard, then veterans who had long served with him, and finally his mother, whom he kissed tenderly. Then he went alone into Josephine's room. Nothing had been changed since her death. He spent a long time there, thinking of the past, and then, in tears, went back to his study.

Half-past five. The suffocating heat became less oppressive. The Emperor glanced around him, walked through the Council Chamber, the dining room and the reception room, crossed the ha-ha, reached the park and then the little 'south gate' which led into the woods. A yellow four-in-hand, preceded by an outrider, was waiting for him. He was swallowed up in it, together with Bertrand, Savary and Beker; Saint-Denis climbed to the box.

By way of the Butard Woods, Rocquencourt and Saint-Cyr, they reached the road to Chartres.

Chapter V

UNCERTAINTIES

EN ROUTE

They had left, all travelling expenses paid: Countess Bertrand and her children, Montholon, his wife and son, Las Cases and his son, Lallemand, Gourgaud, Marchand, Maingaut, the doctor, a complete household, the servants, the anxious, the chatterboxes: sixty persons in all. Rendezvous: Rochefort.

On June 30th Major von Colomb, Blücher's brother-in-law, alerted by him the day before to go to Malmaison and seize the Emperor, dismounted at Montesson to give his hussars a breather and learnt that Napoleon had left!

Napoleon was at Rambouillet by nine in the evening. Preceded by the courier Amodru, who was to look after the relays, the carriages bowled swiftly along. The weather was stuffy. The sound of guns could be heard. The Emperor and his companions, immersed in their thoughts, did not exchange a word. They feared an ambush. On the box, Saint Denis had four pistols; two loaded guns were within reach of each of the travellers.

At Coignières, two stages after Versailles, there were no horses. Amodru had disappeared; he had not passed that way. The courier Santini replaced him and spurred on to Rambouillet. The berline avoided the town and entered the drive of the château; there was no longer any reason to fear the Prussian patrols and the Emperor, physically and morally exhausted, decided to stop. The caretaker, Hébert, his former valet during the Egyptian campaign, opened the gates. Hébert and Saint-Denis served supper. After a quarter of an hour, Napoleon went to his rooms without saying a word. Bertrand had several books and maps from the library packed up, registered them in the inventory and told the librarian Barbier that bookcases and two thousand volumes from the Trianon should be sent to Rochefort.

A feverish night. What were those guns they had just heard?

Was a battle going on? Might someone rush to the Emperor and ask him to lead his troops once more? Gourgaud, arriving very late at night, was sent back along the road to Paris to get news.

Nothing. No one came, except a messenger whose despatch the Emperor read.

'It's all over,' he said. 'It's all over for France. Let us go.'

At eight o'clock the carriages of the Emperor, Gourgaud and Marchand reached the Chartres road, crossing the park in order to avoid the people of Rambouillet, who pressed against the gates of the château.

Epernon, Maintenon, Chartres, Beauce; wheat burnt by the sun, not a bird in the sky. Sunburnt peasants, leaning on their scythes, watched the clumsy carriage pass in a cloud of dust, without suspecting that it was bearing away the former master of Europe.

Silent and drowsy, he stifled in that rolling cage, invaded by the flies; gadflies bloodied the horses, covered with foam under their harness. At other times, the Emperor's postillions received double pay. This time they were paid at the usual rate, so as not to attract attention. At Château-Regnault (Châteaurenaud) two gendarmes appeared. 'These are generals,' said Saint-Denis from his high box. The horsemen offered to escort the carriages; highwaymen had been reported near Monnaie. Savary thanked them. There was no need . . .

Night fell, without freshness. Midnight. They passed through Tours. Then a halt outside the town and a ten-minute meeting with the Comte de Miramont, prefect of the Indre-et-Loire, a former chamberlain of the Emperor. What was happening? Had those in power sent some blackguards to play a dirty trick on him? No. Should anything of that sort happen, the prefect would delay them for twenty-four hours and would let His Majesty know.

Montbazon, Sainte-Maure; relay after relay, shouts from the grooms, the whinnying of horses, the stirrup-cups of the postillions, local inhabitants asking for news. What had happened to the Emperor? Had they harmed him? The travellers listened to these sincere tributes. Though moved, the Emperor remained impassive. Dawn broke on July 1st.

At Rochefort, messages from Decrès came in rapid succession; the last one specified that the 'ambassador' previously announced was 'he who used to be our Emperor'. In a top-secret instruction intended for the captains of the frigates the minister ordered: 'All men-of-war must be avoided. If it is necessary to fight, then the frigate on which Napoleon has not embarked will sacrifice itself to hold back the enemy and allow the one on which he is aboard to escape . . . The frigates must get under sail in twenty-four hours if the enemy blockade does not prevent departure.'

It was therefore not a question of breaking the blockade but simply of self-defence if they were attacked 'on the high seas'. A message dated June 27th, but presented to the port-admiral the following day, confirmed the last sentence of the instructions: 'The frigates will sail if the disposition of the enemy ships allows them to do so without imperilling them.'

Meanwhile on board the *Saale* and the *Méduse* all preparations were being made to set sail. The weather was fine: variable winds N.E. to E.N.E. Captain Philibert, coming from Rochefort where he had been given his orders, had the cutters swung inboard, studsails and royals bent; the artillery commissioner came on board at three o'clock to make his inspection; the gundecks were painted. Supercargoes and clerks loaded wines, including 100 bottles of cognac, 192 of red Bordeaux, 6 barrels of beef stew, 24 hams, 1,000 eggs, etc. The day before, the officer and the men sent as a deputation to Paris for the ceremony of the Champ de Mai (June 1st) had returned on board.

In the roads, in the narrows, the *Bellerophon* fired salvoes to celebrate the victory of Waterloo; an English brig hove to and moored nearby. It was the *Myrmidon*.

At the prefecture, Port-Admiral Bonnefoux was sick and above all uneasy about what he had to do: to receive the Emperor, to keep strict secrecy and to take security measures. The semaphore waved its arms: 'Napoleon will avoid passing through Rochefort; keep boats ready at Vergeroux and other points on the coast . . .' As soon as embarkation has taken place 'all communications between the frigates and the mainland will be forbidden. Departure within twenty-four hours . . . if it can be done in perfect safety . . .'

What did all that mean? If the Emperor wanted to slip away to America, why had the minister chosen Rochefort as port of embarkation, which was very difficult to get away from? Furthermore the presence of the English ships seemed very equivocal. Bonnefoux suspected a trap.

The government's intentions became clear: to isolate Napoleon from the mainland, perhaps in order to make another 'flight of the eagle' impossible; in any case to prevent the Emperor from breaking through the line of enemy ships moored within sight of the coast.

It seemed that the government wanted to gain time until the English security service, warned by the repeated demands for safe-conducts, could take up position.

It was done. The day before, June 30th, Captain Maitland, commanding the *Bellerophon*, had received from an 'agent' in Bordeaux:

'Having learnt from a trustworthy source that Bonaparte, coming from Paris, has passed through the town (?) last night accompanied by the new mayor of Bordeaux, perhaps with the intention of escaping by the estuary or by way of La Teste (Arcachon), the writer of the last note sent by Monsieur X . . . has taken note of the plan in order to allow the British admiral to take immediately the necessary measures to have him apprehended. The town has five thousand men. It would be a good thing to stage demonstrations on the coast with at least eight thousand men and to keep a close watch on all American ships, especially the *Susquehannah* of Philadelphia, Captain Caleb Cushing, and to block all the entrances to Bordeaux and La Teste.

'I assume that the bearer of this present note will bring a line or two from the admiral or from the officer commanding the station.

'As I write these lines, there is a widespread report that the Duke of Berry and the Duke of Wellington are in Paris.'

Not yet! But the situation there was worsening and the disorders increasing hourly. At the La Villette Gate, in the shanty which served him as a headquarters, Davout felt discouraged. Grouchy, who had rushed thither without even taking off his top-boots, was no less so. To prevent the occupation of Paris, they must accept the King. Which King? And how to do it? The army might perhaps accept the Duke of Orleans, but Louis

XVIII and the white flag . . . never! Moreover, on Davout's orders he too had written to the Allied generals to try to end hostilities.

It was complete confusion. The envoys Fouché sent to Blücher and Wellington to negotiate an armistice followed on one another's heels, but could not get through the outposts. Weighing up the military men who were uncompromised and those who were agents of the King, Fouché considered that Grouchy, Vitrolles, Oudinot, Kellermann and one or two others might be able to succeed. Davout replaced Grouchy's name by that of Tourton, Chief of Staff of the National Guard.

Then, in broad daylight, one of Fouché's gigs dropped M. de Vitrolles and Marshal Oudinot at headquarters. The political discussions, begun at once, were soon interrupted by an aide-de-camp announcing a deputation from the Chambers, come to offer its congratulations to the army: Arnaud, Jay, Pouget, Marshal Lefebvre, Generals Gazan, Fressinet and Dejean. These gentlemen, 'wearing their tricolour sashes', had come by decision of the Assemblies to be present at the reading of their address to the army.

Davout make excuses; he had done nothing about assembling the troops under arms. He outlined the situation, tried to explain the presence beside him of M. de Vitrolles, 'who could ease the agreements with the allied armies'. He got confused, did not end his sentences, talked of 'the country's interests'.

The deputies were astonished and grew excited and angry! Vitrolles, at whom Fressinet shook his fist, slipped away to Paris. 'We will never put up with the Bourbons,' shouted General Dejean. Davout tried to calm the uproar, sent orders to the troops to retire to their tents. The deputies inspected the lines of the 1st, 2nd and 6th Corps, from Belleville to Saint-Denis.

The Guard greeted the representatives with shouts of 'Long live the representatives!', 'Long live Napoleon II!' The officers declared that they had fought for freedom for twenty-five years and that they would never accept a King brought by the English and the Prussians. But Bülow's cavalry was at Le Bourget, Ziethen at Blanc-Mesnil, Thielmann at Dommartin.

Pushed to the limit, Davout took a few measures of defence. He had at his disposal 75,000 men, plus the Federals, the National Guards, the veterans, the cadets, etc., that is to say another 40,000 combatants. The heavy cavalry and the Guard were posted from Auteuil to La Chappelle; Reille and Pajol were at La Villette; Vandamme's and Beaumont's dragoons were posted from Belleville to Vincennes. Exelmans was at Gentilly. The advance-posts were strengthened by artillery; an infantry brigade was at Saint-Denis.

The Prussians attacked on June 30th at dawn, but faced with the strength of the defences and the fanatical resistance of the troops who were cheering Napoleon II, Blücher gave orders, about eight o'clock in the morning, to break off the fighting.

*   *   *

On July 1st at nine in the morning Napoleon stopped in front of the Hôtel de la Poste, just outside the walls of Poitiers, and went to a room prepared for him by the innkeeper, Berlaume, 'freshened up', had something to eat, rested for a little and then, through Beker, sent a courier to Rochefort to find out the state of the frigates *Méduse* and *Saale* and how closely they were being watched. Would he be able to set sail as soon as he arrived?

By four o'clock, the hour of departure, he was rested and seemed to have recovered his self-confidence. The people of Poitiers had not recognized him, but talked of him with enthusiasm and asked for news of him.

Night had fallen by the time the carriage entered Saint-Maixent, having covered fourteen leagues. There were many people at the posting-station. There was no hostility, but a large and inquisitive crowd. The National Guards asked for their papers and took them to the Town Hall, whence they did not return . . . Time passed; the travellers grew impatient . . . and so did the people of Saint-Maixent. Beker found a gendarme officer to go and look for the documents and bring them back, together with a *laissez-passer* from the municipality. At last, the postillions spurred on their horses.

At eight, perhaps ten, the Emperor, exceedingly tired, stopped at Niort and decided to spend the night at the Hôtel de la Boule d'Or, next to the posting-station. It was a single bedroom but large enough; the generals slept in the rooms next to his, opening on to the landing. Saint-Denis served supper laid out in one of them. There was great uproar on the ground floor which prevented them from sleeping.

Advised by Savary, the prefect Busche arrived at two o'clock in the morning to place himself at the Emperor's orders and ended by inducing him to take a room at the prefecture. It was a Sunday. The people were still strolling in the streets. An officer recognized him and spread the news of his presence. He was Major Voison, commanding the 4th and 5th squadrons of the 2nd Hussars. Then, followed by several officers of the Army of the Loire of General Lamarque, he appeared at the gates where a large crowd was growing rapidly. There were shouts of 'Long live the Emperor!' but Napoleon refused to appear.

During the afternoon he received the notables with great cordiality; to the civilians who implored him not to abandon them, to the soldiers who wanted to take him to Paris, he replied: 'I am nobody now.' Visitors came, one after the other. Captain Kerengal, in charge of ship movements in the port of Rochefort, brought a reply from the port-admiral to the letter from Poitiers: 'The roadstead is closely blockaded by an English squadron . . . It would seem to me exceedingly dangerous for the safety of the frigates and those on them to try and force a way through. The forces blockading us leave no hope of success to get our ships clear of the harbour . . .'

Was he sincere?

Admiral Hotham had only two ships-of-war to guard 300 miles of coast, from Brest to Arcachon, the *Superb* (at Quiberon) and the *Bellerophon*, a limping old seventy-four-gunner, three frigates, a dozen corvettes, brigs, sloops, etc., so that the blockade of the channels which led from Rochefort to the open sea was entrusted to the *Bellerophon* alone. To send the report of his Bordeaux agent to the Isle of Yeu, Maitland had to use his whaler; he then ordered the *Myrmidon* into the Gironde and the *Cephalus* to Arcachon. At the end of the day, the *Phoebe* having left for Bordeaux on the admiral's orders, he recalled the *Myrmidon*. These movements of the smaller ships of the squadron were frequent. They would have to wait for a favourable moment to escape.

That evening, after a dinner for the Niort notables in honour of the Emperor, the prefect brought a message sent by telegraph from Paris on June 30th: 'There has been an engagement under the walls of the capital which seems to improve the situation.' Spirits rose. Major Voison stated that if the blockade of Rochefort delayed the departure of the frigates, His Majesty should take command of the troops of the South-West (General Clausel with 10,000 men and General Lamarque with another 10,000), make a levy from the regimental depots and march with 50,000 soldiers and 100,000 fanatical workers and peasants. General Lallemand, who had come from Paris, supported his comrade's views. The Emperor seemed to regain confidence; according to Montholon who was, it is true, absent at the time, if he wrote to Clausel and Lamarque it was only to give satisfaction to those about him, for he was reluctant to assume power again and, despite the disgust inspired in him by the French leaders, he refused to believe the Provisional Government capable of letting Louis XVIII enter Paris.

Illusions!

*   *   *

Fouché was busily preparing for the King's return. He manoeuvred flexibly between the Commission of Government, which he dominated, the Chambers, which he kept at arm's length, and the army, through Davout who was on his side. Meanwhile, through his commissioners and messengers, special or secret, he kept the Allied marshals informed about the course of events and of public opinion.

Wellington, who had preceded and protected Louis XVIII and his court ever since they had entered France, carefully perused the information he received and forwarded it to London; but he was in no way convinced of the sincerity of Napoleon's abdication. Afraid lest it might conceal a reorganization of the army, he refused to consider any request for an armistice. He approached Paris warily, fearing danger from the garrison and the fortified camp, and let Blücher operate in advance of him.

The day before, he had told Fouché's emissary, Colonel Macirone: 'Tell the Commission that the best thing they can do is to proclaim the King immediately. I cannot negotiate for an armistice on any other condition. The King is here, quite close; let them send their submission . . .'

The old 'Vorwärts' had no truck with political subtleties; he wanted 'to have Napoleon seized by the advance-guards', to enter Paris and to sack the city. He had with him instructions signed on June 26th by Nesselrode and Metternich, and stuck to them :

'The Allies will grant no truce before Napoleon's departure and nothing must be allowed to halt the operations now going on . . . They will not negotiate with him, nor with any member of his family. They will not recognize any authority set up by him, not even the Chambers which owe their existence to him. The deputies are to be arrested at the outposts and their despatches confiscated . . . As for the government which France is to have, this question will be postponed until later, in order to judge what may be called the will of the people and its wishes in favour of this or that individual (Louis XVIII!), since it is difficult at this stage to ascertain the true feelings of the majority of the people.'

For Blücher only one phrase of the document counted : nothing must be allowed to halt the operations now going on. On June 30th his army began to advance. Leaving Bülow's corps north of Paris to await the English whose advance guards stretched from Senlis to Bourget, he sent Ziethen and Thielmann across to the left bank of the Seine at Maisons and Pecq (Pirch's corps guarded the lines of communication) and, by way of Saint-Germain and Versailles, launched Colonel Sohr's light brigade to cut the road to Orleans and isolate the capital.

It has been written that this was a dangerous manoeuvre, since it exposed his flank to the army at Paris. But in reality Blücher had not much to fear; he held the bridges which, in case of a check, allowed him to retreat towards the English, but he considered that, since Napoleon was no longer at its head, the French army was incapable of launching an attack.

However, the French were eager to cross swords with the enemy on that dawn of July 1st, a day pregnant with every sort of incident. At the Chamber of Representatives there were angry scenes after the return of the delegation sent to establish contact with the troops; there were cries of 'Long live Napoleon II!' Malleville, author of a royalist pamphlet, was branded as a madman by the former regicide Garreau. Terrible scandal! M. de Vitrolles had been seen talking with the Minister of War! Fouché pretended to be astonished, did not defend himself and let Vitrolles be arrested, after giving him due notice of what he might expect.

'Fouché is a traitor,' shouted General Dejean. 'The first thing to do is to hang him in the courtyard of the Tuileries.'

'I have just come from a scene with Quinette, Carnot and Caulaincourt. Didn't they too talk of treason? Of denouncing me?' retorted Fouché, very calm. 'This is what I told them: "Ah! So you are telling me! You are telling me that M. de Vitrolles is a royalist; I've known that a very long time. You're telling me that Davout is about to turn traitor. Very fine! Go and arrest him in the midst of his army! I won't be responsible!" As for me, listen to Carnot; get up on the rostrum and accuse me. I am used to this sort of thing ever since the Convention . . . Come on! No half-measures; get up on the rostrum, Carnot. I'm waiting for you.'

A man of the Convention and the committees, Fouché spoke of his life as 'a matter of indifference'! He continued to keep in touch with Vitrolles, who was now in hiding, through Hyde de Neuville, a very loyal royalist agent, who, gone to earth in the house of Caron, a perfume maker in the Rue du Four, had his papers sent to him by his daughter, little Victoire, concealed under perfume bottles.

Meanwhile, Davout denied one thing after another; he had signed a 'proclamation to the army' drawn up by General Fressinet, his former Chief of Staff: 'They want to force the Bourbons on us, despite the fact that these princes have been repudiated by the majority of Frenchmen . . . They have treated as rebellious the army which, for twenty years, has been the palladium of French liberty.' Seventeen generals signed their names under Davout's: Vandamme, Pajol, d'Erlon, Pelet, Christiani, etc. But when the Chamber decided to print the 'proclamation' in 'twenty thousand copies', Davout declared publicly that he had been 'surprised into signing', insinuating that he had feared that 'if he had abstained, it would have created dissension among the generals and demoralization in the army'!

Civic courage has nothing in common with military courage.

In fact, having learnt that the Duke of Albufera had concluded a truce with the Austrians on the Alpine front, Davout had used this agreement as a pretext to send Wellington yet another demand for an armistice, the sixth in a week! But he did not take part in the 'Extraordinary Council' which had been in session at the Tuileries since nine o'clock that morning.

Faced with the choice of fighting or surrender, Fouché, the contriver of the situation, refused to shoulder the responsibility and tried to gain the consent of the Chambers, the support of the marshals and of certain generals. Scenting the trap, Davout did not reply to Fouché's urgent demand.

As do those in power when searching for approval of a policy too heavy to bear alone, Fouché put to the members of the committees of the Chambers and to the generals, united under his chairmanship, a number of loaded questions:

'Can you defend at the same time all the approaches to Paris, even those on the left bank of the Seine?'

'Can you risk a battle on all fronts, without imperilling the fate of a million men?'

'For how long can you assure the fate of the capital?'

It was impossible not to reply 'No' or 'I don't know'. Which, of course, was just what Fouché wanted.

After some interruptions from Carnot and Grenier, who judged defence to be difficult, and from Soult, who declared it to be impossible, Lefebvre spoke up for resistance. Many representatives were astonished that after so many promises by the authorities about the state of the army 'they had reached such a pass in so short a space of time'. But as the members of the two Chambers, any more than the government, did not want to shoulder responsibility for a catastrophe, they declared themselves incompetent to judge military matters and the Council asked for the advice of the Council of War. Fouché at once sent orders to Davout to summon the marshals, whose replies he already knew in advance, and the 'generals able to throw light on the deliberations of the government' to his headquarters at La Villette; he added a questionnaire and demanded a report.

Enchanted with the result already attained, Fouché was, at that very moment, being violently taken to task in the Chamber of Representatives by Colonel Bory de Saint-Vincent: ' . . . an invisible hand is trying to influence the negotiations of your envoys in the interests of the faction that it serves . . . This parricide hand will make it impossible for you to await the results of these negotiations . . . '

The Chamber knew very well that this meant Fouché but, forgetting what they had said the day before, the representatives, once more overcome by fear, listened with indifference to the prophetic peroration of the deputy for Lot-et-Garonne: 'If you do not open your eyes, you will inevitably become the victim of this system of defeatism, ambiguity and falsehood . . . '

After which they approved the appeal to the nation whose flabbiness they had repudiated the day before; rejecting almost unanimously the proposal moved by Saussey 'inviting the government to make a report to the Assembly on all that was happening . . .'.

To put the finishing touch to its cowardice, the Chamber did not even dare to suspect Fouché of abuse of authority! 'There is a sort of superstition in favour of a dictator,' wrote Henry Houssaye. Nor were they aware that, at that very moment, a part of the army was fighting at Villacoublay and Rocquencourt.

Fouché would not hear of any military operation at any price. They might imperil his political plans and worsen his situation by annoying the Allies and, through them, the King, but Davout felt the suspicion of the army weighing heavily upon him. In his *Mémoires* he says: 'I had a good army, with high morale. Everything that a general commanding could foresee was in my favour . . . I was sure of beating the Prussians and throwing them back in disorder on the English before the English army would be in a position to help them.'

Following in Fouché's wake and compromised by his policy, Davout, with his magnificent military record, hesitated. He felt the need of reinforcing his prestige and giving satisfaction to his troops—without compromising his position. If he sent any orders to this effect, they are not to be found in the War Archives.

Had he given verbal 'instructions' to Vandamme who commanded the corps on the left bank of the Seine? It is probable, even though no order from Vandamme, uniting his cavalry with those of Exelmans for an attack on the Prussians who were passing through Versailles, has come down to us, but only Exelmans' orders to his subordinates. It was a cavalry skirmish, supported by two battalions of infantry and three guns. A phrase in Exelmans' order alludes to the 'troops of the Prince of Eckmühl, which must cross the Seine by the Neuilly bridge'.

But the outposts had received from Vandamme orders 'not to

leave their positions'. Pasquier notes in his *Mémoires*: 'Davout agreed with Fouché to avoid a general engagement'. No military historian of the time, Jomini, Clausewitz, Dönitz, etc., makes any allusion to preparatory movements nor to an eventual battle.

However Count Exelmans, great grandson of the marshal, has in his family archives a copy of the 'Report to the Minister of War by General Count Exelmans commanding the 2nd Cavalry Corps' on the operation which was to take place on July 1st at Rocquencourt, and which begins thus: 'Sir, In accordance with your orders, I left the cantonments occupied by my cavalry . . . '

So Exelmans really had received an order—perhaps verbal—from Marshal Davout.

Furthermore, in Davout's 'political and military archives' there can be found:

1. Letter from General Vandamme to the Prince on the cavalry movement on Versailles on July 1st.
2. Letter from General Vandamme to the Prince (July 2nd, two o'clock in the morning) on the movement of General Exelmans.
3. Letter from the Commission of Government to the Prince acknowledging receipt of the report of General Exelmans (July 2nd, nine o'clock in the morning).

In any case, it was only a question of a demonstration, a sop to the army hotheads. Successful or not, it could not involve a general conflict nor compromise the plans of the Provisional Government, that is to say those of Fouché.

So at dawn on Saturday, July 1st, by Blücher's orders, von Sohr, followed by the 3rd Brandenburg and 5th Pomeranian Hussars (800 to 900 horses, whose shoes were in bad condition), left Saint-Germain and moved towards Versailles, Longjumeau and the Orleans road. According to Branderstein, on the staff of the 3rd Corps, there should have been infantry at Versailles during the morning. The Sohr brigade was reputed to be the best light cavalry in Europe. However, on June 19th, Exelmans' dragoons and a part of Grouchy's corps had marched past them less than two leagues from their positions, on the road from Wavre to Namur, without even a platoon leader having had the curiosity to send out an advance patrol.

Five o'clock in the morning. The leader of the advance guard parleyed with the National Guards at the Porte Sainte-Antoine and reached the Place d'Armes where, a little later, the brigade dismounted. Plenty of people there: idlers, royalists, Bonapartists, National Guards, also the mayor who tried to calm down tempers heated by sun and alcohol. Sohr guaranteed the safety of the inhabitants in exchange for 'everyday supplies', cloth, horses, 2,000 horse-shoes, etc., then the brigade moved away down the Rue des Chantiers. The hussars vanished in the direction of Sceaux. It was then three o'clock in the afternoon.

Sohr had lost precious time, for Exelmans was on his way.

Well informed about everything that had happened at Versailles, the general gave orders: Domon and his chasseurs to skirt Versailles to the south and move on Fontenay-le-Fleury; Vallin (hussars and lancers) to march on Versailles and Le Chesnay; Piré (chasseurs and lancers) to move on Rocquencourt by way of Ville d'Avray. An ambush to be laid at this point with the infantrymen and the guns, with the 1st Chasseurs as decoy; all to be ready to receive the enemy when I drive them back on you.

Exelmans with his dragoons, hefty louts, the best swordsmen in the army, with skins tanned by the sun of Spain, moved on Versailles by Villacoublay and Vélizy. Sohr was in a noose. Surprised at about four o'clock between these two villages, attacked in front by the dragoons and on the left flank by Vallin, the Prussian hussars only escaped by the skin of their teeth and retired on Porchefontaine, Versailles and the Rue des Chantiers, their only possible way out. The infantry promised by Brandenstein was not there.

At six o'clock Sohr rallied his men and, by a counter-march, cleared the Boulevard du Roi with a sabre-charge; his rearguard closed the park gates and the brigade hurried off towards Rocquencourt.

At six-fifteen the head of Sohr's column came upon fifty French chasseurs of the 1st Regiment in the act of sabring the brigade's supply-train, about fifty yards from Marie Antoinette's hamlet. They were wearing the black chenille-covered helmets of the Chasseurs du Roi of 1814. Led by Colonel Simonneau, they had been through the Waterloo campaign wearing this headdress, so that, from a distance, the Prussians had mistaken them for English dragoons!

F

A quarter of an hour later Sohr's hussars came under the fire of the French infantry and the guns in ambush behind the hedges and spinneys on the road. Decimated, they dashed into the scrub at Chesnay and were mopped up by the sabres of the squadrons.

'An incredible fight!' wrote Blücher. 'Insignificant,' wrote Clausewitz. Not so insignificant as all that! Sohr, the sons of Yorck, Kalkreuth, Manteuffel, Messerschmidt, etc., all the fine flower of the Prussian nobility, were killed, wounded or taken prisoner! During the night Exelmans' cavalrymen returned to the French lines with their booty. There has never been such a sabre affray since July 1, 1815. With such soldiers Napoleon would have saved Paris, and perhaps France.

* * *

At Niort the evening ended with a general discussion. 'The government is not aware of the spirit of France,' said the Emperor without enlarging on it. 'It was in too much of a hurry to get me away from Paris and, if it had accepted my last proposal, matters would have been vastly different. I could exercise, in the name of the people, a great influence on political affairs by supporting the government's negotiations with an army which would have had my name as a rallying cry.'

However, 'playing on two tables', he sent Gourgaud to Rochefort to find out 'what were the chances of getting away, whether the road by Maumusson (between Oléron and Marennes) were free and if use could not be made of an American ship, to be joined by pinnace when about five or six leagues out at sea'.

Dismounting at the Hôtel du Pacha on July 3rd about six o'clock in the morning, the aide-de-camp went to the port-admiral's office at Rochefort and told M. de Bonnefoux of his instructions. The Emperor was following.

Before leaving Niort, he had dictated to General Beker: 'We hope that the capital will be defended and that the enemy will give you time to see the outcome of the negotiations entered into by your envoys and also to reinforce the army to cover Paris. If the English ships prevent the frigates from going out, you can make use of the Emperor as a general, whose sole concern is to be of use to his country.'

This was added to the letter addressed to the government by Beker.

On his arrival at Niort, Napoleon was informed by the port-admiral at Rochefort that from June 29th the English squadron had doubled the blockade and its watchfulness and had thus made the departure of the frigates impossible. 'The Emperor desires that the Minister authorize the captain of the frigate which he is about to board to communicate with the commander of the English squadron if extraordinary circumstances make such an approach essential, as much for the personal safety of His Majesty as to spare France the sorrow and the shame of seeing him taken from his last refuge to be handed over to the discretion of his enemies . . . '

Then the general, in this remarkable despatch, gave an account of the arrival of the Emperor at Niort, of his fatigue and anxiety, as well as of all the events of the past twenty-four hours.

PARIS CAPITULATES

The events which took place at Paris on July 2nd and 3rd, as recounted by Henry Houssaye with as much care as talent, were most dramatic.

Davout was deeply humiliated. To his request for an armistice General von Ziethen replied : 'I dare not refer this request to His Highness Marshal Blücher; but if the representatives of the government tell my aide-de-camp that they are willing to surrender the city and if the army also is willing to surrender, I will accept a cessation of hostilities.' Must he then surrender before being granted an armistice?

On Sunday, July 2nd, at four in the morning, Davout sent to the government an account of the meeting of the War Council held at La Villette. Opened at midnight it had ended disconsolately about three o'clock. Eighteen marshals and generals were present, with Davout as chairman: Masséna, Soult, Moncey, Mortier, Kellermann, Lefebvre, Sérurier, Oudinot, Gouvion-Saint-Cyr, Grouchy; also Vandamme, d'Erlon, Reille, Drouot, Gazan, Deponthon, Valée. Macdonald, who had been summoned, refused to attend. Discredited since his speech in the House of Peers, which it was suspected had been delivered at the demand of the Duke of Otranto, the Prince of Moscow had not been called upon to take part.

Six questions prepared by Fouché, two of them technical, were on the agenda. To the technical questions, concerning the state of the defences, and the arms and munitions available, General Valée, commanding the artillery, had given satisfactory replies:

On the right bank. Work completed. At Montmartre work still in progress. Four hundred guns in position, in addition to those belonging to the army corps.

On the left bank. Some trenches and batteries. Forty-three guns in position; a large reserve of twelve-pounders. General Vandamme has, in addition, eighty-three guns at his disposal.

Munitions available: 200 rounds per field-piece, 300 per fixed piece; five mobile parks behind the lines; 2,000,000 cartridges in reserve; daily production of 300,000 assured. Full complement of artillerymen.

The other questions, similar to those already asked on July 1st, were, as several generals said forcibly, 'absurd, vague, captious or loaded in such a way that honest, sincere and practical men could not reply to them'. That was just what Fouché wanted. 'Could one fight on all fronts at the same time?'

Absurd! The enemy had 110,000 men and could not attack everywhere at the same time!

'In case of reverses, could the Prince of Eckmühl collect sufficient means to oppose a forcible entry? Could the fate of the capital be assured and for how long?'

Absurd! What general in command could guarantee the success of an operation or of a battle?

'Could the approaches to Paris be defended, including those on the left bank?'

Certainly; but the left bank was not fortified. Fouché knew this very well. He had caused work on the fortifications to cease by stopping the credits for it.

The discussion became more general; it went on from the possibility to the purpose of defence and to political matters. Making preparations for his future, Soult said that 'the return of the Bourbons being inevitable and therefore necessary, he did not think that blood should be spilt to delay the solution for a few days. Better invite the King to come than have him imposed by the Allies . . .' Masséna said that ' . . . the town could never be taken if the inhabitants were willing to make it a second

Saragossa, but there was not enough unanimity in feeling to dream of any long resistance'.

The French had really only once shown a unanimous resolution: on July 14, 1790!

'For whom, for what, are we fighting?' one marshal dared to ask. As if that mattered!

Lefebvre, Valée and d'Erlon protested; Vandamme stigmatized the 'moneybags' who 'didn't want to fight any longer'! They were too old . . . 'They feared crises,' Père Bugeaud was to write later. 'They awaited salvation from their enemies. It was cowardly . . . But that was how it was.'

Davout remained silent. In his *Mémoires* he estimated that he could still win one more battle under the walls of Paris, but 'such a victory would only have served my own ends. The political and military situation would not have been greatly changed . . .'

What did he know about it? Politics are not for soldiers. Davout, with his legendary past, should have read once more: 'Any governor or commander-in-chief guilty of having surrendered to the enemy or relinquishing the post entrusted to him without having exhausted every means of defence at his disposal and without having done everything that duty and honour demands of him . . .'

Instead of being the soul of resistance, he became the promoter of surrender. With his flabby and indecisive report to Fouché he enclosed an insolent and insulting letter from Blücher, which called on him to surrender so as not to inflict upon Paris the suffering he had inflicted on Hamburg, and one from Wellington expressing a desire to stop the bloodshed. After that, secure in his knowledge of the cowardice of the Chambers and the weakness of the generals, Fouché undertook the final negotiations for the surrender of Paris.

In his name Bignon sent to the commissioners accredited to the Allied marshals three proposals for a convention, drawn up by Caulaincourt: the cessation of hostilities, the evacuation of the capital by the army, its eventual occupation by the Allies and non-victimization. Meanwhile Fouché summoned his special messengers, Colonel Macirone and General Tromelin. The first, half-English, half-Italian, aide-de-camp to Murat from 1813, certainly a spy and probably a double if not a treble agent, was, naturally enough, one of Fouché's agents and was described to

Wellington as his 'man of trust'. The second was to go to
Blücher. To each of them he personally confided two documents,
which he amplified by 'a verbal explanation'.

The first was an extremely clever letter, intended to cover
himself in the eyes of the Chambers, the army and the King,
while showing that it was in the interest of the Allies to conclude
an armistice:

'The legal state of France is a government with the grandson
of the Emperor of Austria at its head. But if the Powers regard
him as incompatible with peace, would the taking of Paris forward the views that you might have for the restoration of Louis
XVIII? Would the increasing of the evils of war, which could
only be attributed to this motive, be a means of reconciliation?
It is in the King's interest that everything remain in suspense.
What is more reasonable than to conclude an armistice?'

The secret message, in his handwriting but not signed,
attached to the letter, ran as follows:

'The army resists because it is apprehensive; reassure it and it
will be loyal. The Chambers are opposed for the same reason;
reassure each of them and you will have everyone's support. In
order to be understood, some explanation is needed; consequently
do not enter Paris for three days, so that everything may be
made ready. The Chambers will be won over, will believe in
their independence and will consent to everything.'

According to Macirone and Tromelin the 'verbal explanation'
was as follows:

'The Duke of Otranto and his friends must reckon with the
army, where there is much suspicion . . . Davout is won over to
the Bourbons. He assures the Duke that the army will yield if
there are promises of good treatment and that it will readily
become loyal to the King. Fouché and Davout pledge themselves
to send the army out of Paris to any point, no matter how far,
that may be assigned.

'Once the army and the Chambers are separated, both will
quickly agree to accept the proposals of Fouché and Caulaincourt

to recognize Louis XVIII, on condition that the King guarantees the Charter and promises an amnesty.'

At the Tuileries the Commission of Government sat uninterruptedly throughout the night in dread of a general attack by the Allies.

When at dawn on July 3rd the envoys took carriage— Macirone for Le Bourget and Tromelin for Versailles—at Montmartre there were reports of firing between the advance posts. The previous day, the Allies had increased their pressure on the capital; the English from Pierrefitte to Bondy, facing d'Erlon and Reille who were defending the line from Saint-Ouen as far as La Villette.

On the left bank Vandamme, with the 3rd and 4th Corps, occupied Montrouge, Vaugirard, Vanves, Issy and Les Moulineaux, with advance patrols reconnoitring towards Arceuil and Gentilly. The Huet division held Bellevue. Davout had reinforced Vandamme with the Guard and Kellermann's cuirassiers and transferred his headquarters to the Barrière d'Enfer.

About midday, Ziethen's advance-guard, marching from Marly by way of Sèvres, flushed Hulot's patrols who, step by step, withdrew, on Vandamme's orders, towards Vaugirard. The Saint-Cloud and Sèvres bridges were energetically defended against Jagow by the 2nd Line Regiment, the dismounted Polish lancers and the local inhabitants on the orders of Colonel Trippe. In the evening Thielmann, advancing from Versailles by way of Le Plessis-Picquet, occupied Châtillon; Ziethen threw back the French towards Vaugirard.

But during the night Wellington had had second thoughts. Now sure that Napoleon had left for Rochefort and fearing lest the French army, driven by desperation, might leave its entrenchments and fearing its strength and valour, also feeling that his distance from the Prussians might become a danger to him, he at last understood that an armistice might lead to the surrender of Paris and the return of the King. The English commander therefore sent a letter to Blücher through the Prussian General von Müffling, who was attached to Blücher's staff, in which he pledged him to consent to a suspension of hostilities.

'It seems to me,' he wrote, 'that to attack Paris with the forces that you and I have at present under our command would be to risk much and to expose ourselves unnecessarily to the possibility of serious losses . . . The conditions could be that we remain in our positions, that the French army withdraw behind the Loire, that the guarding of Paris be entrusted to the National Guard until new orders from the King of France . . . Doubtless we should not have the useless glory of entering Paris at the head of our victorious armies, but . . .'

Impossible! The old Prussian held firm. He was ready to sacrifice anything to avenge Jéna and staunch his hatred of the French. A second and more urgent letter from Wellington, together with the letter from Fouché sent to him by Tromelin who had been held at the outposts, made him reflect; less so, however, than Gneisenau's advice: exhausted troops, out of touch with the English who were across a river and at least four leagues away, exposed to a flank attack and committed, in case of a check, to a hazardous retreat in order to assure his line of communications. The English did not seem ready to cross the Seine and no one knew whether a French army from the south was on its way . . . with Napoleon at its head!

To Ziethen: order to remain in his present position between Meudon and Issy; to Thielmann: to remain on a line from Bagneux to Châtillon; to Bülow: not to leave Versailles.

Tromelin received 'a clamorous and dramatic welcome'; cessation of hostilities within twenty-four hours on condition that the Prussian army should not be attacked. The Prussian positions would remain between the Bièvre and Issy. 'The Orleans road by Arpajon shall be left open for the movement of the French army to the Loire.' After which Gneisenau handed Tromelin a document which he read several times in order fully to understand it. It was the memorandum signed by Nesselrode and Metternich on June 6th.

On July 3rd, when he made his report to Fouché, the sun had already long risen and cannon were thundering on the left bank. Issy was occupied by Ziethen's troops who, perhaps, had not received Blücher's orders.

Davout was expecting a battle. He ordered Vichery to re-take Issy. The 3rd and 4th Army Corps, the cavalry and the Guard were under arms. Lefol was straddling the Orleans road, Teste was at Grand-Montrouge, Berthezène and Habert were moving on Vaugirard where Pêchoux and Vichery already were, Hulot was on the Seine, Kellermann and Milhaud were mustering on the plain of Grenelle, and the divisions of the Guard were holding the road leading to the military school at Petit-Montrouge. The reserve batteries and the artillery park, coming from the Barrière du Trône, were in position in front of the Invalides. Reille was summoned to the Champ-de-Mars. D'Erlon remained alone on the right bank facing the English, who made no move.

Everywhere the flames were springing up. Officers and soldiers, ardent, excited and burning with enthusiasm, vigorously attacked the Prussians, who defended themselves with energy. Vichery was wounded. A little behind the lines, Davout, on horseback, watched through his spyglass the regiments' advance. Here and there rose shouts of 'Long live the Emperor!'

Napoleon heard similar shouts on leaving Niort. They came from Major Voisin, eighteen officers of the Legion and the 2nd Hussars who had come to render him military honours on his departure.

Six o'clock in the morning. Other cavalrymen were trotting in the Montrouge plain. They were escorting carriages. From them dismounted Bignon, acting Minister of Foreign Affairs, Bondy, Prefect of the Seine, and General Guilleminot, Davout's Chief of Staff since June 29th. Uneasy at receiving no news, Fouché had sent them to the Prussian general commanding the front-line troops. Warned by the following letter, Davout listened to them . . .

'Paris, July 3rd, one o'clock in the morning.

'My dear Marshal, the Commission of Government advises you that it has appointed Messieurs Bignon, de Bondy and Guilleminot as commissioners to treat for a suspension of hostilities and to draw up a military agreement for the surrender of Paris. The outline of this agreement will be given you by the commissioners, for whom you will provide the documents and passports necessary to enable them to carry out their mission.'

It was signed by Count Grenier, Duke of Otranto, Carnot, Quinette, Duke of Vicenza.

In front of them the soldiers were advancing singing, while the guns of Valée and Vandamme pounded the Prussians at Issy.

What inner drama did Davout's impassivity conceal? He hesitated to reply, said that the situation seemed favourable . . . 'he could gain a success if he ordered a general attack'. Bignon bore a terrible responsibility and seized the chance to rid himself of it. Moved by the energy and enthusiasm of the soldiers, whom he could both see and hear, he wrote in his report on the negotiations: 'Sir,' he said, 'if you have hopes of a success, a patriotic feeling drives me not to press you too hard in a contrary direction. It is for you to judge what is best to do.'

'That was not what he wanted,' the minister commented. 'He felt that something should be done. He wanted it, but in order not to lose his popularity with some of the hotheads and the crowd under their orders, he would have liked to have had his hand forced . . .'

Without replying, Davout rushed off at full gallop towards Vaugirard and passed along the whole line of battle. Coming back after an hour, he announced that he had sent General Revest, Vandamme's Chief of Staff, to parley with General von Ziethen.

At eight o'clock firing ceased along the whole line. 'Do you want to dishonour us?' several generals—Exelmans, Flahaut, etc.—shouted at Bignon. There was a great lull. French and Prussian truce envoys went to and fro with proposals for an agreement.

The Commission of Government met in permanent session. Unaware of what the future held for them, but never losing sight of their own interests, Fouché had a resolution passed—unanimously, one may be sure—that 'the sum of one hundred and forty thousand francs allotted for the expenses of the month of "July" be paid at once to those to whom monies are due', and then awaited news from the commissioners.

Nine o'clock. A messenger from von Ziethen announced that they would be received by Prince Blücher and the Duke of Wellington at three o'clock that afternoon at the Château of Saint-Cloud.

A wave of revolt spread along the whole line. An immense clamour invaded the entire front. Angry infantrymen fired into the air; rebellious artillerymen fired at the enemy. They mobbed Davout: 'We have been sold!' 'Treason!' 'Death to the Bourbons!' 'Long live the Emperor!'

ROCHEFORT

It was also about nine o'clock when a yellow four-in-hand without armorial bearings entered Rochefort, passed with a noise like the rattling of old iron under the Tonnay-Charente Gate leading to the port, followed the Quai des Vivres, the Rue des Fonderies and the Rue des Grandes-Allées, turned into the courtyard of the Marine Prefecture and stopped in front of the steps. Saint-Denis leapt down and opened the right-hand door. A man in a green top-coat descended laboriously. The port-admiral and Gourgaud, who had arrived about six o'clock, hurried forward.

'I thought you were ill, M. Bonnefoux,' said the Emperor, mounting the steps.

'Sire, I am no longer ill and would have been much distressed if I had not been able to welcome you . . .'

'I thank you for that and would rather be welcomed by you than by anyone else.'

Respectful greetings, bows, courtesies . . .

The long and tiring journey was over. 'During the journey from Malmaison to Rochefort,' wrote Beker in his account of his mission, 'heavy thoughts must have weighed upon his august brow. But his face never betrayed any emotion and he was always calm and majestic . . . A gloomy silence reigned inside the carriage . . . Everyone drowsed or pretended to do so; no one dared to interrupt the Emperor's train of thought.'

He often reached out for General Beker's snuff-box, on which there was an excellent portrait of the Empress Marie-Louise carved in ivory. Once he took the box in his hands, examined it for a minute and then handed it back without a word. Taciturn and wrapped in thought, he exchanged only a few broken sentences with his companions and it could be seen that in his imagination he still thought that he could be the master of events.

On the staircase, its walls faced with red marble, the Emperor saw once again the words he had carved there in 1808 when he had halted at Rochefort on his way to Spain. Here too was his room, luxuriously furnished; he recognized the great four-poster bed, a marble table supported by swans' necks, Josephine's emblem. She had been with him then, seven years ago. She had done her hair in front of the mirror.

The baggage was all there, brought by Gourgaud, who was acting as orderly officer. The safe-conducts? And the frigates?

They were there in the roads, moored under the guns of the Ile d'Aix, six miles from the port, ready for him. The *Méduse*, a fine seaworthy ship, had recently arrived from Martinique. She was commanded by Captain Ponée, aged forty, who had joined the navy as a sailor in 1790, had been promoted ensign in 1794, lieutenant in 1802 and captain in 1811. He had won all his promotions in action, had been three times prisoner of the English, and owed everything to the Emperor. The *Saale*, formerly the *Amphitrite*, a fine frigate of the line, very seaworthy, heavily gunned, had been ready to leave for the Indies. She was commanded by Captain Philibert, forty-one years old, a naval volunteer, promoted lieutenant in 1803, captain of a frigate in 1811 and captain of a ship of the line in 1814 under the King; an experienced officer. He had distinguished himself at Trafalgar by re-taking the *Algésiras*, captured by the English. He was a Chevalier of the Legion of Honour and of Saint-Louis. He commanded the squadron.

Ushered into the Emperor's room, Bonnefoux announced that all was ready to set sail. Presented a few minutes later, Philibert, 'a cold, brave and sincere man', very conscientious, replied to a few questions about the English. 'Sire,' he said, 'the two frigates await your orders. They will leave when Your Majesty gives the word. They will do everything possible to elude or break the blockade and if they are attacked they will let themselves be sunk rather than cease fire before Your Majesty gives the order . . . '

This was military language, without emotion, the words of a man ready to do his duty. After which Bonnefoux, whose orders and instructions received from Paris we already know, repeated to the Emperor that the winds were contrary and that the Antioche, Breton and Maumusson channels were blockaded.

This last item of information was false. The *Bellerophon* had been alone there since the morning and would still be alone there the following day. Furthermore, she was an old ship. She had fought on August 1, 1798, at Aboukir and had for a time struck her colours to the *Tonnant* (Captain Dupetit-Thouars). At Trafalgar she had fought ship to ship with the *Aigle*. Both captains, the Englishman Cook and the Frenchman Gourrège, had been killed. Dismasted, the *Bellerophon* had had to leave the line of battle. A bad sailer, she was unfitted for a long voyage. Were the French unaware of this?

Gourgaud, who in 1811 had known, studied and inspected Rochefort and its roadstead, sent to reconnoitre, returned to say that it was possible to get out by the Breton channel. But Bonnefoux was a man of honour! False information . . . mistake? Or a secret instruction sent by the government that the Emperor should not be allowed to escape?

The Emperor dined alone and then asked Bonnefoux to summon several naval officers to a discussion, amongst them Vice-Admiral Martin, who had retired in 1810 and was living near Rochefort.

It was a hot day. Bare-headed, hands clasped behind his back, plunged in thought, the Emperor paced up and down the covered terrace near his room. Since June 23rd there had been so many intrigues, deceptions, hypocrisies, irritating restrictions, treasons, woven by Fouché about his departure! The army and the people —would they rise against these wretches who were handing him over to the enemy?

He was still waiting, hoping. Were not all the 'waverings of Napoleon' since leaving the Elysée merely the shifts and changes of his thoughts which now seemed less decisive? Was it a diminished faculty of decision? Or wishful thinking? Or was he awaiting the arrival of a courier bringing news of an appeal from the nation?

From the gardens facing the Prefecture rose cries of 'The Emperor! Long live the Emperor!' The people of Rochefort had heard of his arrival and rushed to see the man who had once held the destinies of France in his hands and who had been so generous to those who were now harrying him. Everyone knew that if he had 'the misfortune to fall into their power they would hand him over to infamous executioners'. He had been recognized along the road from Niort; at Mauzé, at Surgères, the people had cheered him. At Muron two veteran grenadiers of the Guard, Breuil and Bennessée, had come to greet him at the posting-station.

Recalling the irrigation works which he had ordered in 1807 and which had transformed those unhealthy marshes into green meadows, he said to Beker : 'You see, the people are pleased with me for what I did. Everywhere I go, I find proof of their gratitude . . . ' At that moment the crowd was cheering with so much insistence that he went out onto the balcony overlooking the garden. All were quiet. Smiling and moved, he made a friendly gesture with his hand and went on with his pacing.

Did they really believe in Paris that he was no longer strong enough to wield a sword?

Three o'clock. Seated in one of the armchairs at the table, he meditated, and without taking anyone's advice, put his thoughts down on paper and sent them hot-foot to Paris by courier . . . Too late.

At this time the French commissioners were arriving at the Château de Saint-Cloud, Blücher's headquarters. The Prince, Gneisenau, Nostitz, Wellington, Müffling and Colonel Hervey were waiting for them.

Together with Caulaincourt and Fouché, Bignon had drawn up a proposal for an agreement. It was immediately rejected.

Blücher was determined to enter Paris at the head of his troops, Wellington to impose the restoration of Louis XVIII. Both demanded the immediate withdrawal of the French army south of the Loire, the dismantling of the *barrières* and the defence works at Montmartre, etc. They pledged themselves to respect the government and to see that it was respected, even though provisional. Also to respect public property, 'save such as was concerned with war' interposed Blücher, as well as 'individual persons and property . . . until such time as the authority of the King shall replace that of the government' interposed Wellington, who also demanded that passports be refused to 'all persons wishing to leave France in order to flee the King's justice'.

The commissioners signed the capitulation.

Lord Arthur Hill, Wellington's aide-de-camp, took the good news to London.

After reading through the terrible document that crowned his work, completed the humiliation of France, ensured the surrender of the army and the abandonment of so many Frenchmen to partisan fury, Fouché knew very well how to get it approved by the Assemblies. He edited the message in vague and obscure terms, replaced the title 'Capitulation' by that of 'Convention' as less hurtful to national pride, added to it 'some papers concerning earlier negotiations and two proclamations of Louis XVIII', and sent the whole thing to the two Chambers meeting in joint secret session.

Félix Desportes, deputy of the Haut-Rhin and future mayor of Montmartre, the man who on June 28th, during a visit to his home town, had accused Fouché 'of treason and connivance with the country's enemies', tried to restore some vigour to the Assembly. 'Alarming rumours are abroad,' he said with emotion, but murmurs rose from the hall. 'Get back to the agenda and let the Assembly get on with its committees.'

'They want us to carry out measures of public safety,' shouted one representative from his seat, 'and then they tell us to get back to our committees. We must, first of all, save the country!'

Shattered by fear and cowardice, the Chamber refused to listen to Desportes, but decided to hear Sibuet, who proposed a method of shortening the discussions on the Constitution!

'Public safety lies in the quickest possible completion of the Constitution,' concluded the president, Lanjuinais.

In public session on July 4th the deputies listened impassively to the shameless message from the government. 'Having exhausted all means of defence,' wrote Fouché, 'it is impossible to prevent the Allies from making an entry into Paris by force ... ' He expressed his satisfaction that 'in preventing bloodshed the Commission of Government has not had to sacrifice either the principles of political independence or national honour or the glory of French arms'.

And General Solignac had a proposal adopted 'to thank the army, whose firm and courageous stand has made it possible to obtain an honourable agreement which was more than could have been hoped for'. It only needed a motion of thanks from the Chamber to Fouché!

But in Paris the army was snarling. At four o'clock, and again at eleven o'clock, the Commission of Government, threatened by rebellious troops and Federals yelling 'Long live the Emperor! Death to the royalists!', demanded from Masséna the protection of the National Guard, whose duties at the crossroads were far from heavy. Carnot, sent to Montrouge, was the only one who could appease the soldiers. Naturally, they would go but at least they should be paid. The government was afraid. Finally Laffitte agreed to advance the monies necessary. It was the three millions in gold handed over to the banker by the Emperor after his visit to Malmaison which was used to pay the troops.

It is useless to speculate on the feelings of the Guard when they read: 'The former Imperial Guard will march at once and retire behind the Loire, where it will be disbanded. It will take with it its arms, its baggage-train and all its equipment. The wounded may remain in Paris under the protection of the English and Prussian generals. None of the corps commanders, generals, senior officers, officers or non-commissioned officers of the former Guard who have fought against the Allied forces on the 16th, 17th and 18th June last will in future be allowed, on any condition whatsoever, to form part of the new army which will be organized . . . '

Such were the decisions of Wellington and Blücher, approved by Davout. The fury which had driven these men to revolt, indiscipline, desertion, misery and suicide was succeeded by a gloomy resignation since, with the aid of Drouot, military duty and discipline prevailed over their feelings.

July 4th. 'The army retires behind the Loire . . . ' It was to march in two columns. It was to start the next day.

The veterans wept. These men of war, rough, nomadic, indifferent to well-being and careless of passing sentiments, united by the spirit of duty and self-sacrifice in a military family whose father was the Emperor, felt that evening that they had become orphans and foundlings. Accustomed to unforeseen catastrophes, cradled by their dreams, the men of the Guard had believed that the Guard would remain to guide the King of Rome. But 'the traitors' had recalled the Bourbons, bringing misery and humiliation.

Slowly, on July 5th, Vandamme's column began to move off towards Montrouge, Longjumeau, Etampes, Orleans, Jargeau. The Guard followed.

On the 6th Reille's column moved off towards Oysonville and Saint-Péravy-la-Colombe. There was considerable disorder and many desertions, 'since the Emperor was no longer there'! Eighty per cent in the 33rd Line Regiment, eighty-seven per cent in the 86th, all Berthezène's artillerymen, except for six soldiers, took their leave; the Young Guard was reduced to nothing. 'It is no longer possible to serve in such chaos,' wrote the colonel commanding the 6th Hussars. 'Please accept my resignation.'

The generals were prodigal of promises, but the soldiers no longer trusted them; threats, sentences and punishments were without effect.

At Saint-Mesmin (near Orleans), at La Ferté-Sénectère (La Ferté-Saint-Aubin), 'the Old Guard is awaiting the outcome of the promises made to it,' wrote Davout, 'but its calm is like a fire smouldering under ashes'.

'He is smarter than they are,' said the grenadiers. 'He too has withdrawn behind the Loire . . . We are going to him . . . He will return.'

That was what Wellington, Louis XVIII, Blücher, Fouché, the government and a section of the Chambers feared most of all. Learning from one of Beker's letters, sent from Niort on July 1st, that the Emperor had stopped in that town, the Duke of Otranto was thunderstruck and proposed to the Commission measures that betrayed his panic. 'The one fear of the Allies both within the country and abroad,' wrote Carnot, 'is that Napoleon will ride once more, that he will return at the head of the Army of the Loire'.

At Rochefort he still hoped. Perhaps there would be a rising of the people. He watched the arrival of the couriers, hesitated. Would the safe-conducts be granted?

That day, July 4th, he took the chair at the 'Admiralty Council' summoned by Port-Admiral Bonnefoux to discuss the situation and the means of going to America. Admiral Martin was announced. A Canadian, short, thick-set, lively, energetic, very intelligent, a little superficial, he had gone into retirement near Rochefort on his property, La Brulée. The Emperor had known him a long time; twenty years before, they had collaborated in the defence of the coasts of Provence, the one with his guns, the other with his ships. When Napoleon expressed surprise to see him so alert, even though retired, Martin replied that 'princes cannot verify everything for themselves and do not see the wiles of the ambitious, who make use of every means to eliminate their rivals . . .'

In 1809, after the destruction of Admiral Allemand's fleet in the roadstead of the Ile d'Aix, due far more to the admiral's incapacity than to Colonel Congreve's fireships, Decrès had sacrificed Martin, then port-admiral at Rochefort, and sent him into retirement. He had been a *Grand Officier de la Légion* since 1805 and was a highly skilled naval officer. He had had nothing to do with this affair but had offended the minister.

'I wanted to appoint you commander of the fleet before Villeneuve left Cadiz to go and fight at Trafalgar,' remarked the Emperor bitterly, 'but Decrès dissuaded me . . .'

That was in the past. As far as the Emperor's departure was concerned, Martin's advice was: if the commission, on Bonne-foux's advice, considered that it was impossible for the frigates to get out, then the Emperor must go in a small boat as far as the Seudre; he could then reach Royan on horseback and would take ship in the estuary of the Gironde where two corvettes were moored, the *Bayadère* of thirty-two guns and the *Infatigable* under the command of Captain Baudin. He knew Baudin; wounded six times, one arm lost in the fight of the *Sémillante* on March 15, 1808; a sailor and a good one, brave and energetic, he would take the Emperor safe and sound to America. Martin would answer for him.

Consulted immediately by Bonnefoux, Baudin replied on the 5th: 'The Emperor may rely on me; I was opposed, in will and deed, to his attempt to remount the throne because I considered that it would be fatal to France and events have justified my forecast only too well. Today there is nothing I am not willing to undertake to spare our country the humiliation of seeing her sovereign fall into the hands of our most implacable foe. My father died of joy on hearing the news of the return of General Bonaparte from Egypt. I would die of grief to see the Emperor leave France if I thought that, by remaining, he could still do something for her. But he must leave here only if he may live in honour in a free country and not die the prisoner of his enemies . . . The Emperor will embark on the *Pike* or the *Ludlow*, American privateers of exceptional speed. In the case of an encounter, I will sacrifice myself with my two corvettes to bar the enemy's way; however superior he may be, I am sure that I can delay him . . . Let the Emperor hasten; we shall all leave at the same time . . .'

In principle the Emperor accepted the proposal, but he was waiting for his horses, his carriages, his staff and all those who were to accompany him to the United States. His brother Joseph was expected; he wanted to consult him. Sometimes confident, sometimes discouraged, he above all watched the couriers, bearers of news which might 'change the course of events'. He was in no hurry. If the winds were favourable, he would leave on board the frigates as 'more in keeping with his dignity'. Safe-conducts had been asked for. He could just as well go to England; he had spoken of this possibility ever since the day of his abdication, to Hortense, to Bassano, to La Vallette, to Carnot. Later, at Malmaison, he had expressed the wish to surrender to the blockading fleet 'if circumstances compelled him to do so'. In that solution he saw a certain grandeur.

On July 2nd Beker told Bonnefoux of these intentions, which kept coming up in conversation. Perhaps he had been over-persuaded. But on July 4th, in the evening, Napoleon was still hoping that the French would call upon him to place him at the head of the army, while the government, on tenterhooks, feared lest he accept that command.

That afternoon Gourgaud announced the arrival of the suite and the convoy, with Montholon and his family, Las Cases, the orderly officers Planat de la Faye and Autric, the page Sainte-Catherine, the intendant Baillon, some colonels, the 'Mouth', the 'Chamber', servants, chambermaids. The huntsman Chauvrin and the 'Stables' were lodged in the Cordeliers barracks at La Rochelle, with seventeen riding horses, forty-five carriage horses, one *dormeuse*, three berlines, one *pourvoyeuse*, one travelling-carriage, some wagons; in all about sixty men and women, all dead-beat, talkative, peddling news, true or false, collected by hearsay at the posting-stations, uneasy about their future.

They were not to see the Emperor more often than at the Tuileries, for he insisted on preserving sovereign's etiquette and took his meals alone. Bertrand asked to be made an exception, but was refused. The entourage became worried; if the Emperor accepted Admiral Martin's proposal, a great part of it, excluded from the voyage, would be exposed to royalist reprisals. Madame Bertrand and her husband wanted the Emperor to go to England. The Emperor was always thinking about this but kept silent. He dreamed of organizing his 'House', chose Gourgaud and Montholon as orderly officers and asked them for information on the capabilities of Las Cases who could, perhaps, act as *chef de cabinet* . . . to replace Maret . . .

'The senior naval officers have declared that it is impossible to get out of the roadstead of the Ile d'Aix as long as the English keep so strict a blockade within sight of our ships . . . ' Beker wrote to the Provisional Government. 'A corvette is being made ready in the Gironde and a brig is being fitted out so as to profit by one or other of these occasions should the blockading ships, by stationing themselves in front of the channels, leave the estuary of the Gironde unguarded, which would favour the escape of the corvette . . . As the success of this manoeuvre is by no means certain, it is urgent to get the passports, which the English, anxious to see Napoleon depart, can hardly refuse . . . '

Was Beker sincere? Was he in collusion with the port-admiral? Was he under his influence?

Bonnefoux, a brave sailor but an official without initiative, dreaded the responsibilities heaped upon him. Without wishing to betray the Emperor, he wanted to serve the present government, while making provision for tomorrow's; he exaggerated the obstacles in Napoleon's way, quadrupled the smallest skiff sent by the four observation posts, etc. 'To read the reports by telegraph,' wrote Henry Houssaye, 'one would think that all the English squadrons were cruising in sight of Rochefort.' Bonnefoux, worried, full of care, perhaps sincere but certainly panic-stricken, impressed the 'Admiralty Council', Beker and all those around the Emperor. In reality it was no more difficult to get out of Rochefort than to leave the Gironde, and Baudin offered to see to it. Martin, the old sea-wolf, advised this solution.

Chapter VI

THE MOUSETRAP

WHIMS

Joseph had just arrived. He had left Paris with passports bearing false names. The Spanish doctor Unzaga, the American interpreter J. Caret and the valet Maillard were with him. He had come from Saintes, where a 'royal' had mistaken him for the Emperor and had thrown himself at the horses' heads, calling for aid. He had taken refuge in the Hôtel de France, whence he had been rescued by the arrival of some energetic Federals.

Welcomed and lodged at the Prefecture, he had stated his wish to go to America and had forcefully protested against handing Napoleon over to the English. He had suggested that he leave with him, with no other suite than the good Bertrand. The Emperor did not refuse. However, he did not want to run away like a fugitive, abandoning all those who had followed him. Joseph insisted. The essential thing was to leave for the United States; then, with the help of gold, it would be easy to get his real friends to come to him.

The two brothers argued, walking up and down the gallery, while in the garden below the local people cheered them. The ex-King of Spain showed the cool-headedness and decision that the Emperor seemed to lack. Napoleon made no final decision, saying that his situation and his brother's were quite different. However, at Niort he had said : 'I am going to Rochefort and will go on board the first ship I find for America, where others may come and join me . . . ' as Marchand wrote in his *Mémoires*. The 'Admiralty Council' met every day and Napoleon did not accept or refuse the proposals made by Baudin, Joseph or those brought by Lieutenant Besson who offered to take him to America on board the *Magdeleine*, a merchant ship which he commanded and which was due to sail for America with a cargo of brandy.

What had happened to the Emperor since Niort? Why didn't he accept one or other of the proposals which had been made by highly experienced sailors? Montholon also wondered: 'The reasons for our stay at Rochefort are a mystery that nothing can explain,' he wrote, 'for I will always refuse to believe that we stayed five days in this town to await the trunks and wagons sent to La Rochelle by mistake and which contained objects forming part of the service of the Master of the Household at Elba!'

This sally, directed at Bertrand and his wife, was similar to the opinion expressed in his notes by General Lallemand, former vice-commander of the Chasseurs of the Guard who, wounded at Waterloo, had now joined the Emperor: 'Several officers who accompanied the Emperor, and especially those who, being trusted by him, had free access to him and influence over him, were not in favour of this last proposal (Baudin's) and, seeing nothing but obstacles to all the proposals suggested, caused delays. The luke-warmness with which they welcomed these proposals, the lack of resolution which they continually showed, were due to their desire, clearly shown even before the departure from Malmaison, to see the Emperor decide to go to England . . . It was strange and pitiful to see men who had given the Emperor proofs of sincere loyalty acting in the same way as his enemies and those who desired his downfall . . . Such was, however the secret of the Emperor's destiny; such were the causes that thrust him, still living, into the tomb. He could have retained his freedom and reached a friendly land . . . ' In fact, Joseph and Besson reached America without difficulty.

'Unfortunately,' concluded Lallemand, 'now that there was no longer any question of high political interest, now that there was no longer any glory to be won, the Emperor became indifferent to everything that concerned his personal affairs. He paid too little heed to his own interests and entirely abandoned the responsibility to those about him.'

'The Emperor is calm and seems more or less indifferent to what happens . . . ' wrote Marchand. Meanwhile, all round him there was suddenly more and more consternation.

*　　　　　*　　　　　*

From some old tub leaving Rochefort, the commander of the

Bellerophon learnt that 'Buonaparte is at the Ile d'Aix' and that the frigates in the harbour had taken their powder aboard. The Emperor would certainly try to escape. He therefore came as close inshore as possible, kept look-out boats circulating all night, and kept a hundred picked men ready to board the fugitive.

Countless orders and messages came from the British Admiralty. Rear-Admiral Sir Henry Hotham, on board the *Superb*, in the roadstead at Quiberon, made the best possible use of the weak means at his disposal between Cape Finisterre and Bordeaux. He was kept advised of numerous projects for Bonaparte's flight. Which was the right one?

July 6th. Order to Maitland : Buonaparte intends to go to the United States. Port of embarkation uncertain. Redouble vigilance. 'I believe that he will leave from Rochefort, either with a squadron or on a merchant ship. The commander of the *Bellerophon* will keep under his command all the ships to be found there until there is news of his capture . . . The peace of Europe may depend on this . . . If you take him he should be brought to me; I have orders about how to deal with him. You will transfer him from the ship on which he may be found to one of His Majesty's ships. Hold the messenger . . . '

It was the *Slaney*.

A little later there was another letter from the Admiral, brought by a coasting lugger. Lord Keith had sent to Hotham by the *Ferret*: 'During the night of June 30th the government received from the French authorities a request for a passport and a safe-conduct to allow Buonaparte to go to America. The reply was negative. The *Pactolus* has landed an agent in the Gironde . . . Use the best available means to capture the fugitive . . . '

At Rochefort, an order to Bertrand to take Lieutenant Besson's proposal into consideration. A native of Angoulême, aged thirty-four, enlisted as cabin-boy and then accepted as midshipman, he had been promoted assistant ensign in 1804, commissioned in 1811 and appointed brevet-lieutenant by Rapp in 1813 for his conduct at the siege of Danzig. He had been recommended to the Emperor for further promotion but had not been gazetted until January 6, 1815. Married to the daughter of an Altona ship-owner, he now commanded the *Magdeleine*, belonging to his father-in-law. He would make, on this boat, a hiding-place for the Emperor in a sound cask, in case of an unexpected search.

On July 6th Las Cases signed a contract with Besson and advanced him the funds he needed. Meanwhile the Emperor's baggage was loaded on to the schooner *Sophie* . . . Order to Gourgaud to go to the Gironde to make contact with Baudin and to inspect the *Bayadère*.

Was a decision imminent? In haste Savary cashed 100,000 francs worth of bonds for gold pieces. These were divided into twelve buckskin belts made by Marchand and entrusted to twelve members of the suite . . . The papers announced the entry of the English into Paris. There was dread of what would happen next. The guard at the Hôtel de la Marine was strengthened. Las Cases believed that Napoleon would resume the throne . . . The Bourbons could not be accepted in France!

On July 6th Beker wrote to his family: 'Today is the third day since our arrival with no prospect of getting out as long as the English ships block all the channels. No news from Paris and no passports, thanks to which it would be possible to seek refuge in some country or other. I can see no favourable chance for the Emperor's departure. We await our fate from Paris, in the hope that the Provisional Government, speaking in the name of France, will be able to obtain suitable conditions to ensure the imperial family a refuge and the means of existence. I am longing to know the fate of our unhappy country and that of the unfortunate monarch whom I have been appointed to guard . . . This state of affairs may still last several days without our position getting any better, unless the attitude of the army and the capital influences the enemy and forces it to recognize the government chosen by the people . . . As we are far from the theatre of events it is impossible to hazard any guess what the intentions of the Allies towards France may be . . . '

However, the telegraph brought some news: 'Hasten the departure of the Emperor . . . Louis XVIII is on his way to the capital . . . Forthcoming convention with the English . . . The government refuses the books from the Trianon and the furniture demanded by Bertrand . . . '

Was this a good or bad sign? The Emperor read in the papers the proclamations launched from Cambrai by the King on June 28th: 'I learn that the door of my kingdom is open: I hasten to win back my misled subjects.' In that of the 25th there was: 'In the period when the most criminal undertaking backed by the most unbelievable defection, etc. . . . We will then put into effect laws against the guilty . . . ' There seemed to be a distinction between the 'instigators' of the revolution of March 20th and those who were 'misled', but how was that distinction to be made? Twenty thousand, 50,000 Frenchmen were threatened . . . Was this an amnesty? . . . The Emperor expressed his sorrow, waxed indignant, when he found that the emissaries of Fouché and Davout, Gaillard and Périgord, had already left for Cambrai. 'He denounced the intriguers and the lickspittles, the scourge of princes, castigated the hypocrisy of the King, harshly criticized his family.'

*   *   *

July 7th. The telegraph announced the entry of von Zeithen's Prussian corps into Paris by the Barrière de la Cunette (at the farther end of the Quai de la Grenouillère—Quai d'Orsay—at the point where the Ile des Cygnes ends).

Davout and the army had left Paris; the Chambers were at their last gasp, still discussing the Constitution! Fouché was the sole authority existing in France, able to arrange her future as he chose. Wellington, acting for the King, sent him a verbal invitation through 'Colonel' Macirone to come to his headquarters at Neuilly.

A written memorandum: Dissolution of the Chambers created by Buonaparte and the Commission of Government appointed by them . . . Loyal address to the King.

A note dictated by Talleyrand announced the maintenance by His Majesty of the ancient Charter . . . an appeal to the electoral colleges . . . formation of a new chamber, etc. . . .

No mention either of the tricolour or of an amnesty.

Fouché did not want to go alone to the rendezvous 'like a conspirator'. To accompany him he chose the deputy Manuel, 'his tool', Molé, aiming to become a King's minister, General de Valence, member of the Chamber of Peers, former equerry of the Duke of Chartres, son-in-law of Madame de Genlis . . .

The interview took place in the evening of July 5th. The English were everywhere; the Allies had occupied the northern suburbs. Alongside Wellington were Talleyrand, Pozzo di Borgo, Goltz and Sir Charles Stuart. Wary, cold and maintaining an extreme reserve, Fouché, pretending to represent the Chamber, stressed the bad impression produced on the country by the threats from Cambrai, and its desire to preserve the flag. France would accept the King's return on condition that His Majesty granted a general amnesty and accepted the tricolour flag. They argued until four in the morning of July 6th, but Wellington and Talleyrand refused both the amnesty and the tricolour.

On July 5th, at the Château d'Arnouville (near Gonesse, three leagues from Paris), Louis XVIII welcomed the royalists: Crussol, Pasquier, Macdonald, Vitrolles, etc. and then Talleyrand, Baron Louis, Jaucourt—and Wellington. They could get whatever they liked from Fouché in exchange for the post of Minister of Police. The next day, July 6th, the King signed the appointment of the regicide.

Fouché had made everything ready for the 'restoration', which meant the 'reconciliation'; but everything was not yet over. He had still to gull those who had supported him and to master the others . . . to have his portrait painted for his fiancée, Mlle de Castellane, whom he was to marry on August 1st, by which time Louis XVIII, who owed his throne to him, would have agreed to sign the marriage contract!

Dressed in full court costume and adorned with all his orders, the old Jacobin posed for his miniaturist before going to dine with Talleyrand. Then the Prince of Benevento, leaning on Fouché's arm — 'vice supported by crime' as Chateaubriand put it — entered the King's study to take the oath! Fouché's oath!

The royal proclamation, placarded on the walls, ended: 'So now there is amongst us the father and friend of the people, the angel of war, the guarantor of our happiness . . . ' And in the last paragraph: 'News has just been received that Buonaparte has arrived at Rochefort. The two frigates which were waiting for him in the roads were closely blockaded even before his arrival there. It has been judged wise to withdraw them into the port, but, in order to put the English fleet on the wrong scent, a corvette and a sloop have been hastily fitted out and it is on board one of these that Buonaparte will try to escape. Justice, both human and divine, is on his trail; it is to be hoped that he will not escape . . . '

It was a paraphrase of the letter sent to the provisional government on July 4th by Beker, while that sent him the same

day by Fouché had just reached him and had left him thought-
ful:

'Napoleon must embark without delay. The success of our
negotiations depends mainly on the assurance of his embarkation
that the Allied powers demand and you cannot imagine how
greatly the safety and tranquillity of the state are compromised
by these delays. If Napoleon had only made up his mind . . .
We have before us a report from the port-admiral of Rochefort,
in which he says that departure would not have been impossible
on the 29th . . .

'The Commission therefore places the person of Napoleon in
your charge. You must use every means that may seem necessary, while preserving the respect due to him. See that he arrives
at Rochefort without delay and see to it that he embarks at once.
As to the services which he offers, our duty to France and our
engagements with the foreign powers do not allow us to accept
them and you must not refer them to us again. Finally, the
Commission finds it unsuitable that Napoleon should have any
communication with the English squadron. It cannot grant the
permission asked of it in this matter.'

[Signed] Duke of Otranto, Count Grenier, Quinette,
Duke of Vicenza, Carnot.

By the same courier Davout ordered the generals commanding
at La Rochelle and Rochefort 'to give every assistance to Beker
and to support him by all means and measures judged suitable'.
The navy, Bonnefoux, the Ministry of the Interior and the
prefects had been advised!

It will be noted that it was a question of getting Napoleon to
embark, if needs be by force, but not of letting him leave.
Although Fouché knew of the presence of the English ships and
the impossibility of the frigates leaving safely, he did not rescind
the order 'only to set sail if the situation allows this to be done
without exposing them to any danger' and, since he forbade
Napoleon to communicate with the English squadron, it must
be assumed that he wanted to keep the Emperor shut up in a
floating prison in order to hand him over to the English or to
Louis XVIII, as his interests might require.

July 8th: a day of decisions—or almost! At Paris the members of the Commission of Government had met the previous evening and had learnt from Fouché that that meeting was to be their last, the Allies having decided to restore Louis XVIII. Caulaincourt had acquiesced; Carnot, Grenier and Quinette had protested, proposed to join the army and to re-establish themselves at Blois. The Prussian drums of a detachment of the 4th division of Ziethen's corps, entering the court of the Tuileries with two fieldpieces, matches alight, had put an end to the discussion.

The message of dissolution addressed to the Chambers was listened to without emotion by the representatives; the order of the day was passed unanimously. Manuel spoke of 'the will of the people'. One heard 'the will of the people!' ... 'permanently' ... 'let us await the enemy!'. Then Lanjuinais went to the door, saying: 'History will judge!' History has judged.

The same day, at three o'clock in the afternoon, white flags replaced the tricolour on the public buildings. His Majesty King Louis XVIII made his entry into Paris in a coach, preceded by Marshals Gouvion-Saint-Cyr, Macdonald, Marmont, Oudinot, Victor, Moncey, Lefebvre, and Generals Maison, Reiset, Rochechouart, Bordessoulle and Beurnonville ... 'all heroes *sans peur et sans reproche*' ...

At the former Empress Theatre, which that evening reverted to its earlier name of the Théâtre de l'Odéon, a comedian put on a piece: *La Journée des Dupes*!

Castlereagh wrote to Lord Liverpool: 'I learnt this evening from the King (of France) that he has given Fouché orders to make every effort to have Buonaparte arrested ...'

At sea. Hotham wrote to Maitland that the Lords of the Admiralty believed that Napoleon was thinking of flight and of going to America with his family: 'I require and order you to keep the strictest watch and to intercept him. You will search thoroughly every ship you may encounter. If you have the luck to apprehend him, you will take him on board with his family, will keep strict watch on him and will make your way as swiftly as possible to the nearest English port (Torbay in preference to Plymouth) ... All communication with the land is forbidden. Absolute secrecy ... If there is no flag-officer at the port

. . . send express letters to the Secretary of the Admiralty and to Lord Keith.'

At Rochefort, at six in the morning. Gourgaud was sent by the Emperor to the frigates. All day long the wind was inshore and during the night off the land, but at three leagues distance it died out. At reveille the winds were variable N.W. to N.N.W. Philibert and Ponée, visited one after the other, were of the same opinion; the English fleet blocked the channels as far as Les Sables. There was little hope of being able to get out.

But on Gourgaud's return to the Hôtel de la Marine everything was topsy-turvy. The Emperor's entourage was alarmed. Beker had come to show the Emperor the letter from Fouché dated the 4th and received the previous day.

'What do you think, General?' asked the Emperor in astonishment.

'I am not in a position to give Your Majesty advice,' Beker replied. 'The risks that Your Majesty may run are too great. The only advice I can permit myself to give is to take an immediate decision and then carry out as swiftly as possible whatever Your Majesty may have decided. The fate of France may depend on it, unfortunately; the new government may send agents to seize Your Majesty. From then on my powers will be at an end and Your Majesty may be exposed to dangers whose outcome it is impossible to foresee.'

Were these threats or loyalty? Had Beker and Bonnefoux received secret instructions?

'But surely you would never hand me over?' the Emperor asked sharply.

'Your Majesty knows that I am ready to give my life to protect your departure, but by sacrificing myself I would not save you, for the commanders of the frigates, should circumstances change, would take their orders from the ministers of Louis XVIII and would not recognize mine . . . '

HESITATIONS

In order to gain twenty-four hours over his enemies in Paris, the Emperor made his decision known only after the post had left! He would go to the Ile d'Aix with the evening tide; he would be nearer the frigates. 'I will be able to embark at once if the wind is favourable,' he said.

On board the *Saale*. In the log: 'The port-admiral's barge came to warn us that, perhaps, the Emperor Napoleon might come on board this evening . . . ' The whale-boat and the rest of the ship's boats were sent to Fouras, where the boats from Rochefort would meet them.

Four o'clock. After bolting his lunch, Napoleon said farewell to Bonnefoux. He offered him his carriages and harness which he could not take with him. The port-admiral refused them, but accepted a gold box with the monogram 'N' in diamonds.

'Are you afraid it may have something in it?' said the Emperor who had noted a certain hesitation on Bonnefoux's part. 'Don't worry; it's empty and worthy of you.'

Outside, the carriages were ready; the company got into them and they left at a sharp trot, with an escort of horsemen, by way of the Rue Saint-Charles. On the Place Colbert a respectful crowd was waiting. The carriage-blinds were lowered, but there were shouts of 'Long live the Emperor!' The guard at the Rochelle Gate presented arms. But he was not there!

A closed caleche, belonging to the prefect, had left the coach-house and stopped in front of the terrace running along the front of the house; a few moments later, still wearing his green over-coat and cocked hat, the Emperor came out with M. Bonnefoux. He looked upset. He walked hurriedly, crossed the terrace and went down the steps. On the pavement he turned to Bonnefoux, moved his left arm as if to reveal his heart and bade him farewell. The door closed and the carriage crossed the garden, reached the gates and turned into the Rue des Fonderies and then along the quay, towards the Charente Gate. Where was he going? To the army? To the Loire?

No. Those who were watching the caleche saw it turn left just outside the town and join the waiting line of carriages on the La Rochelle road. The dusty track led to Fouras, crossing the plain of Aunis, between marshes over which droned clouds of mosquitoes. A flat, monotonous landscape; here and there hedges and clumps of trees bent by the wind, which seemed to be trying to escape from the ocean and its storms.

Buried in his corner, alone, lost in his thoughts, the Emperor remained indifferent. They passed through a few red-roofed villages: Vergeroux, Saint-Pierre. The peasants greeted him . . . without realizing what was happening.

Five o'clock: Fouras. Scarcely 800 inhabitants; strong, thick-set, stout-hearted fishermen grouped around the little port at the mouth of the Charente. The Emperor and his suite avoided the village and moved towards the cove of La Coue, a beach shut off on the south by a cliff dominated by the château and the keep of the Sire de Maumont. In the sun, just beginning to set, it was like a scene from the Orient. The tide was out, surging; the wind rather strong. The boats sent by Bonnefoux, the prefect's barge flying the imperial colours and the frigates' boats were waiting, without being able to come alongside; on the beach were officers, soldiers and fishermen. Halting on the shore, the Emperor stepped out and walked down to the water's edge by a little path; welcomed by the officers, he stood on a stone and climbed on to the back of 'Père Beau' who carried him out to the *Saale's* long-boat; Beker, Savary, Bertrand and Gourgaud took seats beside him. The ladies, the officers and the servants were also carried out to the boats in the same way.

Half-past five. The boats pushed off. A great shout of 'Long live the Emperor!' arose for the last time. Napoleon, greatly moved, made a gesture with his hand and an almost inaudible 'Farewell, my friends . . . '

'We wept like girls,' said an old coastguard, who later carved in the stone on the jetty the word 'Napoleon'. On the golden sands of the south beach where he made his last steps on the French mainland, on the verge of the quay that bears his name, a truncated granite pyramid, the gift of Baron Gourgaud, recalls:

HERE
ON JULY 8TH 1815
NAPOLEON I LEFT
THE MAINLAND FOR EXILE
THE EMPEROR WAS CARRIED TO
THE WHALEBOAT BY THE SAILOR
BEAU OF FOURAS

The crew of the imperial longboat struggled against the wind and tide to reach the open sea. The passengers were drenched; several times they nearly capsized. After an hour and a half's effort they reached the Enet deep; the fort stood out against the red sky. About a quarter of a mile to the west the *Méduse* and the *Saale* lay at anchor.

In the frigate's log is the following entry:

'From four to eight o'clock fair weather; wind from the N.W.

'Six o'clock. Enemy frigate seen abeam near Oléron, running N.N.W. under topsails. She went about and ran S.W. until seven o'clock and was then lost to sight.

'Sighted several boats coming from Fouras, one of them with the Emperor on board, as we judged from the colours it was flying. We at once made arrangements to receive him.'

Since the weather was again favourable, the Emperor gave up his idea of disembarking on the Ile d'Aix. Perhaps it would be possible to leave with the frigates. A little after seven o'clock he had the *Saale* hailed. She was anchored, with her consort, near the little island of Enet where a fort had been built in 1810.

At seven-thirty the log-book reports: 'His Majesty has come on board. The crew was drawn up to starboard and greeted him with cries of "Long live the Emperor!" The guard presented arms and rendered him the honours due to him. His Majesty was accompanied by Generals Bertrand, the Duke of Rovigo, Count Lallemand and Count Gourgaud. The other boats brought the ladies, and the gentlemen's baggage.'

There were no artillery salvoes because of the proximity of the enemy. After the officers had been presented to him by Captain Philibert, the Emperor inspected the ship. He asked about the crew, the armament, the direction of the wind and what measures had been taken. Everything was ready to set sail if, during the night, the winds should be favourable. Napoleon went into the main cabin, divided into two by a curtain, one part of which was intended for him and the other for Beker. The generals were housed in the officers' cabins; Bertrand and his family in a deck-house.

After supper, consumed in a quarter of an hour in the captain's cabin, the Emperor called for Gourgaud. What did they talk about? Then he walked for a little before going to bed. Everyone remained at his post, ready to set sail at a moment's notice.

About eleven o'clock the wind died down; boats came alongside with passengers and baggage so that, on July 9th, at reveille at five o'clock in the morning, there were:

6. The meeting of Wellington and Blücher at La Belle-Alliance

On board the *Saale*: the Emperor and his 'Household', the generals and their servants, in all about forty persons.

On the *Méduse*: General Montholon and his family, the officers de Résigny, Schultz, Piontkowski, Autric and Rivière; secretaries, clerks, valets, cleaners, as well as Joannis, second quartermaster of the Naval Guard, born in America, and Hébert, from San Domingo, cavalryman of the 2nd Hussars! What on earth were they doing there? That is to say twenty-six passengers; in all sixty-six persons.

As for the personal safety of the Emperor, wrote Beker to the Commission of Government on July 8th, all precautions were taken against enemy action. 'However difficult my mission may be, under the double commitment of my duty to the Emperor and to the government, I will, I hope, fulfil it to the satisfaction of both, taking as my code of conduct the recognized principles of honour.'

*   *   *

The sun rose. The weather was fine. The crew breakfasted, then began cleaning ship. On the poop Ensign Luneau, on the morning watch, scanned the horizon.

The Emperor came up to him. 'Which way is the wind? Is there any sign of the enemy?'

'Sire,' the officer replied, 'the wind is still poor and contrary . . . Over there by Chassiron I can see two suspicious-looking ships.'

'Let me look,' said the Emperor. Leaning on Luneau's arm, who before dying as a lieutenant in 1832 often used to speak of the emotion that made his heart beat faster at that moment, the Emperor climbed on to a gun-mounting and watched through his glass the masts of two ships just above the north point of Oléron. They were the *Bellerophon* and the *Myrmidon*, blocking the channel.

He strode pensively about the deck, then again turned to the officer. 'Let us visit the Ile d'Aix,' he said curtly.

Luneau had the Emperor's longboat made ready and informed the Captain, Bertrand, Las Cases and Gourgaud who, still half-asleep, arrived without his sword and was reproved. At half-past five the longboat set out for the Ile d'Aix.

It is a crescent-shaped island facing the mouth of the Charente,

G

a league in length, 700 yards wide and thirty above sea level. Neither the landing stage nor the coastal wall facing Fouras existed at that time. The Emperor landed in English Cove, on a rocky beach emerging from the mud, of which the present 'Petit Boucard' is the last remaining trace. He crossed the Montalembert fort, reached the drawbridge and went on to an open space on which, being a Sunday, the 14th Marines, newly formed from naval ratings of the 27th and 28th, were drawn up for church parade. Their leader, Captain Coudein, was absent; the inspection was being taken by Captain Cuvillier commanding the 27th. Beyond, in the three streets of the village, the inhabitants crowded to watch the parade.

Eight o'clock. The Emperor?—they were not aware of his presence in the roadstead but he was soon recognized. The official report by Coudein, addressed later, it is true, to the King's minister, does not allude to the demonstrations which might have caused him trouble with the authorities, but a contemporary says that Napoleon 'was welcomed with enthusiasm' and that the 'cheering was unanimous'. In any case, walking down the ranks while the drummers beat 'general salute', he asked Captain Bancal, who replaced Captain Cuvillier at the head of the 27th, 'to order a few drill movements'. All were carried out enthusiastically and correctly, after which, satisfied, he took his leave to cries of 'Long live the Emperor!'

Accompanied by artillery and engineer officers, Napoleon then inspected the island, the village laid out by Vauban, surrounded by ramparts and ditches and pierced by streets named Marengo, Napoleon, etc., the Arcole quarter, the fortifications he had planned, the batteries on the rock-bound western coast. They passed close by the house which he had ordered to be built for the local commander. Then he reached the Coudepoint battery, begun in 1812, and stopped for some time at the Liédot fort. He had chosen the site in 1808 and laid out the plans with his own hand. The two fortifications were intended to cover the Basques roadstead where the *Bellerophon* was now lying, out of cannon range.

Napoleon discussed technical matters with the officers, pointed out a mistake, noted a badly sited fortification and looked from a distance at the Boyard fort, begun on his orders but never finished . . . to 'defend with twenty-six 36-pounders' the area between the islands of Aix and Oléron. 'He seemed at the height of his powers.'

What was he thinking? Of his visit to these parts on August 5, 1808? Or perhaps, considering that he might not be able to escape on the frigates, was he afraid of being seized and was thinking how he could defend himself? The visit ended. Beker arrived. He had not been told of the Emperor's departure. Very uneasy, fearing lest he might escape him, Beker had demanded a boat from the sailors who had launched a sort of two-oared 'coracle' which amused them greatly. Shaken and seasick, Beker landed just as the Emperor was getting into his longboat to return to the *Saale*.

'Don't abandon us!' shouted the inhabitants, crowding to the jetty to see him off.

* * *

'Has he abandoned us?' asked the soldiers who had arrived at the Loire.

To avoid desertions, mutinies and dissensions, the generals had told them that, since the Executive Commission and the Chambers were at one with the army, nothing would be changed, neither the form of government nor the flag. Davout, the commander-in-chief, had let it be said—though the deception could not be prolonged without danger of a catastrophe, as the generals warned him in countless letters.

On July 6th, during a short visit to his château at Savigny-sur-Orge, he had summoned Generals Haxo, Kellermann and Gérard, the last not yet fully recovered from his wound received on June 18th at Bierges, near Wavre, and had ordered them to go to Paris to negotiate the adhesion of the army to the royal government just about to be set up. He thus wanted the 'army itself' and not merely its commander-in-chief to offer 'to recognize the King', in exchange for which His Majesty's government would accord certain guarantees . . .

On the 7th Haxo was in Paris with Gérard, 'still unable to dress himself'; Kellermann, who was unwilling to leave his cavalrymen, would join them a few days later. But since the Provisional Government had been dissolved, the mission of the envoys seemed to them to have ended.

General Grundler spread bad news; the Prussians wanted to

invest Vincennes, the English the northern fortresses, above all
Le Havre, Cherbourg and even Brest . . . naturally! The National
Guard still kept the tricolour cockade, which the King would
not hear of. It was said that the Count d'Artois had had the flag
dragged through the mud at Saint-Denis 'which made reconciliation very difficult', Haxo wrote in a letter to Davout.

Maison, governor of the 1st military area at Paris, said that
the King would deal very leniently with the army, that Talleyrand was favourably inclined to the tricolour and that he wanted
to hand in his resignation . . .

Some bodyguards had been stoned on the Quai de la Grande-
Galerie. On his return to Paris four thousand persons coming
from Saint-Denis had wanted to shout 'Long live the King!' but
the National Guard had closed the barriers.

'From all that I have seen and heard today the army is more
anxious than ever to put a stop to the ambitions of the English
and Prussians.'

That day, July 10th, the commissioners had seen Fouché. 'The
army,' he had said, 'will be treated with honour and in accord
with its interests, but the tricolour flag must be renounced.'

With Maison they had encountered a certain amount of military *esprit de corps*, but Marshal Gouvion-Saint-Cyr, the
Minister of War, had been chilly, arrogant and imperious. He
had refused to admit anything except total submission of those
whom he called 'the brigands of the Loire'.

General Haxo wrote at once to Davout: 'A council of the
most important leaders must be summoned at once to lay down
certain very modest fundamental conditions, on the basis of
which we could negotiate with the King.'

Davout himself preferred to draw up his 'instructions and
powers given to the envoys to make known to the King and the
minister of war the submission of the French army which has
withdrawn behind the Loire'.

'The motives which have led the army to take this step are a
guarantee of its good faith,' he wrote. 'These motives are those
of the most absolute devotion to our unhappy country and the
desire to spare it civil war. For this reason the generals, the
officers and the soldiers will sacrifice their glory and their most
cherished interests.

'The army believes that by submitting freely to the govern-

ment of Louis XVIII, based upon the laws, it gives that government a great power against the foreigners who want the destruction of France, of her national existence. It is a powerful force
to contribute to the reconciliation of all Frenchmen.

'The army is therefore disposed to swear loyalty to the King
and to the laws which govern the country; it only asks what is
consonant with honour: that no Frenchman be proscribed nor
deprived of his rank or his civil or military employment, that the
army be preserved in its present state so long as the foreigners
remain in France.

'The commissioners must quickly obtain replies to these
demands, so that the generals and senior officers may reconcile
the other officers, the non-commissioned officers and the men to
the King and preserve his army for him.'

Sent for signature to the regiments, Davout's 'instructions'
were signed by twenty-two marshals, twenty-two generals and
fourteen other senior officers. General Valin refused; so too did
Delort. 'I would be massacred by my cuirassiers,' he said.
Milhaud, the regicide, in order to avoid banishment, without
consulting anyone in the 4th Cavalry Corps, tendered the submission of all his officers and men, and followed this up in
writing with lies and treacheries, boasting of having, the year
before, 'anticipated Marmont's action without his treachery' . . .
since he had only sent his adhesion to the royal government
after the first abdication of the Emperor!

When the envoys presented these 'Instructions' to the Minister of War, Marshal Gouvion-Saint-Cyr, haughty and arrogant,
replied to them that 'this matter cannot be ended so quickly . . .
The King's Council will not hear any talk of conditions . . . '
The envoys wrote to Davout: 'We are told on all sides that any
resistance on our part only favours the plans of the Allies and a
conditional submission would not be enough to halt them; it
would only be considered a ruse and a proof of further bargain-
ing after their departure.' That was what they had been told by
the Foreign Minister, the Minister of Finance and the Prefect of
Police. Gouvion-Saint-Cyr had added: 'Be sure that the King
will do more than you ask of him . . . '! Blackmail?

In any case, fearing for the fate of the army 'whose destruction
would please certain people', the envoys suggested that Davout
'induce the army to make a pure and simple submission, the only

way left, in our opinion'. The collapse was complete, the army divided. What could Davout, who had handed Paris over without striking a blow, do? Would the army fight against the enemy forces who were acting as the King's bodyguard? The Chambers no longer existed; Napoleon II was in Vienna. The Emperor was a prisoner.

*   *   *

Almost.

On his return to the *Saale* Napoleon was greeted by Port-Admiral Bonnefoux, who brought a letter from Decrès. This was to be his last before he handed over his portfolio to the new Minister of the Marine appointed by the King, the Marquis de Jaucourt:

'It is of the utmost importance that the Emperor leave French soil as soon as possible. The interests of the state and the safety of his person alike urgently require this . . .

'If circumstances do not permit the frigates to leave, it might be possible for him to leave on a despatch-boat, without the knowledge of the English ships. In case this way suits him, such a boat should be put at his disposal as soon as possible, so that he may leave within twenty-four hours.

'If this does not suit him and he should prefer to go on board one of the ships of the English squadron, he is requested to make a formal and positive demand to you in writing and, in this case, you will appoint a parliamentarian to be placed at his disposal so that he may carry out whichever of the two solutions he may choose . . .

'It is essential that he does not set foot again on French soil . . .

'It is understood that if it is possible for the frigates to leave, the orders given earlier for his transport to the United States by this means remain unchanged.'

This letter paraphrases a decree of the Provisional Government dated July 6th. In it, in Articles 4 and 5, it is stated that 'in any case, the commander of the ship destined to take Napoleon cannot, on pain of high treason, land him on any point of French territory . . .

'If the commander of the ship be forced to put into port, he will take all measures of security that may be necessary to ensure that Napoleon does not disembark. If needs be, he will call on the civil and military authorities to give him every assistance.

'General Beker must not leave him until he is outside the channels and, if Napoleon has asked to be transported on board the English fleet or taken to England he must not leave him until after he has been put on board the said fleet or has landed in England.'

Was this a tardy, but more liberal, manoeuvre by Fouché?

RENUNCIATIONS

A despatch from the British government dated June 30th, announcing that the safe-conducts asked for by Napoleon had been refused, reached Boulogne on July 2nd or 3rd and Paris on the 5th or 6th. Fouché could now, without risk, let Frenchmen believe that he had provided Napoleon with the means to escape and that, if he had not made use of them, it was his own fault. Naturally the documents received from Paris were silent about the refusal of passports; we do not know the extent of the knowledge of the Emperor's entourage or even of the Prefecture of Rochefort, but there is no doubt that the Prefecture at La Rochelle where the prefect, Richard, was one of Fouché's creatures, was certainly well informed.

On board the *Saale*, Bonnefoux and Beker drew up fresh instructions to Captain Philibert:

'For the mission entrusted to you, you may make full use of all the facilities available at the port ... and of the two frigates, in strict compliance with the instructions of the minister; also of despatch-boat No. 24 and the brig *Epervier* (Lieutenant Jourdan de la Passardière) moored in the roadstead of the Ile d'Aix since July 9th. You may make use of them for either one or the other mission, after reference to General Beker.

'In the event of your sending the *Epervier* under a flag of truce, you will have all her guns, as well as all ammunition, unloaded into lighters, retaining only one piece and a few blanks to summon help in case of need.

'Having full reliance on your common-sense and experience, I approve in advance any measures you may think it necessary to take in order to ensure the success of the missions entrusted to you, reconciling in every possible way the views of the government with the personal safety of Napoleon.'

Nervous and scowling, the Emperor strode up and down the deck, weighing up his chances; then he climbed to the poop, came down again and wandered about. He questioned the officer of the watch about the enemy and about the wind. Breeze from the N.W. Weather good.

Eleven o'clock. A meal was served. Universal despondency. Philibert and the other diners vouchsafed their opinions. Napoleon had not asked for them and paid no attention to them. 'His Majesty was in a brown study,' wrote Gourgaud. Had he made a decision?

Let us think it out. The Emperor had to leave within twenty-four hours. There was no despatch-boat at Rochefort ready to set sail for the United States. To get one fit to undertake such a journey would take several days. Then, too, a midshipman had been given the task of making a reconnaisance along the coast; he reported the presence of three English ships in the narrows. Therefore the departure of the frigates, authorized in principle, was impossible without a fight. On board the *Saale*, whose commander could not 'under pain of high treason' allow Napoleon to set foot on French soil, how could the Emperor reach the *Bayadère* or the *Magdeleine*, now in the Gironde, if he were not to sneak away like a common criminal?

There were these alternatives left: either to reach America on the frigates, if the safe-conducts had been granted, or, if not, to surrender to the English.

Time was pressing. The telegraph announced the entry of Louis XVIII into Paris. 'Fouché had advised us that the English government would probably send the passports through the squadron keeping watch on Rochefort,' wrote Savary.

After supper, during a discussion with Beker and Bertrand, the Emperor decided to send Las Cases and the Duke of Rovigo (Savary) under a flag of truce to the *Bellerophon*. 'We are risking nothing by finding out if the passports are on board.' It might even be possible to find out the extent of the English naval forces and, above all, their feelings towards the Emperor. On a demand made in his name by Bertrand and on the requisition order of Beker, the commander of picket-boat No. 24 was summoned and given the task of parliamentarian. The boat that brought him would collect his arms and place them aboard the frigate.

'At half-past three in the morning,' according to the log of the *Saale,* 'picket-boat No. 24 was made ready and left for the narrows, with the Duke of Rovigo and M. Lascase (*sic*), Grand Chamberlain (*sic*) of his Majesty, on board, to parley with the English ships in the channel. The wind was E.N.E., a strong breeze. Good sea and fine weather.'

Las Cases was the bearer of a letter addressed by the Marshal of the Household to 'The Admiral in command of the squadron before Rochefort'. It informed him that 'passports should have arrived from London for the Emperor and to find out if they had come . . . ' The two envoys, in civilian dress without orders, were to say little and hear much. Las Cases knew English perfectly but was 'not to let this become known'.

Taking advantage of the tide, the picket-boat passed outside Chassiron, on the tip of the island of Oléron, where the *Bellerophon* (Captain Maitland) and the corvette *Myrmidon* (Captain Gambier) were lying. The English ships, with the flag of truce at the mizzen masthead, gave a lee to the Frenchmen who came alongside about seven o'clock. The welcome was courteous. Maitland, a thirty-eight-year-old Scotsman, thin, pale, with tousled hair and big bright eyes, received Bertrand's letter from Las Cases; the chamberlain explained the Emperor's situation, spoke of his abdication and his plan of going to America. Then he brought up the matter of the passports. His Majesty did not want any encounter between the ships of the two nations and wished to go to the United States, if needs be on an American ship, to live there in peace.

'I am unaware of all the things you have told me,' Maitland replied in French. 'I only know that the battle of Waterloo has been won. I cannot reply to the demand which is the object of your message, but if you would not mind waiting a few minutes, I shall know more about it, as I can see a corvette manoeuvring to come alongside. The signal it is flying shows that it has come from England and that it has letters for me . . . I, for my part, will manoeuvre to make its approach easier; in the meantime, let us dine.'

It was the *Falmouth* (Captain Knight). In fact, it had come from Quiberon and was bringing Admiral Hotham's despatches; according to Maitland, who reports the interview, they had nothing to do with the object of the French mission. The Captain would therefore give a report of its visit to the Admiral; he would forward General Bertrand's letter and let him know the reply.

'That would take a long time and it is to be regretted,' replied the Frenchmen, 'and in any case . . . what would happen if before receiving your news the wind should be favourable, and the Emperor go out on the frigates or on some other ship?'

Maitland replied that he would attack them, attempt to seize them and Napoleon would be a prisoner. That was why he was quite right to ask for passports.

After lunch the conversation became general; there was more talk, perhaps too much. Las Cases pointed out that the Emperor was not yet reduced to such a state that he had to leave Europe; he still had much support. If he wanted to go to America it was to avoid bloodshed. It was in England's interest to let him go. He understood then that Maitland had told Captain Gambier that he had had orders to arrest Napoleon.

'But,' objected the commander of the *Bellerophon*, 'what guarantee would England have against a return which would force the nations to pour out blood and money just as they have already done? . . .'

'Circumstances have greatly changed,' replied Savary. 'The Emperor has abdicated of his own free will and has renounced power. His influence on France now seems exhausted. He wants to retire to some obscure place and live on his glorious memories.'

'If that is so,' Maitland retorted quickly, 'why doesn't he ask for asylum in England?'

Las Cases and Savary hesitated and seemed surprised at the question which in fact they had expected. They raised objections to the climate and the proximity of France; he would be suspected of wanting to return there. 'Furthermore, the Emperor looks on the English as his worst enemies and they look on him as a "monster deprived of all humanity".'

'I do not know the intentions of the English government,'

replied Maitland, 'but I have no reason to believe that Napoleon would not be well received.'

Las Cases closed this discussion by saying that they had no instructions to discuss the matter.

Did the English captain add, as the chamberlain wrote, that 'the Emperor would not have to fear ill-treatment'? The accounts of the three men present naturally do not agree. Savary's *Mémoires* are tendentious and Maitland's account a tissue of lies. He knew perfectly well that the Emperor had abdicated and that the safe-conducts had been refused. From the orders he had received from Admiral Hotham he knew roughly the intentions of the government towards Napoleon since, if he managed to capture him, he had been told to take him on board the *Superb* 'where there are instructions concerning the disposal of his person . . .'. 'It is up to you to take every possible means to intercept the fugitive, on whose captivity the peace of Europe depends,' as the admiral had written.

In fact, Maitland was trying to gain time; he had not enough force at his disposal to guard all the channels and wanted to keep Napoleon waiting for the reply he had asked for from the admiral, in order to get reinforcements for the *Bellerophon*.

* * *

Two o'clock. The parliamentarians had returned.

Meanwhile, the log of the *Saale* reads: 'The enemy frigate and man-of-war have moored in the Basques roadstead. We have made all preparations to repel boarders.' Would there be an attack?

No. The English, now certain that Napoleon was there, were drawing in to mark their prey, while on board the frigates the crews grumbled, the crew of the *Méduse* especially.

The preparations, the comings and goings under the flag of truce, the boats between Rochefort and the moorings, all led them to believe that the Emperor, betrayed, would surrender to 'that old tub', the *Bellerophon*, guarding the channels almost alone, since the patrol-boats between Chassiron and Le Verdon amounted to little or nothing. Ponée, commanding the *Méduse* and devoted heart and soul to the Emperor, was disgusted and heaped insults and reproaches on Montholon who was on his ship. A native of Granville, he had knocked about the world since the age of fifteen, had fought everywhere and now had a fine eighteen-gun frigate under his feet with a well-tried crew.

'I speak in the name of all my officers and men, as well as in my own,' he said. 'This is what should be done; tonight the *Méduse*, in advance of the *Saale*, will surprise the *Bellerophon*, which has just dropped anchor, in the darkness. I will lie to windward of her and prevent her from moving. I can go on fighting for two hours. Afterwards my frigate will be in a pretty mess but the *Saale* will have got through, thanks to the off-shore wind that blows every night. It takes more than a miserable corvette and a picket-boat to stop the *Saale*, a frigate with a twenty-four-pounder battery and with thirty-six-pounder carronades on her poop!'

The *Méduse* offered herself for destruction. Ponée would remain on the field of battle but the survivors, officers and men, obeying the orders of their leader, would save the honour of France.

Ponée's heroic offer interrupted the Emperor's reflections and moved him greatly. With such men it should be possible to break his fetters. He sent Savary to give Philibert orders to set sail. A breath of heroism blew over the ships.

Entry in the log of the *Saale*: 'Good breeze from N.N.E. Weather good. At half-past nine in the evening decks were cleared for action and topsails set . . . At half-past ten a boat was sent to Chapus (on the Marennes point) and returned with a pilot for the narrows . . .'

'At midnight,' wrote Jourdan de la Passardière, 'Captain Philibert came over to the brig (the *Epervier*) and gave me verbal orders to be ready to set sail at five o'clock in the morning and to be prepared for action. I took the necessary measures.'

So, on July 11th, shortly after midnight, Captain Philibert's command was ready to set sail. The presence on the *Saale* of the pilot from Chapus proves that the frigate with the Emperor on board would leave that night for Maumusson.

* * *

Three o'clock in the morning. 'He (Philibert) sent for me again,' Jourdan wrote, 'and gave me orders to put the brig's guns in the hold and'—there was no trust between the commander and his subordinates—'to send all the small arms and powder on board his frigate.'

What had happened? Had Beker intervened? Had Philibert himself had second thoughts of the twofold danger for his ships and his epaulettes? According to Montholon and Savary, he had stated that 'he had secret instructions not to go out if the ships ran any danger', and that, out of regard for the Emperor, 'he would not consider the decision of the crew of the *Méduse* as an act of mutiny', and would not listen to another word about it.

So be it. We know those instructions, of which it seems that Savary, Montholon, Gourgaud and the Emperor were unaware. But why, then, the orders to Jourdan to be ready to fight? Why had the decks of the *Saale* been cleared for action? Above all, why had the pilot from Chapus been summoned and brought on board? Why, on the 11th at one o'clock in the morning, had Philibert written to Bonnefoux that 'General Beker had not been able to carry out the mission entrusted to him by the Provisional Government'?

The 'explanations' furnished by the Emperor's watchdog explain nothing. 'The repugnance of Captain Philibert to agree to so rash a project, which endangered the ships for which he was responsible,' he wrote, 'and the aversion of Napoleon himself for an attempt that required the sacrifice of an entire crew for himself alone, made them reject a plan which none the less is worthy of being chronicled in our naval annals.'

His report is silent concerning the all-important decisions taken during the night of July 10th/11th at the moorings of Philibert's command in order to let Napoleon escape on board the *Saale*, whereas the notes of Captain Maitland and the French documents are perfectly clear.

First of all, informers had reported the movements of the pilot from Chapus.

'Tuesday, July 11th, about midday,' noted Captain Maitland, 'a small boat put out from the island of Oléron rowing towards the *Bellerophon*. There were four rowers; two well-dressed peasants were in the boat, who asked for the commander . . . They informed me that there had been a message, that same day, early in the morning, from the Ile d'Aix to a man considered to be the best pilot of the Maumusson channel. He was the only man who had ever brought a frigate through it. He had been offered a large sum to take a ship out to open sea. Evidently, Bonaparte intends to escape by that route . . .

'I immediately got under weigh. The tide was rising. None the less, I managed to get my ships out of the Antioch channel before nightfall. I sent the *Myrmidon* to cruise off-shore in front of Maumusson, with orders to heave to near the entrance, while with the *Bellerophon* and the *Slaney*, which joined me in the afternoon, I continued to cruise between two lights.'

The look-outs on the frigates had clearly seen all these manoeuvres, for the log of the *Saale* reports: 'July 11th. Half-past twelve. A sail in sight — coming from the channel (the *Slaney*). One-fifteen. The man-of-war and the corvette (*Bellerophon* and *Myrmidon*) have set sail, beating up against the wind (N.W.). Seven o'clock. Corvette lost to sight; man-of-war on the starboard tack under topsails . . . '

Thus, during the night of July 10th/11th, the Emperor on board the *Saale* had not left the moorings and the Ile d'Aix in order to escape by Maumusson, guided by the pilot from Chapus. Someone—or something—had intervened at the last moment. Some scruple of Napoleon's? A secret order? Beker? 'The port longboat left for Rochefort at three-fifteen' (log of the *Saale*). Did it bring newspapers announcing the king's entry into Paris?

They had been lulled by illusions. They had believed in the passports, in the English, in Fouché. The Emperor's suite was miserable and discouraged. However, one voice was raised; Lallemand's. He insisted, alone but strongly: 'The Emperor can leave by the Gironde estuary.' Silence. The sailors were consulted and said that it was still possible. Perhaps, but it was a risk. Objections crackled from all sides. 'Lallemand was indignant that everyone dismissed so lightly a means of saving the Emperor.' Summoned to him, Lallemand was authorized to re-establish contact with Captain Baudin.

It was a dangerous mission; agents and informers of all sorts teemed between Marennes and Royan. Here and there white (royalist) flags could be seen. A general's uniform would not pass unnoticed, whereas that of a naval officer might pass unremarked. Sailors have unfettered minds and a taste for adventure. Borgnis Desbordes, a lieutenant on the *Saale*, offered his. The two men had known one another in the past at Brest; it was said that they had even fought a duel but, honour being satisfied, they had remained good friends. First by boat, along the coast and up the Seudre, then by land, Lallemand could reach Royan. It was dusk, with a new moon.

*　　*　　*

Meanwhile, the Paris theatres were crammed. At the Opera, between Acts 2 and 3 of *Castor and Pollux*, Lavigne sang couplets in honour of the King. At Castor's reply to Pollux:

> 'The whole universe demanded your return.
> Reign over a faithful people.'

there was a terrific outburst of applause.

At the Français, Parisians and foreigners stamped their feet as they listened to *Mérope*: 'They bless the king that Heaven has sent us . . .'

The Tsar, the Emperor of Austria and the King of Prussia had come in. In the *Moniteur* of July 11th one read: 'The capital has learnt with the liveliest satisfaction of the presence of the august sovereigns so desired by all . . .

'Davout has disavowed his signature to the so-called address to the army by the Chambers. The Duke of Taranto has been appointed *Grand Chancelier de la Légion d'honneur'* . . .

*　　*　　*

Royan. Baudin was there. He landed when he met a fishing boat with three men on board, one of them, Lallemand, in disguise. 'The Emperor has been dissuaded from going to the United States by persons in his suite who believe in the generosity of the English,' the general explained. But His Majesty had sent him 'to study once more the chances of an escape by the Gironde, for every official departure was now impossible'. Would or could Baudin undertake what he had proposed a week ago?

'I will still do it,' Baudin replied, 'but I can do it less easily than I could have done before. At the Emperor's suggestion I got rid of the means on which I counted, but I can go to Bordeaux to find others.'

'Let the Emperor come with a bag, a valet and one or two friends, men of sense and courage; let him come in a small post-carriage tomorrow morning, but without noise.'

While at Bordeaux Baudin, accompanied by General Clausel,

was obtaining from the American Consul-General Lee a ship anchored in the port, Lallemand was hastening back to the moorings in the same manner by which he had come.

But the Emperor was no longer aboard the *Saale*.

Chapter VII

THE LAST STAGE

THE ILE D'AIX

He was on the Ile d'Aix.

Louis XVIII was at the Tuileries, the Chambers were dissolved, Gouvion-Saint-Cyr was Minister of War, Jaucourt Minister of the Marine, and the regicide Fouché Minister of the King's Police . . . The danger at the moorings in the Enet narrows increased from hour to hour.

The night of the July 11th to 12th was an uneasy one; the Emperor was suffering from abdominal pains. From time to time he consulted with Gourgaud about the movements of his enemies; if he did not surrender to the English they would have him arrested.

In the morning he ordered Marchand to finish packing. Those of his suite who wanted to accompany the Emperor must be ready to go ashore. Where was he going? Anxiety. Uneasiness. Beker and Philibert looked at one another questioningly . . . The Emperor wished to be taken to the *Bellerophon* at sunrise. They breathed again!

The schooner *Sophie* came alongside. 'At half-past four they began putting on board the Emperor's effects and those of the passengers whom we have on the *Saale*,' ran the entry in the frigate's log.

In his cabin, irresolute and dog-tired, Napoleon searched through history for a precedent for his situation. He went back over his memories of classical history, recalled Themistocles surrendering to the King of Persia, welcomed magnificently, loaded with presents. He would say to Maitland: 'Like Themistocles, unwilling to take part in the dismemberment of my country, I come to ask asylum of you . . .'

But surely there was no comparison between him and the victor of Salamis, ostracized by his compatriots on the morrow of his victory. But who just then was thinking of the year 500 B.C.? Of Artaxerxes Longomanus, etc.?

The hours passed. The boat from Rochefort brought the newspapers. The Emperor pored over them feverishly: entry of the King, acclamations, Bourmont appointed commander of the 16th military division of Arras, the supporters of the Emperor treated as conspirators, Wellington 'at home' in Paris in the Faubourg Saint-Honoré!

The newspaper *Les Débats* (formerly of the Empire) wrote: 'It has been decided to retain at Rochefort the two frigates which were waiting for Buonaparte . . . To put the English ships off the scent, a corvette and a picket-boat have been hastily armed and it is on these ships that Buonaparte is trying to escape . . . Justice, human and divine, is on his trail. It is to be hoped that he will not escape.'

Furious, Napoleon hurled the papers to the floor. Better to await Lallemand's return . . . Baudin's reply.

'I tried to surrender to the enemy but was not able to make up my mind,' he was to say later. But he would wait for Lallemand on the Île d'Aix. Only three days before he had been warmly welcomed there. He would be in greater safety; if necessary, he could defend himself. On General Beker's order, Captain Philibert, early in the morning of July 12th, had sent the longboat to the island 'with several members of the suite', entrusted with the organization of 'the Palace'.

It was set up at the local commander's residence at the end of the village. Built in 1808 for the brigade-general in command there, it had two floors of 'general type', seven windows in the façade and in the centre an iron balcony resting on two columns which flanked the main door.

Ten o'clock. Having bidden farewell to the officers and crews of the frigates, the Emperor, loudly cheered, followed by Bertrand, Gourgaud, Beker and Planat, entered the boat which took him to the Île d'Aix. He left desolation behind him. The sailors threw down their caps and stamped on them; Ponée swore like a madman. 'What a misfortune that the Emperor did not come here instead of to the *Saale*,' he shouted. 'I would have got him through, blockade or no . . . He doesn't know the English! . . . In whose hands will he fall? . . . Poor Napoleon! You are lost!'

The welcome of the inhabitants and the troops on the island was like a tonic. Three-quarters of the 14th Marines, at one time prisoners on the hulks at Plymouth and Chatham, regarded the English as mannerless gaolers and shouted 'Long live the Emperor!'

Passing through the entrance hall with its bare walls, he went up the stone staircase of 'the Palace'; a narrow arched doorway led into a small square room, whose window and balcony opened on the garden and the sea. It was very hot; trails of mist hovered over the Basques roadstead.

The furnishings were simple: velvet upholstery in red and green designs. In the alcove between the door and the bathroom a bed with white curtains; in the centre of the room a pedestal table. Four mahogany armchairs covered with blue damask; a few chairs here and there. On the chimney breast, to the right of the alcove, a clock. The house, which now bears an eagle on its façade and is known as 'the Emperor's house', has had many visitors ever since Baron Gourgaud filled it with a valuable collection of Napoleonic relics and made the island the goal of an inspiring pilgrimage.

The Emperor lay down and rested. One by one, Bertrand and his family, the three Montholons, Beker, Gourgaud and Savary settled into their quarters. The suite crowded into the engineers' quarters opposite.

The day was hot and oppressive. The Emperor received the artillery and engineer officers of the garrison, presented by Bertrand. Then those of the 14th Marines in camp on the Jean-Blé peninsula among the broom and the bents. He greeted them with the same graciousness and interest as when he was in power, listened, not without emotion and regret, to their entreaties not to abandon them. The sailors were sure that they could bring him to open sea 'without any risk'. His Majesty must not surrender to the English!

Cannon shots sounded in the Basques roadstead. All sails set, the *Bellerophon* and the *Myrmidon* fired several salvoes. Rejoicings? The white flag flew at their mainmasts. It was a 'royal salute' by Maitland in honour of Louis XVIII's entry into Paris.

His colours now floated over the keep at Vincennes. Daumesnil had surrendered! In the courtyard of the Tuileries 'an immense crowd', wrote the *Moniteur*, cheered the Allied sovereigns, received at the château with shouts of 'Long live the Emperor . . . Alexander!'

Six young officers of the 14th Marines, filled with enthusiasm and overflowing with emotion at the welcome given them that morning by the Emperor, came to see General Bertrand: the naval lieutenant Genty, ensigns Doret, Saliz and Peltier, midshipmen Châteauneuf and Montcousu, and with them Besson. They wanted to save the Emperor; in the roads were moored two decked coasting luggers, two-masted and square-rigged, of twelve to thirteen tons, the *Zélie* and the *Deux Amis*. They should be bought. The frigate could provide rigging and provisions; the crew was guaranteed by the officers, six well-tried petty-officers. The Emperor and two or three persons would go aboard. Thanks to their shallow draft the luggers would hug the coast as far as La Rochelle; thence they could reach Saint-Martin-de-Ré where Besson's smack was ready to go to sea.

Moved by their generous youthful enthusiasm, eagerly described by Bertrand, the Emperor strode up and down his room, looked out of the open window, questioned the wind, halted in front of the mirror in which so many visitors look today, reckoned his chances and discussed them with the Marshal of the Household. These young men must not be discouraged; perhaps their plan was not as crazy as it sounded. Finally he gave orders to buy the luggers, to equip them and to put his effects on board. The women would have to remain in France; a part of the suite would embark. He would leave on Besson's smack.

The young officers set to work, joyous and eager. In the household and on the island everyone soon knew that the Emperor was going to leave. Who would accompany him? Jealousies sprang up; Madame Bertrand wept at the thought of being separated from her husband; if she were left behind she would die. Madame Montholon swore she would slip on board disguised as a man. Gourgaud claimed the place of honour at the Emperor's side . . . so did Bertrand. Napoleon listened to their complaints, heeded none of them, dismissed them all. Had he the right to leave behind him, exposed to reprisals, these men, quick to take offence, these rivals, these whimpering women with their children in tow? Could he himself accept the hazards of a flight on some chance fly-by-night—hidden, perhaps disguised? Was it worthy of him?

If the passports had come he would leave on the frigates, which were, moreover, ready to go to sea, top-gallants loosened, studding sails set; on the afterdecks stacks of provisions and heaps of vegetables could be seen.

He had been brought up to admire the English character. The English had lavished hospitality and monies on Paoli. Lucien, forced to give himself up, declared a prisoner and interned in England in 1811, had been able to acquire the estate of Thorngrove and to live there like a great lord with his wife and children, his own livery, his horses, and a princely table at which the Duke of Norfolk, the Marquis of Lansdowne, Lord Brougham, the leading liberals and the learned men of Oxford, etc. came to dine.

To live like that, far from the tumult of politics and of men, in a pleasant country, seemed that evening to the Emperor infinitely desirable. A year earlier, shortly before leaving Fontainebleau (April 11, 1814) he had written to Caulaincourt 'to sound out Castlereagh to find out if the English government would be willing to give him asylum in England with the guarantee of free and complete liberty, as was the right of every Englishman'.

The British minister had evaded a direct reply, advising the Emperor 'to put his trust in British honour'. Later, the commissioner, Campbell, had guaranteed him the 'fair play' of the English people. Furthermore, at Porto-Ferrajo, he had welcomed and received at his table several English notables, Lord Ebrington, Lord John Russell, son of the Duke of Bedford, etc.; their liberal opinions, the sympathy that they showed for his policy, the vigour and firmness of their principles had greatly impressed him.

On the evening of December 6, 1814, he had had a two-hour meeting with Lord Elsington, the future Viceroy of Ireland.

'You have come from France,' he had said. 'Tell me frankly; are they content there?'

The Englishman only shrugged his shoulders.

'They have been too humiliated by the peace,' the Emperor went on. 'The appointment of the Duke of Wellington must have seemed insulting to the army. What the Bourbons should have had was a young, pretty, witty woman able to captivate the French . . . I know the French character; it is not proud like the English but it is far more avid of glory . . . '

Afterwards, Lord Elsington noted down Napoleon's words: 'Mainly they are his own expressions which I have reproduced,' he wrote.

'John Bull is loyal and steadfast; he holds to his ancient institutions and his character is so different from the French that no comparison between the two is possible. Take your political conscience. In England a man who quits his party save for the best reasons is dishonoured, whereas in France men are continually changing to suit their own interests. I respect the English people; I could easily come to love them.'

'I wager,' he added, 'that in England you thought I was the devil himself but, now that you have seen me, you will have to revise your prejudices.'

Then, speaking of British politics and customs: 'I think that if Mr Fox had lived we would have been able to come to some sort of agreement, for the way in which he began his correspondence with M. de Talleyrand gave us a proof of his good faith . . . '

*   *   *

Since then, Byron, Hazlitt and the English liberals had welcomed 'the flight of the eagle', had applauded this challenge to the aristocrats of the Congress of Vienna, described by Sir Robert Wilson as 'flocks of magpies wheeling above the stricken eagle'.

These were the former Whigs, the irreconcilables, who had not rallied to Pitt when he had fought against the revolution in 1794. They formed a 'Mountain' in the House of Commons because of their Jacobin opinions. Grouped first around Fox, then around his nephew Lord Holland and his disciple Lord Grey, they included aristocrats of high lineage, like the Duke of Sussex, prince of the blood, intellectuals and men of action, Whitbread and the lawyer Sir Samuel Romilly, himself of French origin. In their speeches and writings they condemned 'the alliance of their country with the absolutist monarchies' and the distribution to these powers of enormous subsidies 'often without parliamentary approval, which', according to Lord Lansdowne, the friend of Lucien Bonaparte, 'would have been better employed in alleviating the misery of the poor'.

They demanded that Wellington be recalled from Spain because 'he aroused the worst instincts of a savage and ignorant people'. Later, in 1812, at the time of the war with the United States, the scholarly politician Brougham, champion of the abolition of slavery, who called Pitt an 'enemy of humanity', wanted a reconciliation with Imperial France and tried, together with his colleagues in the opposition, to find a formula of 'peaceful co-existence', so terrifying was the unemployment and the business slump.

The previous May, the liberals — Burdett, Whitbread and others — described the work of the Congress as 'a sacrilege, a virtual provocation for the assassination of Napoleon, handed over to public obloquy' and denounced the schemings of the Allies 'who had had his couriers bearing peace proposals arrested at the frontiers'.

Lord John Russell considered the war against France as 'unjust and impolitic, with the aim of imposing on the French people a dynasty which had already been rejected by them'. 'Has not France the right,' protested Wellesley, brother of Wellington, 'to have her people treated as free to decide and able to choose the form of its government? . . .'

And Lord Grey : 'We are asked to picture Napoleon as recalled on March 20th by the army. But in France the army is not a separate class; it represents the feelings of the people.'

'By what right does the government claim to intervene in the revolutions of a neighbouring country? Does it wish to impose upon France a government that she has rejected?' supported Sir Samuel Romilly, Stanhope and Erskine, ex-Lord Chancellor in Fox's cabinet.

The censure motions in the Commons were of course defeated; but the ranks of the opposition increased weekly; from twenty-seven in March to ninety-two in May.

The stormy and impassioned debates went on. In view of the opposition, Napoleon's authority was based on the surest foundation, for it was based upon the rights of the people and against these 'the principle of legitimacy invented by Talleyrand' could not prevail. 'In contrast to the men of Vienna, he is the champion of democracy and of the modern world; it is aggression from without that has turned his steps from peace.' 'At last,' writes Jules Dechamps, 'in the country which had the most to fear from his power, Whigs and liberals, to say nothing of the radicals, with no propaganda effort and relying on history alone, recognized in Napoleon, long before his downfall, the man of *novissima verba*, as Sismondi, born the citizen of a republic (Switzerland), called him in 1815.'

The Emperor knew the sentiments of the English opposition towards him, the desire of the liberals whose numbers increased daily. Active, impassioned, tenacious, brave and intransigent in matters of conscience, they were ready for anything that maintained the honour of their country. They were far seeing too; they could see ahead of them a terrible social crisis drawing nearer. If he were to go to England, all the liberals would be on his side.

But the *Moniteur* was publishing violent articles, true or false, from the *Morning Chronicle*: 'It is reported in London on July 2nd that M. Otto has again approached the English government to obtain asylum for Napoleon . . . Such a proposal is without foundation . . . The ministers would never willingly saddle themselves with such a guest!'

Another, from the *Morning Post*, considered him 'the most infamous of criminals' and demanded that 'he should be hanged, that he should be handed over to Louis XVIII, that he be imprisoned in the Tower, that after his capture he should be summoned before a European court and sentenced to death . . .'

None the less, Napoleon still believed in the English. At the time of the rupture of the Peace of Amiens, he had said to the Russian minister, Markov: 'It is with regret and with horror that I am going to wage war for, speaking as a European rather than as a Frenchman, I should be as grieved as you if, on rising one morning, you were to learn that England no longer existed.' Did he remember that now in his misgivings?

*   *   *

That evening the circle drew closer around the Emperor.

The English waited for their prey; their ships drew nearer to the coast, to the frigates . . . To arms! There were shouts from the sentries and patrols.

Questioned once again, Savary declared himself in favour of departure on the lugger and on Besson's smack. Gourgaud was unwilling to commit himself. There were grave risks. The boats might be captured. The English would throw the Emperor into the Tower of London. It would be better to try and force a way through on the frigates or get to the *Bayadère*. Every precaution must be taken to leave at night.

By what means?

Savary went on board the *Saale*. To do what?

Shots in the night. Call to arms! False alarm. A patrol boat had encountered a pinnace, which had fired on it . . . The garrison stood to its weapons. Gourgaud, sent as a look-out, returned: wind N.N.W., weather cloudy. There was an English frigate at Maumusson! The *Cyrus*? Another one was reported in the Bordeaux river . . .

The watchers were seeing things.

RIDDLES

Genty's cockle-shells were ready. The commanders of the frigates had provided, willingly, equipment and provisions for several months.

On the *Zélie*: Lieutenant Genty, Ensign Peltier de Saint-Paul, 1st class midshipman Châteauneuf, ship's corporal Abada, petty-officer X . . . , a sailor from the *Saale*.

On the *Deux Amis*: Ensigns Doret and Saliz, 1st class midshipman Moncousu, ship's corporal Villars, petty-officer Y . . . , a sailor from the *Méduse*. Also Ensign Galland from the same frigate.

Two well-armed pinnaces, belonging to the frigates and commanded by Ensign Luneau, would escort the convoy to beyond the narrows. The *Zélie* was fitted up to receive the Emperor; the baggage would be placed on board on the 12th, between eight o'clock and midnight. Marchand was furnished with a money-belt. The aide-de-camp Planat went on board the *Zélie*. Countless comings and goings.

Maitland had observed them. 'There are obvious signs of getting under weigh, well known to sailors,' he wrote. 'I have ordered my ships to clear their hawsers, ready to slip their moorings.'

July 13th, nine o'clock. One of the prefect's boats landed Prince Joseph. He stopped for a moment at the widow Bolla's to change his clothes before presenting himself to his brother. He had come from Rochefort. Letters sent him from Paris by Julie (his wife) had been alarming. She had not yet vacated her house in the Rue Anjou-Saint-Honoré, but the arrival of the King would soon compel her to do so. They feared the worst for Napoleon; the royalists were taking their revenge everywhere. They had demanded the unconditional surrender of 'the Army of the Loire'. It was a good opportunity for Napoleon to place himself at its head and try his luck one last time.

He shook his head: it would mean civil war! Dog-tired, he spoke without energy. Let him take his place on the ship hired by the Sieur de Rochefort, Pelletreu, which was waiting in the Gironde. Joseph would take his place and surrender to the English. Their resemblance would deceive the English long enough to allow Napoleon to reach the high seas.

He must hurry; Joseph's carriage was waiting for him on the banks of the Charente. But the Emperor would not accept this hazardous sacrifice by his brother; he urged him to look to his own safety, embraced him affectionately and bade him farewell. (Joseph was to embark at Royan on July 25th and to reach America without difficulty.) Napoleon felt that Joseph's situation was different from his; he could not lend himself to this deception. His dignity forbade it. It would be cowardly. What would Beker do? Or Bonnefoux? 'He was in one of those fits of depression where one throws oneself at every wave.'

Lallemand was announced: Baudin was at His Majesty's disposal. The corvette *Bayadère* was still awaiting his orders in the Bordeaux river. The English did not keep so keen a watch there as on the Rochefort channels. Captain Baudin was fully armed, equipped and provisioned and was ready to take the Emperor to the ends of the world if needs be. Marchand adds in his *Mémoires*: 'General Lallemand assured the Emperor that he would be able to go by land to the Gironde and embark there; that to outwit the guard it would be sufficient to pretend to be indisposed. Marchand could be left on the Ile d'Aix. He could answer any questions about the Emperor's indisposition and would keep the Emperor's door inviolate for twenty-four hours.'

What guard? Beker? Bonnefoux? The English agents? Lallemand said nothing about danger from the royalists or about the white flags flying in the countryside, about which Beker wrote in his account of his mission, 'but only four persons must accompany the Emperor . . . ' The generals of the suite became more and more uneasy.

'There are a lot of mysterious parleys,' wrote Gourgaud.

The Marshal of the Household said that His Majesty had decided to leave on a Danish ship, whose captain had formerly been an officer in the Marines of the Guard, that a cargo of brandy had just been bought in La Rochelle for this ship and that there was a hiding place and . . . whose captain had all his papers in order, a passport, etc. There were only four sailors on board . . .

Was this Besson's ship? But Besson had never served in the Marines of the Guard! Confusion, uncertainty, apprehension, affectations of mystery. The supposed decisions of the Emperor were announced by those who knew nothing of them, had caught them on the wing, commented upon them . . .

Gourgaud went to His Majesty. Was he among the four called upon to follow him? No. The Emperor would leave Marchand on the Ile d'Aix to guard his door during the first hours of his absence. He would take with him Bertrand, Savary, Lallemand and his personal valet Saint-Denis.

'But Lallemand is not an orderly officer!'

'Lallemand knows the countryside; besides he is "the Danish captain's friend".'

Napoleon expressed his great regard for Gourgaud and tried to console him. 'Once in America he would live as a private citizen. His role was over; he could never return to France . . . It would take a month or two to get news from Europe; the passage there would be at least as long . . . Any return such as that from Elba would be impossible . . . ' Gourgaud was indignant. He did not follow His Majesty for any personal interest or ambition but because he was in trouble . . . 'No one could suppose that he had any other thought than his boundless devotion to a great man, now defeated and abandoned.'

Little by little his jealousy made him brutal and insolent. 'The Emperor would do better to go to England! That noble role would suit him best! He cannot play the part of an adventurer . . . History one day would accuse him of having abdicated out of fear, since he had not made the ultimate sacrifice.' (!)

Intolerable suggestions, which the Emperor appeared to tolerate and even tried to justify. Perhaps that was the wisest thing to do. He was sure of being well treated in England, but 'such good treatment would have something humiliating about it'. Moreover, 'he could not bear the idea of living among his bitterest enemies'.

Two forms of pride tortured him.

What if he were captured en route?

He would kill himself.

'His Majesty cannot do that. A gambler kills himself. A great man confronts adversity.'

Gourgaud boasts of having said all this. Was he telling the whole truth?

'You will come with me,' the Emperor may have said to him, at the end of his patience. 'We can manage five!'

   *   *   *

Half-past three. His Majesty's armed launch, flying his colours and coming from the *Saale*, moored in English Bay. Would the Emperor go on board? They had taken his baggage on to the luggers, now ready to leave.

Everyone in the suite was talking of the *Bayadère* and of Baudin, of the Dane and of Besson, of Genty's boats.

The sea was calm. Cannon shots to the W.S.W. The English ships had just moored to the N.N.W. of the frigates; their ships were standing off. Those placed at His Majesty's disposal began their patrols.

A boat taking Gourgaud to the *Saale* passed among them; the general was to hand over, in the name of the Emperor, a brace of pistols to Captains Philibert and Ponée, and announce His Majesty's decision to surrender to the English ships. Was this to put the rumourmongers off the scent? Or the spies? Or to bewilder Philibert?

'You don't know what you're doing,' said the officers of the *Saale* on taking leave of him. 'You don't know the English! Dissuade the Emperor from any such idea!'

After the return of his orderly officer, had the Emperor been impressed by the flight of a bird which had entered his room and then taken wing towards the English ships? Gourgaud tells of this incident with a certain complacency.

It was time for dinner . . . a somewhat gloomy one. Silence. Bertrand, who had been invited, sat facing the Emperor, who after a quarter of an hour retired to his room and watched the enemy ships through his glass.

All the preparations for the 'secret' departure had been made. To put Maitland and his ships off the scent, Las Cases and Lallemand would go at dawn the next day, July 14th, on board the *Bellerophon* under flag of truce. They were to ask for news of the safe-conducts and try to find out the intentions of the English towards the Emperor. By then he would be far away.

Ten o'clock in the evening! Besson announced that all was ready. About midnight 'our preparations for departure were suspended', wrote Gourgaud without further comment. What had happened? Those were decisive hours, decisive minutes, yet full of uncertainty.

*   *   *

In his account of his mission, published, it is true, in 1841, Count Beker writes, under date of July 13th, about the proposal for departure made to the Emperor by Lallemand:

' . . . Whether the idea of an escape on board the *Bayadère* was really the best, as the naval officers would have it, it was none the less not accepted since it was necessary to enter the river Seudre and then to cover four leagues on land, from La Tremblade to Royan. The white flag was flying over the whole of the countryside he had to cross, which made the journey dangerous for Napoleon and might lead to the failure of the only plan regarded as practicable by the sailors . . . Departure on the *Bayadère* was therefore renounced.'

This cannot have been the real reason, since no one had ever spoken of these difficulties. Then, alluding to the proposals made by Lieutenant Genty, Beker said that this plan 'was approved the more easily insofar as it fitted in with that of the "Danish captain" . . . ' Everything was ready for departure which should have taken place on the night of July 13th to 14th. At eleven o'clock the two luggers had sail set. The greater part of the suite was to be divided between them 'while Napoleon was to embark on the Danish ship, accompanied only by his loyal Marshal of the Household, the Duke of Rovigo, Generals Lallemand and Gourgaud and M. Marchand. The orders for the embarkation had been completed; this plan, which appeared to be the last, seemed ready to be carried out.'

Beker was mistaken. The Emperor was to leave on the *Zélie* and only when on the high seas was he to transfer to the *Magdeleine*, at that time moored at Saint-Martin-de-Ré, while Marchand remained on the Ile d'Aix to keep indiscreet enquirers at a distance. Beker went on:

'But around the Emperor himself preparations for departure advanced more slowly. Scenes of grief and confusion kept "the Household" in a turmoil. The ladies did not want to be separated from their husbands and the resentment of those who could no longer follow Napoleon added to this commotion . . .

'Such was the general impression of that troublous night, when the captain (Besson) announced that everything was ready to receive the Emperor. General Beker went at once to His Majesty's room and told him: "Sire, everything is ready; the captain is waiting for you." He withdrew, convinced that the departure would take place immediately. However, there was a long wait. The general, addressing himself to the Master of the Household, pressed him to tell His Majesty once again of the dangers of a longer delay. Just as Count Bertrand was about to repeat this final warning Napoleon, hearing the movement of all these comings and goings, impressed by the wails and sobs which grief drew from those who could not accompany him, either giving way to the misery around him or because he feared to put himself at the mercy of a strange crew or because he had no faith in so hazardous a venture, told the Marshal of the Household to say that he would not take this way of salvation and would spend the rest of the night on the Ile d'Aix . . . '

Certainly the Countess Bertrand did not conceal her desire that the Emperor should go to England but, wrote Marchand, 'these sentiments had no influence on His Majesty's decisions'. Later, at Saint Helena, skimming through the *Souvenirs* of Madame Durand, maid of honour to the Empress, Napoleon read this accusation, took a pencil and wrote in the margin: 'False!'

In any case, whatever may have been the feelings of those around the Emperor, his mind was already made up.

Beker adds a few comments to his account:

' . . . The attraction of England for his companions in misfortune, the hope of an honourable reception which they flattered themselves they would receive, and finally their fears of being taken prisoner during the long sea voyage, had always made them prefer English hospitality to a passage to America.'

One person who had at one time been in the intimate councils of the Emperor had even approached General Beker to try and get him to advise His Majesty to renounce all hazardous attempts to escape and to 'surrender to the generosity of the British Regent'.

Beker concludes:

'Count Beker vigorously rejected a proposal which he did not approve and which, had he accepted it, would have nullified the role of passive neutrality which he had adopted as a rule of conduct. He would have felt guilty had he tried in any way to influence, however indirectly, the Emperor's decisions . . . '

Was this so sure? Beker was a good soldier. Ever since his arrival at Malmaison he had given the Emperor many proofs of his devotion but, like Bonnefoux and Philibert, he had received strict and precise orders 'not to let Napoleon set foot on French soil again under pain of high treason'. Knowing that a part of the Emperor's entourage was opposed to all hazardous adventures, had he multiplied the objections to improvised departures, exaggerated the dangers of reaching Royan and Baudin's *Bayadère*, even as Bonnefoux had daily told the Emperor and the generals of imaginary English ships in order to prove the impossibility of breaking through the blockade?

In a letter addressed to the minister Jaucourt on July 18th, that is to say three days after Napoleon's surrender, it is true, and when he was no longer to be feared, the port-admiral wrote, perhaps to draw attention to his services:

'General Beker was fully conscious of the importance of his mission and neglected nothing to fulfil it satisfactorily. The interests of the state were always in his mind. As for me, ever since I received the message of July 6th to have Napoleon arrested if he tried to return to the mainland, I kept constant watch on him. I sent gendarmes to every point on the coast. He could not have set foot on shore without being compelled to go back on board. The Ile d'Aix was not in my command, but I took all measures to forestall Napoleon's intentions and to prevent him from escaping if he made any attempt to return to the mainland. General Beker also kept his eyes open. He would have been advised of the slightest movement.'

But Beker had known all about the Emperor's plan of departure since he had gone to warn him that they were waiting for him ! Had Napoleon and those loyal to him tried to envelop their preparations in uncertainty and confusion to conceal their departure from the English and French authorities as well as from their spies?

On the evening of July 13th, having been told by informers and by certain persons close to the Emperor that the plot with Besson and the naval officers was being taken seriously, Beker, according to the royalist author Mayeur de Saint-Paul, 'told Buonaparte that, since he had been entrusted with the safety of his person, he could not allow him to disembark'. It is possible . . . though the prohibition would have been ineffective for if the Emperor had decided to escape, General Alméras, commanding the island, a veteran of Egypt and devoted to the Emperor, would have protected his flight with the fifteen hundred men of the 14th Marines !

But that evening, as so many times over the past three weeks, the Emperor was probably unwilling to undertake anything unlawful. Never confiding his intimate thoughts to anyone, had he perhaps renounced every hazardous departure and decided to surrender to the English? In any case, Marchand, Beker and Gourgaud report in their accounts these words addressed to Bertrand : 'There is always danger in putting one's trust in one's enemies, but it is better to trust in their honour than to fall into their hands as a prisoner . . . Say that I will not embark and that I will pass the night here.'

It must, however, be admitted that this sudden decision may have been influenced by a chance event, for at dawn the six officers of the 14th Marines who were waiting for Napoleon on board the luggers were all arrested !

The night had been eventful. The frigates had armed their pinnaces 'for bivouac', that is to say for night patrol. There were

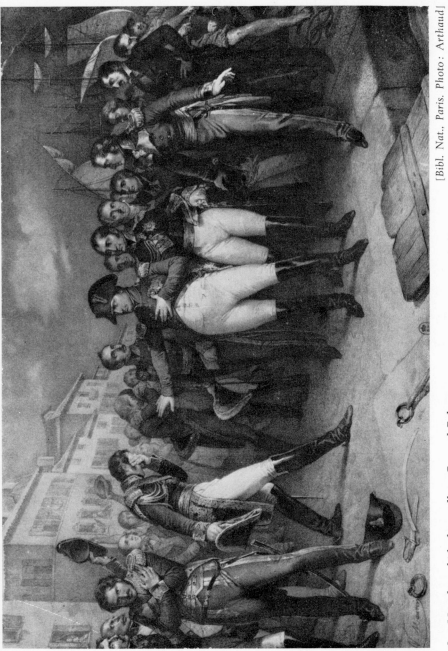

8. Napoleon bids farewell to General Beker

9. Bonaparte is transferred from the *Bellerophon* to the *Northumberland*, August 28, 1815

many shots in the vicinity of the island. The French and English patrol boats were getting nervous. The brig *Epervier* and the harbour-craft *Sophie* were moored in the roadstead; a general (?) boarded the *Saale* about one o'clock in the morning and was taken, two hours later, to the Ile d'Aix in the longboat. Who was it? Gourgaud? Savary?

Four o'clock. With a fresh north-east breeze Las Cases and Lallemand left on board the despatch-boat under a flag of truce. The *Bellerophon* flew the white flag at her mainmast. The envoys were welcomed. With the aid of Captain Sartorius, commanding the *Slaney*, Maitland recognized Lallemand. He had received him before in Egypt, on board the *Camelion*, which he then commanded. The general had been Junot's aide-de-camp. He had been taken prisoner by the English squadron while trying to make his way back to France.

On arrival Las Cases asked if there had been any reply from Admiral Hotham to the letter from the Marshal of the Household about safe-conducts. To his negative reply Maitland, obviously suspicious, added that he was awaiting a despatch at any moment, though he had known for six days that they had been refused and that he 'must use every possible means to capture Buonaparte . . .'

'If that is the only reason for a parley,' went on the Englishman, 'then this mission is quite unnecessary. I told you that, as soon as the reply has been received, I would let you know.'

'The Emperor's wish to prevent further bloodshed is so great,' replied Las Cases, 'that he will go to America in any way that the British government may authorize, even on board an English ship.'

To which, according to his *Memoirs*, Maitland replied: 'I am in no way authorized to accept any arrangement of this nature and I do not believe that my government would agree. I can, however, take the risk of receiving Buonaparte in order to take him to England. But should he accept this, I cannot assume any responsibility for the reception he may receive since, in such a case, I would be acting on my own responsibility with no certainty of being approved by my government . . .'

Nothing but lies . . . but Maitland was consumed by the desire to lure Napoleon on board his ship! Then there was talk of arrangements, of the welcome given earlier to Lucien Bona-

H

parte and the general sentiments of the English people . . .
Knowing that he was playing with fire, Lallemand asked, on his
own behalf, whether, on demanding asylum, 'he would be called
to account for the part he had played'.

'You have nothing to fear,' Maitland replied. 'That sort of
thing is foreign to the English government. You would live in
England at your ease; no authority would pursue you there . . . '

'I do not know what decision the Emperor may take,' Lallemand writes in his *Mémoires*, 'but should he come to England
and should I accompany him I would not like to be exposed to
persecution . . . I have never had any intention of going to
England. Nothing forces me to go there and I assure you that I
would not go, were there the slightest suspicion that I might be
sent back to France. Nor could I run the risk of finding my
liberty restricted or of being harassed in any way.'

'That is impossible,' said Captain Maitland heatedly. 'In England the government is not despotic; it is forced to uphold the
laws and to defer to public opinion. You are under the protection
of the English laws as soon as you are under the British
flag.'

Did Maitland realize that what was true for Lallemand was
equally true for the Emperor?

Las Cases, new to the job but filled with a sense of his own
importance and 'inclined to take the thought for the deed', was
enchanted, ready to believe that courteous phrases were binding
engagements. On leaving, Maitland said that if the Emperor
decided to come aboard in order to go to England, he would like
to be advised beforehand and to receive as soon as possible the
list of persons who would accompany him in order to make the
necessary arrangements to receive each one of them with as little
discomfort as possible.

'Where is Buonaparte?' the Englishman asked curtly, warned
by a spy that the Emperor was preparing to give him the
slip.

'At Rochefort. I left him there yesterday evening,' Las Cases
replied.

'The Emperor is staying at the Hôtel de la Grand-Place,' Lallemand backed him up. 'He is so popular with the inhabitants that
they gather every evening to see him and to shout "Long live the
Emperor!"'

'Why do they tell me such stories?' wrote Maitland, feeling uneasy.

Was the principal, or even secondary, reason for the mission of Las Cases and Lallemand to mislead the commander of the *Bellerophon* and conceal Napoleon's departure from him?

Eleven o'clock. Flying before the storm the passengers returned to make their report to the Emperor. Through the glass he could see the boat with the flag of truce. He must not count on the safe-conducts allowing him to go officially to America but, as Las Cases wrote, 'we may look forward without much uneasiness to the probability that we shall be prevented from leaving England; that is the limit of our fears and forebodings'.

FINAL DECISION

Friday, July 14th, at three o'clock in the afternoon. At Rochefort bad news had reached the Prefecture. The prefect, Richard, confirmed in his duties by the King, brought to Rear-Admiral Gourdon, on duty in the port, the minister's promise that he would replace Bonnefoux, and handed him a message from Jaucourt, dated July 10th:

'On receipt of this message you are to give strict orders, on your own responsibility, that the frigate on which Napoleon has not embarked shall return to port at once with all persons who may be on board and shall, from now on, be independent of any movements made by the frigate with Bonaparte on board.

'No consideration whatever shall be allowed to hinder this movement which must be carried out without any communication with the frigate on which Napoleon now is. This must be carried out with all discretion and speed.

'In accordance with the instructions you have received from the Commission, you should have prevented any attempt by Napoleon, either alone or with others, to disembark; you should also have prevented any communication which he may have tried to make with the English ships or with any others . . .'

Jaucourt was, therefore, unaware of the Commission's decree and of Decrès' message of July 6th, according to which the Emperor was authorized to communicate with the blockading squadron on condition that he requested General Beker's approval in writing. He further increased the confusion by adding: 'I confirm these orders (!) which guarantee me that Napoleon is on board the frigate *Saale*, Captain Philibert.'

Richard let Bonnefoux know that officers were on their way to Rochefort 'entrusted with secret missions . . . ' What missions? To arrest the Emperor?

Overwrought, distressed, warmhearted, Bonnefoux considered what measures to take; rather than provoke what might prove to be irreparable, he tried to gain time . . . he told Richard that he would go on board the *Saale* with the ebb-tide that evening. Then he replied warily to the minister that he would carry out his orders; that he would leave for the roadstead at nine o'clock that evening and that on the 13th Napoleon was still aboard the *Saale*. He knew perfectly well that he had been on the Ile d'Aix since the 12th!

Had messengers been sent to him? In any case several boats had been moving between Rochefort, the moorings and the island. There, the Emperor was listening to Besson's complaints. Besson, very annoyed, was stressing the absolute necessity 'of following up the measures already taken'.

'Were it a question of saving the state,' replied Napoleon, 'I would make every effort imaginable, but since it is my person alone that is at stake I must sacrifice myself.'

To which the future Besson Bey, Egyptian admiral and Mehemet Ali's Minister of Marine, objected that it was not a question of the Emperor alone, but of the sacrifice of all his followers in France and those throughout the world who called on him in the name of liberty. Did he promise once more, and sincerely, to embark on his ship at nine o'clock that evening?

'What strikes one when one studies this man closely, apparently so secretive, calculating and cunning,' wrote Elie Faure, 'is his boundless innocence . . . ' That evening, as throughout his life, he was alone, involved in a struggle between his aspirations towards an unattainable goal and the implacable inertia of events. Once more, all men had their eyes fixed on him . . . A terrible exhaustion weighed him down. 'I have always,' he was to say, 'borne the world on my shoulders and that task, after all, does not permit me to be tired.'

It was this lack of self-interest that he displayed in that monastic room which today attracts so many visitors to the Ile d'Aix. He was thinking only of his companions in misfortune and of France, which, as Lallemand wrote, 'in those supreme moments filled all his thoughts'. Standing with his back to the chimney breast, he watched Las Cases and Lallemand, the harbingers of his destiny, and those whom he had just summoned, Bertrand, Savary, Gourgaud and Montholon, grouped around the table.

On his order, Las Cases recounted his interview with Maitland and 'the whole conversation he had had with him'. One heard: 'British honour . . . hospitable English soil . . . the proposals of the captain of the *Bellerophon* . . . without commitment on his part . . . ' What did they think?

He already knew their replies. For different reasons and different interests, Gourgaud, Bertrand, Las Cases and Savary, whose devotion served him in the same way as his enemies' hatred, declared themselves partisans of reliance upon English honour. Montholon hesitated and would have preferred the Emperor to go to America on Baudin's *Bayadère*. Lallemand protested violently against these suggestions. He had no confidence in the English and their government. They would make Maitland the instrument of their perfidy and then disown him if they found it convenient. He implored the Emperor to leave, with a single officer, on Besson's smack. 'Let Your Majesty,' he said, 'choose the man in whom he has the most trust. Should he honour me by his choice, I would serve him as secretary and personal valet . . . '

The Emperor could equally well join the Army of the Loire. For more than ten leagues around every man was willing to die for him. Even here: General Alméras, the 14th Marines, the 82nd of the Line and the National Guards of La Rochelle, the Naval Artillery Regiment and the 43rd of the Line at Rochefort, the 2nd Hussars at Niort, Clausel, the troops at Bordeaux and Blaye, Colonel Carré's 66th of the Line, the Federals, the Army of the Vendée under Lamarque, etc.

'Were it a question of the Empire, I could try a second return from Elba . . . ' On arrival at the Loire, once in the army cantonments his cause would be won; and that of the King and his allies would be lost.

Davout knew that. Louis XVIII was not unaware of it. The English dreaded it.

During the night of July 13th to 14th, speaking to his commissioners, Generals Haxo, Kellermann and Gérard, who had been sent to Paris and were becoming more and more uneasy at the attitude of Gouvion-Saint-Cyr towards the army, Davout agreed to the generals' suggestion to offer its submission to the minister.

' . . . You have won by your conduct the admiration of all French military men,' he wrote, 'and thus, in the present grave situation, the side that you have taken will have the assent of all. If you consider that a pure and simple submission will be of value to our unfortunate country accept it, but preserve the army's honour.'

Meanwhile (on July 14th) the three commissioners, without further reflection, handed to the Minister of War the loyal address to the King which they had drawn up in advance.

*   *   *

At the Château de la Source (Loiret) near Orleans, the Prince of Eckmühl was trying to convince the generals and colonels of the troops in cantonments in the area that they should sign the act of submission which had been read out to them by Colonel Carrion-Nisas:

'Sire. The army, unanimous in purpose and allegiance, in order to be brought to a pure and simple submission to the government of Your Majesty, has no need to receive any special admonition nor to change its spirit and its sentiments; it is enough that it consult the feelings which have guided it in all circumstances, the spirit that has imbued it throughout twenty-five years of political turmoil.

'The opinions, the actions and the conduct of each one of its members have always had for motive a love of country, ardent, deep and exclusive, capable of the greatest effort and of the greatest sacrifice, worthy of respect even in its errors and divergences which has won the admiration of Europe for all time and which will assure us that admiration for posterity.

'The generals, the officers and the men who rally around their standards and who have been loyal to them with even greater constancy and love in the midst of misfortune are not men whom anyone could accuse of regretting their individual interests.

'It is therefore to other thoughts, to more noble motives, that the silence which the army has guarded up to this day must be attributed. From the humblest soldier to the most senior officer, the French army is composed of citizens, or the sons or brothers of citizens. It is entirely bound up with the nation. It cannot differentiate its interests from those of the French people. Together with the French people, it accepts, and sincerely accepts, Your Majesty's government. It will safeguard the happiness of France by a noble and complete forgetfulness of the past, by effacing the remnants of all hatreds and dissensions and by respecting the rights of all.

'Convinced of these truths and filled with respect and confidence in the feelings manifested by Your Majesty, the army swears complete submission and boundless loyalty. It will shed its blood to uphold the oath that it solemnly swears today to defend the King and France.'

There were murmurs, objections and refusals. To the stubborn, who lacked confidence and wished 'to wait', Davout replied that the submission of the troops was urgent and essential; mass support and signatures would show the union and strength of the army and would give the sovereign the power to halt the devastation of the country and prevent its dismemberment. The marshal called on everyone to rally around him. 'Public interest alone dictates my conduct,' he said. 'No one will ever see me at court or accepting any post. I will live in retirement, devoting the remainder of my days to the education of my children . . .'

They signed. They signed even more freely than had been hoped. But the cavalry general Dejean, son of the engineer general, obstinately refused.

'I order you in the name of your father whom you will distress, in the name of France,' Davout told him violently.

'My father is a fine man and I love my country very much. But I will not sign,' the Emperor's devoted aide-de-camp at Waterloo replied imperturbably.

There were others; however, within ten days the officers' corps was to capitulate, including Reille who 'no longer wanted to tail after Bonaparte', even though he too had been Napoleon's aide-de-camp.

'The intriguers have destroyed France,' the Emperor said to the few faithful gathered around the table in his room on the Ile d'Aix to hear his great decision. 'Corrupt men have played fast and loose with her independence and her glory, but I do not complain of the people; they have not ceased to be stout-hearted and magnanimous.'

He did not wish a single cannon to be fired in his interest alone. 'I do not know the Prince-Regent of England,' he went on, 'but according to all I have heard I have no reason to lack confidence in the nobility of his character. My decision is taken; I will write to him and tomorrow, at dawn, we will go on board the English ships. Once on board the *Bellerophon* I shall be on British soil; the English will be bound by the laws of hospitality.'

* * *

Which was just what the victors of Waterloo did not want at any price: Liverpool, Castlereagh, Louis XVIII. The executor of their designs was the minister Jaucourt. Liverpool had written a letter to Castlereagh exactly a week before (July 7th):

'If we capture Buonaparte we must keep him on board ship until the views of the Allies can be canvassed. The most suitable measure would be to hand him over to the King of France, but then we must be quite certain that he will be tried and that he will have no chance to escape. I have had several consultations with legal experts and they are of the opinion that this would be, in every way, the measure least subject to objections. We should have the right to consider him a prisoner of the French and, as such, we should hand him over to the French government.'

Louis XVIII would have preferred to lay hands on Napoleon himself and this desire was conveyed by Jaucourt's order brought to Bonnefoux by Richard to keep him aboard the *Saale*. But he was not yet absolute master in France and had to submit to pressure from the Allies who, after restoring him to his throne, had forced him to dismiss Blacas, the Count of Artois and his friends, and to accept Fouché and form a constitutional government.

If the English laid hands on Napoleon 'in order to hand him

over to the French government' what would the King's Council do? The execution of 'the usurper' would provoke a terrible revolt which would sweep away the throne and all those near it. Castlereagh feared, indeed, 'that the King of France does not feel strong enough to hand him over to justice as a rebel . . . In such a case,' he wrote, 'we are ready to take upon ourselves the guard over his person in the name of the Allied powers and, in truth, we feel that it would be better if he were handed over to us rather than to any other member of the Confederation.' To which Liverpool replied that 'the best place for his imprisonment would be at a certain distance from Europe; the Cape of Good Hope or Saint Helena would be most suitable . . . '

That was why Louis XVIII, having accepted these 'suggestions' as well as so many others, was to choose as executor of his base designs the Marquis du Jaucourt, Minister of the Marine, former brigadier-general (1792), member of the Legislative Assembly, emigré who had returned to France by the grace of the First Consul, tribune, steward of the household of King Joseph-Napoleon, friend of Talleyrand, Minister of State to the King in 1814 and who, without ever having been a day on a battlefield, had promoted lieutenant-general on October 25th that same year; chameleon, turncoat, opportunist and Jack-of-all-trades.

That evening, July 14th, in the name of the King and by agreement with Sir J. W. Croker, Secretary of the British Admiralty, then resident in the Hôtel du Mont-Blanc, Rue de la Paix, Jaucourt gave his orders to his aide-de-camp, Captain Gauthier de Rigny, nephew of Baron Louis, who had returned from Ghent with the King. This senior officer had served at the age of sixteen in the Egyptian campaign and had been in command of a gunboat of the Boulogne flotilla in 1803. He had served as ensign in the Marines of the Guard and had distinguished himself at Wagram. He had been promoted captain in 1811. He owed his whole career to his own talents and to the Emperor.

M. de Rigny, accompanied by Lieutenant Fleuriau, was to leave immediately for Rochefort. His mission was not only to prevent Napoleon's departure but to take prisoner the man who had violated the Treaty of Fontainebleau and was under the 'ban of Europe'. He must therefore prevent him surrendering voluntarily to the English ships cruising off Rochefort, so that he could not ask the English for asylum by placing himself under the protection of their laws and by that means avoid being regarded as a prisoner.

He must therefore hold discussions with M. Bonnefoux in order to get definite ideas of the position of the ships and of the whereabouts of Napoleon Buonaparte. He was to commandeer the boats he needed to go to the English squadron.

'To make certain that Napoleon is on board the *Saale* . . . He is no longer a passenger but a prisoner for whom the captain is responsible to the King. The frigate must not leave the roadstead save by the King's order. Napoleon Buonaparte is not the prisoner of the King of France alone but of all the sovereigns who were guarantors of the Treaty of Paris (May 30, 1814); all the rulers to whom he has broken his word by bringing war and revolution to France have equal rights on his person.

'That is why the English commander blockading the roadstead of the Ile d'Aix is ordered by his government to summon the captain of the ship with Buonaparte on board to hand him over immediately.

'I therefore entrust you with a letter addressed by M. Croker to the commander of the squadron and add it to my order to the commander of the *Saale* and an order from the Minister of War to the officer commanding the Ile d'Aix. You will go on board the English ships and will deliver the letters with which you have been entrusted.'

To these official ignominies Jaucourt added a note of personal treachery. 'The orders of which you are the bearer,' he wrote, 'are dictated by sentiments of humanity. These sentiments have, in the circumstances, alone determined the intervention of the King's ministers, since the allied sovereigns are able to act without the aid of France.'

Thus, 'by the sentiments of humanity', two French officers were entrusted by their minister with a task so degrading that the English did not dare to carry it out.

* * *

'May the peace of Europe become the pledge of my renunciation of the throne of France,' said the Emperor to General Beker when telling him of his intention to leave the Ile d'Aix at dawn the next day. 'May the Emperor Alexander maintain that character of grandeur and magnanimity that has always distinguished him in the memorable circumstances of his reign; may he never forget that in the present European situation the peace of Russia depends upon the preservation of France. May the sovereigns who now control the destiny of nations keep their word and my desires will be fulfilled . . . '

Beker at once ordered Captain Philibert to prepare the brig *Epervier* to receive the Emperor and his suite at dawn on July 15th.

The Emperor was alone in his room with Gourgaud. 'Write!' he told him: 'To the Regent of England.

'Your Royal Highness,

'Because of the factions tearing my country and the hostility of the greatest powers of Europe, I have ended my political career. I come, like Themistocles, to seat myself at the hearth of the British people. I place myself under the protection of its laws and demand this grace from Your Royal Highness as the most powerful, the most steadfast and most generous of my enemies.'

The note he held in his hand was dated July 13th. In tears, Gourgaud dashed down the phrases jerked out in that abrupt voice he knew so well:

'My aide-de-camp Gourgaud will go on board the English squadron with the Count of Las Cases. He will proceed, as soon as the commander of that squadron may be able to send him, either to the admiral or to London. He will try to gain audience with the Prince-Regent and will deliver my letter to him. If there is nothing against the delivery of passports to the United States, that is what I would prefer; but I do not want to go to any colony. If America is not possible, I prefer England to any other country. I will take the name of 'Colonel Muiron' (Bonaparte's former aide-de-camp, killed at Arcole sheltering him with his body).

'If I must go to England, I should like to be lodged in a country house some ten or twelve leagues from London, where I would like to arrive with the strictest possible incognito. I should need a residence large enough to house all my suite. I would like, if that is in accord with the views of the govern-

the next day. May the Emperor Alexander maintain that
character of grandeur and magnanimity that has always distinguished him in the memorable circumstances of his reign, may
he never forget that it is the respect which he owes to the peace
of Russia depends on the preservation of the crown of Marie, the
sovereigns who now decide the destiny of nations keep their
... and my design will be fulfilled ...

... at once ordered Captain Philibert to repair to the brig
Eurotas to receive the Emperor and his suite, during one
of his ...

... Emperor was pleased to toast with Captain Willett, who
told him: "To the Kings of England ..."

... al Highness,

... me of the factions which any minute ... and to destroy the
greatest power of Europe, I have ended my political
career. I come, like Themistocles, to seat myself at the hearth of
the British people, I place myself under the protection of its laws
and I claim this grace from Your Royal Highness as the most
powerful, the most steadfast and most generous of my enemies.

This note he had his secretary signed July 13th, at
Gourgaud dated it from the triplicate, backed out in that script
voice he knows to well:

"My aide-de-camp, Gourgaud, will go on board the English
squadron with the Count of Las Cases. He will proceed, as you
as the commander of that squadron ... be able to avail himself
either the arrival or to render. He will to go to England
with the Prince Regent, if not and will deliver my letter to him, then
is under the dignity of ... the delivery of passport to the United States
that is his if I prefer he will ... not wanting to go to a
colony ... America is not possible ... I beholden to any other
country. I will take the name of Col. or Musson [Bonaparte],
former de-camp, killed at Arcole sheltering him with his
body.

"If I must go to England, I should like to be lodged in a
country house some ... or twelve leagues from London that
I would like, as much as possible ... privacy ... I
should not ... reference large enough to ... because ... I there
would like, if that is in accord with the views of the govern-

Handwritten facsimile (overlaid):

Attens Royales en but an factions qui' Divisies

en Fi divisai Dem plus grandeur
pui il existe ma carrière
poli stique m'étter

lire comme Themistocle e m'
al seoir comme Bri stannique
Fisis Sermi ne's Sei Serminai
vien comme Bri stannique de
Sur le peuple Bri stannique
On peuple On rapportae's
e'et plus hospita liers
met Sour le payer et
reclame Du Nostre
la le poyn Sour la protection
pui il om's
plu re puis sion De
generosive De
Rochefort 13 Juillet 1815

Napoléon

ment, to keep away from London. If the minister sees fit to appoint an English commissioner in my household, he will do his best to see that there is no suspicion of imprisonment.'

These were his last instructions, dictated to his last ambassador, whose descendants have piously preserved these pages. There was no more Emperor, no more Napoleon, no more Bonaparte. There was only 'Colonel Muiron'. Then there were other letters.

The Marshal of the Household feverishly copied the Emperor's letter to the Prince-Regent and another dictated to the commander of the British ships off Rochefort:

'His Majesty will come, by tomorrow's tide, about four or five o'clock in the morning, on board your ship.

'I am sending the Count of Las Cases, State Councillor, to act as Controller of the Household, with the list of persons included in His Majesty's suite.

'If the Admiral, in reply to the letter which you have sent him, forwards to you the safe-conducts to the United States that have been requested, His Majesty will go there with pleasure but, in default of such safe-conducts, he will willingly go to England as a private person to enjoy the protection of your laws.

'His Majesty has sent Baron Gourgaud to the Prince-Regent with a letter, of which I have the honour to send you a copy, asking you to forward it to the minister to whom you may think it necessary to send him, so that he may have the honour of handing to the Prince-Regent the letter that is in his possession.'

Signed: 'Marshal of the Household, Count Bertrand.'

Half-past four. Gourgaud, Las Cases, a page (Las Cases' son) and the valet François Aubin, coming from the Ile d'Aix, went on board the *Saale*. Forewarned by Beker, Philibert manned his longboat which left for the *Bellerophon* at a quarter-past five with a naval officer, Gourgaud and Las Cases on board. After which . . .

The captain of the *Saale* wrote to the captain of the *Epervier*:

'By order of Lieutenant-General Beker and in accord with the orders and instructions of His Excellency the Minister of the

Marine and the port-admiral which I have transmitted to you, you will make ready to receive on board your ship, at about two o'clock tonight, the Emperor Napoleon and the members of his suite, in order to take them to the English squadron in the Basques roadstead. It is not necessary to remind you of the courtesies due to this exalted person.

'PHILIBERT'

All was ready for the great departure.

Chapter VIII

THE BELLEROPHON

MAITLAND'S WELCOME

Six-fifteen on the evening of July 14th, in the Basques roadstead. Spies, coming from the coast, reported that the *Myrmidon* had joined the *Bellerophon*.

Captain Gambier brought news: 'Bonaparte will try to escape on a Danish sloop, in a vat concealed amongst the ballast; tubes have been placed so that he may breathe . . . '

Order to the *Myrmidon* to take up position N.E. of the *Bellerophon* 'to prevent any ship from passing or landing on the coast'. Patrol boats were lowered. Maitland was extremely uneasy.

Seven o'clock. 'It is quite impossible for you to have been to Rochefort and to have returned since you left me this morning,' Maitland said to Las Cases who, leaving the *Saale's* longboat, set foot on the poop with his companions.

'I had no need to do so,' the chamberlain replied. 'When I got to the Ile d'Aix I found the Emperor there . . . ' Lie upon lie.

In the presence of Captain Gambier (*Myrmidon*) and Captain Sartorius (*Slaney*), Maitland read Napoleon's letter to the Prince-Regent, which according to Las Cases, made a deep impression. The welcome was cordial and eager. 'I had my heart set on seeing this affair through since I had brought it so near to a conclusion,' wrote Maitland.

Before nightfall, the *Slaney* (four guns, eight carronades) set sail. Sartorius took with him a letter from Maitland to the Secretary of the Admiralty. In it he gave an account of what had happened: Las Cases and Gourgaud had handed him a letter from Count Bertrand asking him to receive Napoleon 'who intends to surrender to the generosity of the Prince-Regent'. Considering himself authorized by the secret instructions of their Lordships, he had accepted this proposal. He said that he had 'formally explained that he was in no way authorized to agree to any conditions whatsoever and that he could only transport him and his suite to England'.

Captain Sartorius had orders to make for the nearest port and to have Napoleon's letter forwarded to the Prince-Regent by his first lieutenant while, relying on Maitland's word, Gourgaud was persuaded to go direct to London. Shortly after the departure of the *Slaney*, the *Saale's* longboat vanished in the direction of the Ile d'Aix. The officer in charge brought to the Marshal of the Household the agreement of the 'squadron commander' to his proposal 'to receive Bonaparte and his suite and to take them to England'.

According to the list sent by Bertrand, the suite was a large one. Some would be taken on board the *Myrmidon*, which Captain Gambier had prepared in great haste: Officers: Lieutenant-Colonels de Résigny and Schultz, Captains Autric, Mesener and Piontkowski, Lieutenant Rivière, Sub-Lieutenant Sainte-Catherine. In His Majesty's suite: Maitre d'hotel Cipriani, ushers Santini and Chauvin, in charge of the lights Rousseau, footmen Archambaud, Joseph, Lecharron, Orsini and Fumeau, butler Lisieux. In all, seventeen persons.

On Las Cases' advice, Maitland had the cabins and deck-houses, which had been removed in order to clear the decks for action, put back again and had the gundecks fitted out to house thirty-three passengers:

Five generals: Lieutenant-General Count Bertrand, Marshal of the Household; Lieutenant-General Savary, Duke of Rovigo; Lieutenant-General Baron Lallemand, aide-de-camp to His Majesty; Brigadier-General Count Montholon, aide-de-camp to His Majesty; Count Las Cases, State Councillor.

Two ladies: the Countesses Bertrand and Montholon. Four children: Napoleon, Hortense and Henri Bertrand, Charles Montholon.

Three officers: Lieutenant-Colonel Planat, Maingaut, His Majesty's surgeon, and Las Cases, page.

Five persons in the service of the bedchamber: Marchand, head valet, Gillé, Saint-Denis and Noverraz, valets. Denis, master of the robes. Three persons of the livery: Archambaud, first footman, Gaudron and Gentilini, footmen. Four persons in the service of the table: Totain, first maitre d'hotel, Pierron chief of the pantry, La Page and La Fosse, cooks.

Seven servants of the suite accompanying His Majesty: Bouchart (Marianne), married name Madol, and Barté (Colette), married name Aymond, lady's maids to the Countess Bertrand. Brulé (Joséphine), lady's maid to the Countess Montholon. Lambzer, valet to Count Bertrand. Dowling, known as Dooge, valet to the Duke of Rovigo. Trépied, valet to Count Montholon.

Wishing to show his distinguished guest 'every possible consideration' Maitland reserved for him the whole afterpart of the ship because, as Las Cases said, 'the Emperor likes to be alone and to take some exercise'.

In his room in his last 'palace' on the Ile d'Aix the Emperor dined and then retired; the white bed-curtains were drawn against the buzzing mosquitoes. The night was warm. Outside there were cries, comings and goings. The suite took their places in the boats to go on board the *Epervier*; the pinnaces in which sailors and servants were piling the luggage went to the *Sophie*. They returned empty and left again with fresh loads. The Marshal of the Household loved bustle and confusion; a carriage was embarked, two horses, some furniture, the coronation robes. Little by little, the fishermen, the people of the island, the soldiers, who had at first been kept at a distance, edged closer to the jetty.

He was about to depart.

Ten o'clock at night. A boat from the coast hailed the *Bellerophon*. A man clambered on board, a traitor. He came from La Rochelle. Buonaparte had just reached the Breton channel on board a lugger; the man had seen him, wrapped in a huge sailor's cloak. Sceptical, but suspicious, Maitland knocked at Las Cases' door.

'What time did your informant see the Emperor,' the chamberlain asked.

'Ten o'clock in the morning.'

'On my honour, I left him this evening at half-past five. I do not know what he has done since, but he had the definite intention of coming here tomorrow morning.'

That is what Philibert told the port-admiral, who came on board his ship in the middle of the night (July 15th at half-past one in the morning) with Baron Richard. Bonnefoux certainly knew what was happening, but he continued to play for time. Instead of going to the Ile d'Aix, where he was sure of seeing the Emperor and forbidding him to surrender to the English, he went directly on board the *Saale,* sure of finding no-one there.

Everything took place as if, advised of the minister's orders, Philibert and the two prefects had agreed not to carry them out and to let Napoleon leave. They even sent Borgnis-Desbordes to the Ile d'Aix to urge Beker to hasten his departure and to tell the commander of the *Epervier* to use especial diligence, in case Jaucourt's emissaries should arrive to arrest Napoleon.

July 15th, two o'clock in the morning. He was up; Marchand dressed him. Instead of the terrible green coat which he had been wearing for the past fortnight, he put on his legendary coat of the Chasseurs of the Guard. On his breast sparkled his orders and on his coat golden hunting-horns. He put on the Grand Cordon of the Legion and buckled on his golden sword, picked up his little hat with the tricolour cockade and slipped his 'green riding-coat' over the lot.

The wooden stairs creaked under his heavy tread. He reached the door. Behind him, Bertrand, Savary, Montholon and Beker, followed without speaking. Their steps echoed noisily on the landing. Followed by Mesdames Bertrand and Montholon and their children, the gloomy procession moved towards the rocks of the south point, now know as Grave à Barbotin.

Sad and hushed, the fishermen, hat in hand, saluted him. The tide was out, the sea calm. Three boats were rocking to the rhythm of the short swell breaking on the shingle; the ladies, the generals and a few servants took their places in them.

Just before he embarked, the Emperor turned round towards the island, took a long look at this fragment of French soil, made a weary gesture and, last of all, got into his boat, steadied for him by two sailors. 'When man deserts us,' Queen Hortense had said to him on June 28th at Malmaison, 'it is good to turn to nature, which does not deceive us.'

Strong arms pushed. It was a quarter to four, according to the log of the *Saale*. The stars paled. The dawn lightened. The outline of the *Boyard* could be seen. The side of the *Epervier* loomed large. The sun rose quickly above Fouras, revealing the tricolour flag and the torch, symbol for parley. Napoleon who, behind Bertrand, stepped on to the poop was welcomed by the captain and by frenzied shouts of 'Long live the Emperor!' from a crew shaken by intense emotion.

'Sire,' Beker said to him, 'does Your Majesty wish that I accompany you to the squadron, as the instructions of the government prescribe?'

Perhaps foreseeing what was threatening him, he replied: 'No, General Beker. Go back to the Ile d'Aix. It must not be said that France handed me over to the English.'

That was, however, the wish of his masters, and their agents' carriage was galloping towards Rochefort.

Ollivier Jourdan de la Passardière, thirty-two years old, from Granville, former cabin-boy, midshipman in 1799, ensign on board the *Formidable* which had fought at Trafalgar, interned in English prisons, whence he had escaped to take up service again, commander of the *Epervier*, has left an account of Napoleon's reception on board:

'Enthusiasm and extraordinary emotion. A crew of young sailors, some of whom had gone to the Champ de Mai. I could rely on them.'

To Borgnis-Desbordes, a relation of Philibert, sent 'secretly' when the ship was ready to sail to tell them to be quick since the Emperor might be arrested, he replied: 'Not on board the *Epervier*, at least not while I am alive to prevent it . . . '

Had M. de Rigny, former officer of the Marines of the Guard, been announced?

In the haste, despite the almost mild N.W. wind, the *Epervier* fouled one of her anchors and left it behind.

Meanwhile, a midshipman on the *Bellerophon* wrote: 'All was expectation and excitement . . . Half-past four. We saw a man-of-war brig get under weigh from Aix Roads, and stand out towards us, bearing a flag of truce . . . '

In his usual manner the Emperor inspected the crew of the *Epervier*, then took the seat of the officer of the watch and questioned Jourdan on his captivity, on the character of the English, who had also held two of his uncles prisoner: what was his opinion 'on the decision to go to England'? Jourdan was embarrassed, but since His Majesty told him to speak freely, he thought it would have been better to have tried to get to the United States.

When the Emperor objected that he thought it would not be possible to make the journey because of the presence of the English ships, the officer agreed that it might have been risky;

but none the less he should have 'tried to break through on the frigates, or on the *Epervier*, which was faster'.

Certainly, if it so happened that she encountered the enemy, His Majesty would be considered a prisoner of war . . . but he was sure that he would be treated as such on surrendering to the *Bellerophon*. So, if he preferred to adopt the alternative which still offered some hope of success . . .

'It is too late,' said the Emperor. 'I have sent one of my generals on board the English ship. They are waiting for me and I shall go.'

'He's young!' said Bertrand, shrugging his shoulders. He had been listening to the conversation. A long silence . . . unbearable.

For something to say . . .

'What colour is it? Green? Or blue?' he asked Madame Montholon, showing her the sleeve of his overcoat.

'Green, Sire.'

Eight o'clock. They were becalmed. The Emperor took his coffee on the capstan, leaving a few stains on the copper, which were carefully respected by the sailors. Then he walked on the poop, questioned some old gunners who had been prisoners of the English. He was uneasy.

He walked towards the sterncastle; mounted the ladder, dirtied his hands, tried to clean them, asked for a little water . . . the ensign Pelletreau called a sailor, but already the generals had vanished into the wardroom whence Lallemand, exhausted, would not come out. They reappeared bearing a basin, a jug, soap and a towel . . . 'I have felt angry all my life at not having forestalled them,' Pelletreau says in his *Mémoire*.

The persistent calm held them motionless.

Standing on an ammunition chest the Emperor looked around through his glass, 'examining,' wrote the ensign, 'the white flags that floated over Oléron and La Rochelle'.

Were there any? Not on the public buildings nor on the men-of-war before midday July 17th. Not if the orders of General Butreau, commanding the area, of the port-admiral or of the military commander of the port of Rochefort, Querengal, are to be believed. But it is probable that white flags, hoisted here and there by the royalists, were visible, since Pelletreau saw them.

They made longer and longer tacks. The Emperor asked the captain 'not to go so near the land'. He considered that the brig 'was not going in the right direction'.

'What is its armament?'

'Eighteen guns, Sire. There are no larger made in France.'

'Where was it built?'

'At Bayonne.'

He remarked that the *Inconstant*, which brought him back from Elba, had twenty-two guns, a hundred men and a squad of grenadiers.

'On a ship as small as this, it is impossible to have more than we have (ninety),' replied Jourdan.

At which he murmured: 'Decrès deceived me like all the others . . . ' Bitter recollection of the past. Like all the others! Like Fouché, like Davout, like Carnot, like Talleyrand. The endless list tailed off into shame and forgetfulness.

Like this Englishman who, eager to seize his prey and seeing the *Superb* approaching flying the flag of Rear-Admiral Hotham, wanting to keep for himself alone the profit of an extraordinary prize, lost his famous self-control and sent boats under oars to the *Epervier*.

Andrew Mott, second on the *Bellerophon*, came on board, hesitated, advanced towards the Emperor, saluted. He did not know a word of French. His elbow resting on the binnacle and his head in his hands, Napoleon 'made a slight gesture of disapproval . . . ' then, breaking the painful silence:

'Madame Bertrand,' he said, 'ask this gentleman how long it will take to get to England with these north-west winds.'

'It will take a week.'

'And with a fair wind?'

'About forty-eight hours,' replied the Englishman with a smile.

Then, straightening up: 'Do you feel strong enough, Mesdames, to go on board the English ship?' When they said yes, bowing, he went on: 'Very well, then! Go on board.'

The English officer offered his arm to his compatriot and went to the largest boat.

The Emperor told the officers and crew drawn up to port that 'he would long remember the *Epervier* and its inhabitants (sic)'. Then he moved towards the gangway and went down last.

Seated in the sternsheets, his eyes bathed with tears and his
spirit in turmoil, he plunged his right hand in the sea and three
times sprinkled French water on the *Epervier* in sign of farewell.
The crew cheered him, weeping, until the boat was out of ear-
shot.

On the *Bellerophon* they had been watching him for the past
ten minutes; they could see the sailors of the *Epervier* climbing
into the rigging and waving their hats. A general's guard of
marines was ordered aft on the *Bellerophon's* quarterdeck and
the boatswain stood, whistle in hand, ready to pipe him aboard;
lieutenants, ensigns and midshipmen were drawn up in two
ranks. The commander kept trudging backwards and forwards
between the gangway and his own cabin, sometimes peeping
out at one of the quarterdeck ports to see if the barge was
drawing near.

'Is it possible! The famous Napoleon!' wrote a midshipman.

'Have you got him?' Maitland asked Mott, who arrived
quickly.

A little later, saluted by the rowers, who were perhaps French
prisoners, the Emperor, preceded by the Marshal of the Household, slowly mounted the steps of the ladder and reached the
deck.

It was ten o'clock. The guard did not present arms. Led by
Bertrand and Las Cases to the aftercastle, the Emperor looked
fixedly at Maitland, with a look not to be forgotten, and said in
a firm voice:

'I have come aboard to place myself under the protection of
your ruler and your laws.' Was this a free man surrendering?
Or a hostage whom one seizes?

On the *Saale*, renamed the *Amphitrite* as before March 20th,
they had followed all the details of the drama. As soon as the
curtain fell, Bonnefoux eased his conscience by sending a report
to the minister. Being himself involved he was not able to reveal
the whole truth, but edited generalities, trying to make his lies
plausible.

'To carry out Your Excellency's orders,' he wrote, 'I embarked
on my boat, accompanied by Baron Richard, prefect of Charente-
Inférieure. I had not yet received the reports from the roadstead,
but was told by the captain in command of the *Amphitrite* that

Bonaparte had embarked on the brig *Epervier*, flying a flag of truce, with the intention of going to the English squadron.

'In fact, at early dawn, we saw it tacking towards the English ship *Bellerophon*, commanded by Captain Maitland who, seeing that Bonaparte was making his way towards him, hoisted the white flag on his mizzen.

'Bonaparte was received on board the English ship, together with the members of his suite. The officer whom I left on watch has just given me this important news when General Beker, who arrived a few moments later, confirmed it.'

In fact, Beker had returned on board, greatly moved by the events of the past few minutes, but now at ease since he was free of the responsibilities which had been heaped upon him during the past three weeks, even though a little uneasy at the consequences which might ensue.

The *Epervier* returned to her moorings about three o'clock that afternoon and Jourdan reported on his mission. The Emperor having 'left his ship' to take his place in one of *Bellerophon's* boats, Jourdan, being suspicious and mistrustful of the English, had asked the commander to confirm in writing 'if it were really aboard his ship that the Emperor had gone'.

Some of those in the entourage were afraid lest this lack of trust might offend Captain Maitland! It was not very likely, for Maitland replied at once with this acknowledgment:

'Sir, Napoleon Bonaparte, late Emperor of the French, has, this day, embarked on board His Majesty's ship under my command, from the *Epervier*, French brig of war, commanded by Monsieur Jordin (*sic*) . . .

'J. MAITLAND'

Then, since the swell was driving his ship landward, Jourdan moored and went aboard the English ship, on which the Emperor had invited him to dine. He had hastened the unloading of the *Sophie*, and had chatted with the generals who had seemed impressed by the fear that he expressed that 'the Emperor might be considered a prisoner . . . ' That did not prevent Bertrand from handing him this naïvely optimistic letter for General Beker:

'My dear General,

'We have arrived on board the English ship; we have nothing but praise for the way in which we have been received and we thank you for the careful watch that you have kept. I pray you let Madame the Princess Hortense know that the Emperor is in good health. Please tell Prince Joseph also; he must be somewhere in the vicinity of Rochefort.

'I have sent you a copy of the letter that the Emperor has written to the Prince-Regent. I do not need to remind you not to communicate its contents to anyone for at least a fortnight . . . '

Then, Jourdan went on, the *Superb* dropped anchor nearby and His Majesty sent a message to the Admiral through the Marshal of the Household that he would like the Admiral to dine with him. The meal, a cold one, was served in the English style. The Emperor ate little.

At one o'clock Jourdan took leave of him. On returning to her mooring the *Epervier* met a boat in difficulties, with several members of the suite aboard. He took it in tow and brought it to the *Bellerophon*. 'As we passed under the poop of the vessel, the Emperor appeared on the gallery; the crew manned the yards as a salute. He waved farewell to us and we soon lost sight of him . . . ' Jourdan wrote.

On board the *Bellerophon*, the Emperor, in silk stockings and gold-buckled shoes, expressed his wish to inspect the ship. The veteran of Aboukir, justly escaping the breakers' yard, washed and holystoned, looked fine. The procession was formed : Maitland led, Napoleon followed. The generals, in full uniform, brought up the rear. The captain spoke French tolerably well, save for his Scottish way of pronouncing the Rs, chatted with his guest who complimented him on the good turn-out of the ship, pinched a midshipman's ear and talked with the boatswain . . . narrow-brimmed glazed scraper in hand.

'I hope I see Your Honour well,' said the old red-whiskered sea-wolf, ducking his head as he shuffled up to Napoleon.

Then came the Admiral, who immediately uncovered . . . 'This was the signal which I believe every one of us desired,' wrote the midshipman George Home. 'The captain followed the example of the Admiral, and in future everyone uncovered while the Emperor was on deck, thus treating him with the respect due to a crowned head . . . they treated him with the respect due to the man himself, to his innate greatness, which did not lie in the crown of France, or the iron crown of Italy, but the actual superiority of the man to the rest of his species.'

'I repeatedly observed Napoleon, with his keen, calm, meditative gray eye, watching every movement, auguring therefrom, I suppose, what might be his future fate.'

*   *   *

That evening the Emperor seemed quite at ease, as if he were on a pleasure cruise. He was lodged in the great stern-cabin. The room leading into it served as dining-room and salon in which, every night as in Paris, an aide-de-camp slept. Marchand slept on a mattress in the room itself and Saint-Denis just outside, across the doorway. The officers of the suite had cabins fitted up on the main gundeck. Sofas of flags were improvised on the quarterdeck for the ladies; nets were rigged over the ports to prevent the children from falling overboard.

The Emperor chatted with the Admiral for an hour. Everyone remained standing. They noted the animation of his expression. The conversation was mainly about America. Then he moved towards the dining-room 'as if in his palace'. The foreigners, the suite, led by the Marshal of the Household, took their places. Madame Bertrand was on His Majesty's right, the Admiral on his left. Dinner was in the French manner, served on the imperial dinner service by the 'Household'. They spoke little. Coffee was served in the stern-cabin. His Majesty, very tired, retired early, after accepting an invitation to a dinner to be given by the Admiral the following day.

Sunday, July 16th at ten o'clock. Cloudy weather. The Emperor came on deck. Inspecting the guard of honour, he praised the men's bearing and returned their salute. Then he put them through a few drill movements, had them fix bayonets, corrected a stance, straightened an arm, took a gun and carried out the movements in the French manner, analyzing it.

Never had the English seen their sovereign 'let himself go' like this among his soldiers!

Then, turning to Bertrand: 'What couldn't one do with two hundred thousand fine fellows like this.'

He was to say it again, on March 10, 1819, to Montholon,

when summing up his views on the peoples of Europe. 'The English are really of a calibre superior to ours . . . If I had had an English army, I would have conquered the world; I could have gone right round the world without it losing its morale . . . If I had been the man chosen by the English in 1815 I could have lost ten Waterloos without losing a single vote in the legislature or a single soldier from my ranks . . . '

'Aye, and so you might well say, my most redoubtable Emperor,' a midshipman on the *Bellerophon* wrote that day. 'For, give you two hundred thousand such fine fellows as these, and land you once more at Rochefort, and I shall be sworn for it, that in three short weeks you have Wellington and the Holy Allies flying before you in every direction, and in ten days more you have the imperial headquarters at Schönbrunn, and in quiet possession of your tame Marie-Louise, and that beloved boy over which thy imagination so fondly dotes.' (!)

'But it could not be,' concluded the midshipman, coming back to realities on the deck of the ship which looked like 'the warrior court of Napoleon'. The crew had been won over.

'How is it, Las Cases, that you too are a man of war?' asked the Emperor, seeing his chamberlain in a captain's uniform.

'Sire, before the revolution I was a naval lieutenant and, since I think that a uniform earns you more respect in a foreign country, I have put mine on again!'

'He was a midshipman! He was wearing the Cross of the Legion of Honour which he hadn't had on leaving! . . . Vanity of vanities!' wrote Gourgaud.

*   *   *

The *Superb*, a seventy-two-gunner built in 1798, had had a face-lift; on the deck a tent of flags, having as ceiling the great English ensign. On the poop a band was playing. The soldiers rendered military honours. The sailors, in blue shirts and white trousers, manned the yards.

Bareheaded, Admiral Hotham greeted the Emperor with courtesy and deference. Aged thirty-eight, he had been in the service since 1790 and at Trafalgar had captured a small French squadron which had escaped the disaster. In command of the *Northumberland* from 1810 to 1812, he had taken part in the blockade of the French coast, after which he had participated in the American war. Rear-Admiral in 1814, he had hoisted his flag in the *Superb*. He showed the Emperor over the ship and asked him to stay aboard; His Majesty thanked him but refused, so as not to offend Maitland. Then he received the flag-officers, chatted with the chaplain and moved towards the after-deck, where dinner was served in the English manner. Saint-Denis was astonished at the welcome, but the Frenchmen ate little. Despairing of the situation of his master, to whom he was deeply attached, Colonel Planat could not hold back his tears.

About midday, after graciously thanking the admiral for his frank and cordial welcome, the Emperor returned to the *Bellerophon* which, about half-past one, set sail for England.

'Accompanied by the *Myrmidon*,' the admiral ordered, 'you will set course as quickly as possible for Torbay, where you will land the officer from my flagship who has been entrusted by me with a message to the Secretary of the Admiralty, as well as one of your own officers. The latter will take coach for Plymouth with the enclosed message to Lord Keith and a copy of these present orders which you are to hand over to His Lordship. He will await orders concerning your further movements.'

About six o'clock the *Bellerophon* sailed out of the Antioch channel.

THE BIRD HAS FLOWN!

Meanwhile a port pinnace from Rochefort came alongside the *Amphitrite*. It brought torches and white royalist flags. Next day, July 17th, at midday, all the troops at Rochefort would be wearing the white cockade.

Metternich wrote: 'According to an arrangement made between the Powers, Napoleon will be held prisoner at Fort St George in the north of Scotland . . .'

At Paris a royal decree regulated the disbandment of the army. Cut off from the capital by the Prussians, threatened by an Austrian offensive against the army cantonments, the Prince of Eckmühl gave way to despondency and perhaps remorse. Soiled by dubious intrigues, he had had to put up with humiliating compromises, had denied his Emperor, had handed Paris over without a fight, had abandoned his flag, had deceived his companions and had lost the respect of his soldiers . . . but he had preserved the army for the nation.

But the sovereign, whose good intentions towards the army Gouvion-Saint-Cyr had guaranteed, had decided upon its destruction, thus completing the disarmament of France and delivering her over to the enemy soldiers. It was what the marshal, using a phrase that was widely quoted, called 'the reorganization of the army'. Without stating his reasons, the victor of Auerstädt asked the King to accept his resignation.

Fouché prepared the list of proscriptions. There was talk only of punishment, severe punishment. All the soldiers who had come from Elba would, it was rumoured, be shot.

'The King will leave for Péronne, so as not to be in Paris at the time of the proscriptions,' one of his hirelings wrote to Wellington on July 17th. 'Names are raining down from the gutters of the Tuileries,' the Duke of Otranto remarked, to cover his own villainies and those of his agents.

The agents of his colleagues, Jaucourt and Gouvion-Saint-Cyr, Captain de Rigny, Lieutenant Fleuriau and General du Coëtlosquet, arrived at Rochefort on the morning of the 18th. Too late! Napoleon had gone freely to place himself under the protection of the British flag.

Had it been impossible—or had no one wanted—to carry out the preliminary order of July 10th? What did Rigny think, that former officer of the Marines of the Guard, or du Coëtlosquet, former aide-de-camp of Lasalle, promoted general by the Emperor at the age of thirty now and appointed commander of the Charente-Inférieure district to watch over the Emperor's arrest? No one has reported the conversation between the port-admiral and the messengers, whose mission now seemed pointless.

Perhaps thinking that his reputation and that of the French government would gain nothing if his instructions became known, Captain de Rigny decided to keep in his pocket the messages to Captain Philibert and General Alméras and to send Fleuriau on board the *Superb* to inform Admiral Hotham of this decision and to hand over to him the letter from Croker.

In acknowledging receipt of this document, 'whose aim is now pointless since Napoleon has embarked on one of His Majesty's ships', the admiral goes on: 'In the present circumstances may I express my view that you have acted wisely in holding back the messages for the commanders of the *Amphitrite* and the Ile d'Aix . . . '

Were the two officers so ashamed of the mission entrusted to them that they agreed on the necessity of suppressing every trace of it? However, one cannot think of everything. The minutes of Jaucourt's orders, written in his own hand, still exist in the Naval Archives, crossed out in red ink, it is true. Perhaps in order to let it be believed that they had been cancelled! Here they are:

'Napoleon Bonaparte, who is on the frigate under your command,' the minister wrote to Captain Philibert, 'is merely a prisoner whom all the sovereigns of Europe have a right to claim. It is not only the King who claims him. The King of France is not acting in his private interest alone when he pursues Napoleon Bonaparte. His cause is Europe's cause. All the forces that attack Napoleon act in the King's name. Consequently Frenchmen who do not wish to be in rebellion against their King and country must treat as friends and allies the commanders of all naval and military forces which, should occasion demand, will fight to lay hands on Napoleon.

'I therefore advise you that the commander of the English squadron now blockading the roadstead of Rochefort is authorized to demand from the commander of the frigate where Napoleon now is that he should be handed over immediately. This demand will not be made in the name of His Britannic Majesty alone; it will be in the name of the King, your legitimate sovereign . . . You must therefore not regard the commander of the British naval forces who will execute this order as merely a British officer. He represents all the sovereigns allied to His Majesty. He also represents the King of France. I order you, therefore, to hand over to the English commander who will execute this order the person of Napoleon Bonaparte as soon as he shall demand him from you.

'If you are guilty enough or blind enough to resist this order, you will be in open rebellion and responsible for any eventual bloodshed and the destruction of your ship . . .'

To this letter, which could not be read without 'a blush of shame', was attached one from Marshal Gouvion-Saint-Cyr to the commander of the Ile d'Aix. After some general remarks similar to those in the letter to Philibert, the former comedian of the Marais ends: 'I forbid you to assist with your forces the captain of the *Saale* should he refuse to hand over Napoleon Bonaparte to the English commander. I further order you, should Napoleon Bonaparte attempt to escape or land on the Ile d'Aix, to seize him and hand him over to the English commander.'

Neither Bonnefoux, nor Philibert, nor Alméras, were aware of the trap laid by Fouché—so Henry Houssaye thinks. One lends only to the rich. In any case, only the Minister of Police could have told his colleagues of the Emperor's plan to ask the English commander for asylum. The plan was a good one: the *Méduse* was to leave her moorings according to the order received and remain in the Rochefort river so that the two French officers would only learn that they must deliver the Emperor when they received the demand from the English admiral entering the Basques roadstead with his squadron. And lest in a moment of despair and indignation they might refuse to hand over the proscribed man, Captain de Rigny and Admiral Hotham should open fire with all guns on the *Amphitrite*, guilty of treason and rebellion, until they sank her . . . involving in her loss, now that Frenchmen had tasted blood, the throne and Louis XVIII.

The future victor of Navarino had had a narrow escape!

'Luckily for the agent of the Restoration, he was advised of the Emperor's departure before he arrived on the Ile d'Aix,' wrote J.-M. Feillet, former naval paymaster and at that time quartermaster of the 14th Marines. 'For if he had been advised a few hours earlier that the reason for his mission had become known, there is no doubt that the wheel of Fortune, which was later to raise him to the highest flights of power, would have been broken with his life by those very men whose uniform he had the honour to wear.'

It only remained to dictate a report and find scapegoats. An enquiry was entrusted to Captain Coudein, Colonel of the 14th Marines. It was to cover all that had happened in the Rochefort area since the arrival there of Napoleon Buonaparte, his conduct, his attempts to escape, his accomplices, the state of mind of the inhabitants, etc. There was a rush to come in out of the rain.

The 14th Marines had behaved correctly. The men had remained indifferent to Bonaparte's advances when he had come to the Ile d'Aix. The drums had not beaten the 'general salute',

no drill movements had been ordered. At the moment of departure there had been a few shouts—nothing more. The colonel
had not been present, nor had one of the frigate captains; the
other one had learnt later that some officers had been received
by General Bertrand. Ensign Doret had inveigled several young
men to help in an attempt to get Bonaparte away. This Doret
was an agitator; he had sent to the Chambers a protest against
the abdication of Napoleon and then had an address drawn up
to the Prince of Eckmühl. This document had been signed by
several officers of company rank, but those of the staff had, of
course, abstained . . . Doret and his accomplices had been
arrested.

Bonnefoux, Beker, the prefect Richard, Admiral Gourdon,
Generals Butraud and Alméras, the officers of the port, of the
frigates and of the gendarmes, all made reports, to say nothing
of those who, in hope of a reward which they claimed, pretended
to have brought information 'at the peril of their lives' to the
French and English authorities about 'the traitors' and the
presence and movements of Bonaparte . . . 'For sixteen years,'
wrote Vaulabelle, 'to have betrayed gave rights to honours and
fortune . . . '

*   *   *

A report by M. de Rigny appeared in the *Moniteur* of July 23,
1815. In it there is a brief account of the events and the reception at the Ile d'Aix 'of Joseph Bonaparte who brought news of
the dissolution of the Chambers and the King's entry into
Paris . . . Up till then Bonaparte had often expressed the opinion
that the Chambers would recall him, either because he wished
to impress the authorities around him or because he really
cherished such a hope . . . '

Rigny then gave an account of the Emperor's attempts to
leave:

' . . . On the 12th, Napoleon landed on the Ile d'Aix with his
suite and baggage and, on the night of the 12th/13th, some
half-decked boats arrived there from La Rochelle. It seems that
Napoleon had bought them with the intention of embarking on
them and reaching, under cover of night, the Danish smack
with which it is presumed he had come to some sort of agree-

ment and which was to wait for him about thirty or forty leagues out to sea. It is not known why he did not take advantage of this arrangement; doubtless it seemed to him too risky . . . '

This opinion tended to prove that the Emperor's decision not to leave had not been influenced by Bonnefoux or by Beker, who would not have been slow to make the most of their opportunities in such a case.

'On the night of the 13th/14th he (Napoleon) went on board the French brig *Epervier*, and during the evening of the 14th, after General Beker who had gone to parley with the English squadron had returned, Napoleon had his suite and baggage transferred to the *Epervier*. On the morning of the 15th this ship was observed making sail under a flag of truce towards the English flagship; since the state of the sea did not allow it to approach, the English boats came to meet it and took the passengers on board the *Bellerophon* . . .

'In these circumstances, Lieutenant Jourdan, commanding the *Epervier*, thought it right to ask for, and in fact obtained, from the captain of the *Bellerophon*, a written certificate confirming the transfer of Bonaparte to his ship.'

There are several errors of fact and of date: Napoleon did not board the *Epervier* till the morning of the 15th: Beker had never gone to the *Bellerophon*. Was there some confusion on Rigny's part? Had Beker and Bonnefoux, in order to 'justify' their disobedience of the orders of July 10th, advanced by twenty-four hours the time of the Emperor's boarding of the *Epervier*? Jourdan's attitude towards Maitland is, in every case, stressed in an unfavourable manner. A timid allusion is made to the measures taken by 'the port-admiral and the brigadier-general Butraud'. 'They should have,' wrote Rigny, 'foreseen the intentions of the malefactors.'

But on his return to Paris, the sanctions began. Bonnefoux was dismissed; he died in 1838. Beker, having written to Fouché on the 21st to ask for the Grand Cordon of the Legion of Honour 'as a reward for his services', was on the same day 'authorized' by Gouvion-Saint-Cyr to withdraw to the department of Puy-de-Dôme and to remain there! Reinstated, it is true, in 1818 he was to receive in 1825 the red ribbon of St Louis but not until 1831 that of the Legion. 'All that was left to him was his life,' wrote Frédéric Masson.

Thanks to Fouché, Richard, exempted from the law that struck at the regicides, received a salary of six thousand francs. Jourdan was retired and only reinstated in 1817; promoted captain in 1827, he commanded the *Superbe* during the Algiers expedition and died at Cherbourg in 1860 as man-of-war captain in retirement. Coudein, relieved of his command, was put on half-pay. The officers 'who took the most active part in the escape plans of the Usurper and deserted their corps to embark on the ships intended for that escape' were dismissed the service.

Genty disappeared. Doret took service in the merchant marine and was to be reinstated after the July revolution. Captain in 1844, he was, under Napoleon III, governor of La Réunion and then senator. Saliz left for the Indies. In September 1815, Peltier addressed a violent letter to the port-admiral: 'I have done my duty. I am far from repenting of an action which my heart approves. You see me ready to begin again.' Montcousu, son of a captain killed on the quarterdeck of the *Indomptable* at Algeciras in 1801, was to leave for the colonies, where he died. After the departure of du Coëtlosquet, recalled to Paris on August 4th to enter the Royal Guard, General Butraud, a native of Rochefort, once more took over the command of the 10th department. Captain Philibert died in 1824. Ponée, commanding the *Méduse*, was to be promoted in 1820 and placed on the retired list in 1831. Captain de Rigny was promoted in 1816, became a rear-admiral in 1825 and a vice-admiral after Navarino. He was to become Minister of the Marine to Louis-Philippe and ambassador to Naples. He died in 1835. De Fleuriau, seriously wounded on the *Atalante* at the Cape of Good Hope, then prisoner of the English, was to end his career as captain of a man-of-war and a Grand Officer of the Legion of Honour.

* * *

That evening, July 18th, in light winds, the old *Bellerophon*, creaking in all her planks, slowly reached the open sea. It was wonderful weather. Seated to port, the Emperor watched the French coast vanish in the mist.

I

The day before, Fouché had informed Castlereagh of Napoleon's intention.

A new life began. Except for Savary, former chief of the information service and Minister of Police, Bertrand, Marshal of the Household, his wife, a distant relation of Josephine, and Gourgaud, orderly officer, those who accompanied the Emperor were almost unknown to him. United by interest, fear or devotion, they revealed their characters, little by little.

Las Cases, weasel-faced, wrinkled, grizzled, cultivated, patient, reflective, put himself forward as the Emperor's historian. He had brought with him his eldest son, Emmanuel; his wife had agreed to join him later. Lickspittle and courtier, he was known as 'the fusspot'.

Montholon, thirty-two years old, of limited means, hard-working, ambitious, had been appointed chamberlain by Josephine; a colonel on Berthier's staff, but without passion for the military career, he had entered the diplomatic service thanks to his father-in-law, Simonville, and then had compromised his career by marrying his mistress, Albine-Hélène de Vassal, a clever, coquettish, penniless young woman about whom there had been much, perhaps too much, talk. The couple had everything to gain in the entourage of the fallen Emperor.

Gourgaud, brave and sensitive, ambitious and jealous, intelligent and loyal, was a former student of the Military Academy. First to enter the Kremlin, orderly officer to Napoleon, he had run to the Bourbons, who had confirmed his rank as colonel, then returned to the Emperor the following year and had been appointed general on the eve of the abdication. Believing his head to be in danger, he saw no other way of saving it than by following Napoleon.

The British press was exultant, but the *Morning Chronicle* of July 22nd displayed a certain apprehension. The editor wrote:

'The possession of Buonaparte is a great point gained. The choice he has made of England for an asylum is a refutation of all the calumnies that he has tried to spread against her. This latest development is a fresh triumph which we owe as much to the nobility as to the heroism of our national character.

'The detention of Buonaparte and his removal from the scene

(which are officially confirmed) give rise to several problems which it is far from easy to resolve.

'What effect will this have in France on the conduct of the Allies? On the behaviour of the French armies? Or on that of the King? Will the war go on against the armies which have submitted to the King? These are the questions that are on everybody's lips. There are some who say that this is not the time to consult reason and justice, nor the time for being consistent; that which is expedient is just and the law of the strongest is the only law applicable. We do not know how to reply to such questions.'

Thwarted by heavy seas and uncertain winds, the *Bellerophon* rolled and pitched. The French were mostly seasick, but Napoleon held out, inspected the forecastle, chatted with the captain and the ship's doctor, the Irishman O'Meara.

Sunday, July 23rd, at four o'clock in the morning. Steadying himself on the arm of a midshipman, the Emperor stumbled on the wet decks, sat down on a gunslide and thanked his supporter with a smile.

'Ushant? Cape Ushant?' he asked.

'Yes, Sire.'

Through his pocket-glass, he looked eagerly at the land; then, paying no heed to what was going on about him, paying no attention to his suite standing behind him, he went on looking, until midday, at that land where men had worshipped him in his glory but had basely deserted and betrayed him in the hour of his bitter adversity. Did he catch there a last glimpse of that life of brilliance, of his soldiers, of his Empire, of his youth with Josephine, of his son? . . . He watched it to the last minute, till it was no more than a speck in the distance.

Better that it should be so and that he could not see what was going on in Paris. On July 20th, in an audience with the Minister of War that did not end until seven in the evening, 800 generals and senior officers brought certificates of submission and white flags, kept by those who 'foresaw the future'.

Then Napoleon turned, stepped from the gunslide into Bertrand's arms; without a word he went down the poop-ladder, his head drooping, unaware of the looks that followed his movements, and returned to his cabin.

By evening another land was in sight.

*   *   *

On deck, the daily routine. Without apparent care for the future, Madame Bertrand's children came to play with the Emperor, tugging at his coat-tails. He smiled and tapped them gently on the cheek. They went to dine. He never removed his hat, except for meals; he even sat down at table with his head still covered. Marchand came up to him, took his hat and replaced it at the end of the meal, apparently without him taking any notice. Back on deck, surrounded by his intimates, watched and admired by the young officers whose eyes had their fill of gazing at the great man, he walked up and down, his gold snuff-box in his left hand, his right in the opening of his waistcoat or in his trouser pocket.

'But these are trifling matters,' wrote Home, who saw everything and noted everything, 'only worth recording of one man in a thousand years, and Napoleon being the most remarkable man of the last four thousand, being thus particular in such trifles may be pardoned.'

PRISONER

'A lovely land! It reminds me of Porto Ferrajo on Elba!' he said, when the *Bellerophon* entered the Torbay roadstead on Monday, July 24th, in the afternoon. He looked at the coast dotted with charming houses and said that he would like to live there in solitude.

Scarcely had they dropped anchor before an officer came on board with orders from Admiral Viscount Keith, commanding the Channel fleet. They were to remain in Torbay and await further orders from the Admiralty. The passengers were not to go ashore. No one was allowed to go on board the ship.

That was not so easy. The news of Napoleon's arrival had spread through the countryside. The officers in command of the picket-boats had their work cut out to defend themselves from inquisitive sightseers. One of them was dragged by a score of young ladies to 'a fine house in the little town, regaled with tea and clotted cream, and bored with five thousand questions about Napoleon'.

What does he look like? Is he really a man? Were his hands

and clothes covered with blood when he came on board? Is it true that he foundered three horses running away from Waterloo to reach the *Bellerophon*? Does his voice sound like a thunder-clap? The royalist propaganda had crossed the Channel! Could one see the monster? No! Just a glance . . . a tiny little peek? No!

Napoleon took his regular stroll on the afterdeck and saluted the ladies of fashion crammed into countless boats which milled around the ship. Bands played French airs. In order to let the inquisitive know about Napoleon's movements the sailors chalked on a blackboard held up for them to see: 'Has dined', 'In his cabin', 'He's coming on deck', etc.

'Don't let Napoleon lack for anything; nor those with him,' Keith wrote to Maitland. 'If you need anything, refer to me; I will send it to you at once . . . ' And in another letter: 'Present my respects to Napoleon; tell him that I personally am under the greatest obligation to him for his care and attention to my nephew who was taken prisoner at La Belle Alliance, who was brought to him and who would certainly have died had not Napoleon ordered his surgeon to see to him on the spot before sending him to a first-aid post . . . ' The Emperor remembered perfectly well the young cavalry captain, Elphinstone, seriously injured and in danger of being trodden underfoot by the cavalry. He expressed his satisfaction at the gratitude of both nephew and uncle.

Everything, therefore, seemed favourable to him. He was being treated as an Emperor. The marks of sympathy, even of respect, multiplied. Napoleon chatted with the officers, asked 'many questions about English customs and laws', repeated that he 'must get as much information as possible, so that he might be able to conform to them, since he would probably end his days among the English'.

*　　　　*　　　　*

Meanwhile, that morning in Paris the English troops, with the regiments of Brunswick, Saxony and Nassau, marched in parade order the whole length of the Champs Elysées and as far as the Neuilly bridge. They marched past the Allied sovereigns from eleven in the morning till six in the evening—to the cheers of the Parisians . . .

Eight o'clock. Gourgaud, allowed to go on board the *Bellerophon*, went to the Emperor's cabin. He had arrived on the *Slaney* in the evening of July 22nd. The commander, like Maitland, had deceived him. Both had led him to believe that he would be taken to London, so that he could hand the Emperor's letter personally to the Prince-Regent. But as soon as the anchor was dropped, Sartorius had demanded the document from him in order to take it himself. On Gourgaud's refusal, Sartorius had left for London with a copy of it in his pocket.

At midnight, the second-in-command of the *Slaney* had received an order from the captain to set sail immediately for Torbay. They had left at three o'clock, flying the quarantine flag; their isolation was complete. English generosity and hospitality were mere figments of the imagination.

The Emperor said that Admiral Hotham had sent an officer who would see that the present situation was changed. Was that so sure?

The newspapers carried bad news. Even if the *Morning Chronicle*, the opposition paper, published some protests from the Duke of Sussex and Lord Holland against the government, the other papers fulminated, describing Napoleon as 'the most infamous of criminals'. *The Times*, the *Morning Post* and the *Courier* demanded 'the hanging of the monster' or his imprisonment in the Tower or at Fort St George, or deportation to the other end of the world . . . to the island of Saint Helena!

It was an old idea of the English Conservatives. As far back as 1800, when the government was paying hard cash to the French royalists to seize the First Consul, Pitt, the implacable enemy of the Republic, of the First Consul Bonaparte and then of the Emperor Napoleon, wanted to intern him there. At Vienna, Talleyrand had suggested the Azores as the place of detention, but the other members of the Congress were generally in favour of Saint Helena.

'We have been spared the shame of handing over Napoleon to the King of France to be shot,' wrote Lord Rosebery. 'But, by going aboard the *Bellerophon* to demand asylum from England, he has caused all the plans of the Cabinet at St James' to collapse and everything has to be revised.'

What was to be done with Buonaparte? It was urgent to make a decision. The plenipotentiaries of the Allied sovereigns, meeting in Paris, expressed the wish that Great Britain, the head, heart and purse of the Coalition, be responsible for his person, and that she make it impossible for him to escape a second time.

England had never refused hospitality to the most humble suppliant, but could she welcome Buonaparte on her territory only a few miles from France where that Bourbon was reigning, who by the malignity of fate had become her ally? Would the new 'Colonel Muiron' behave as a gentleman-farmer in the English countryside? Even if his thoughts, his wishes, his health, prevented him from taking up the struggle again, would he not become for his supporters, and even for his adversaries, an object of temptation, still able to shatter the nervous system of Europe?

In England he would be a source of trouble. Interpreting the feelings of the army and the navy, the Conservatives expressed their hatred and jealousy of him, stirred up public opinion, recalled the incident of Captain Wright who had earlier landed Cadoudal on the French coast, accused the Bonapartist police of having had him killed, evoked the Duc d'Enghien and the shootings at Vincennes. On the other hand the liberal and radical opposition, Lords Russell, Holland, Grey and Stanhope, the writers like Hazlitt, etc., raised cries of protest against the government and openly took Napoleon's side. Supported by Brougham, Hobhouse and Wellesley, some procedural lawyers were working to keep him in England by indirect manoeuvres.

Buonaparte's home in the English countryside would rapidly become a centre of intrigues and discord fiery enough to create currents of opinion to which he could not remain insensitive. Napoleon could not be left free. Considered, moreover, as a prisoner of the European powers, Russia, Prussia, Austria and England, it was to be feared that his imprisonment in the Tower, or at Fort St George, would make a martyr of him, provoke protests, attempts at liberation, assassination, etc. It only remained to send him far away—to intern him at Saint Helena—which the Conservatives regarded as an act of leniency.

On July 20th Liverpool wrote to Castlereagh:

'We are all of the opinion that it is not expedient to imprison him in this country. His presence here, or anywhere else in Europe, would keep alive a certain amount of ferment in France

. . . Very delicate legal questions could be raised on this matter which would be particularly embarrassing. Over and above these considerations, you know enough of feelings in this country not to doubt that he would immediately become an object of curiosity and, within a few months, of compassion . . . '

Liverpool judged Napoleon well enough. Learning later at Saint Helena of certain revulsions in French public opinion, the Emperor let fall: 'Oh! If only we were in England!' Liverpool was also a good judge of his compatriots who already did not trouble to conceal their sympathy, and even admiration, for Napoleon.

The aureole of the Emperor shone over Torbay.

Sightseers, coming from all parts of England, milled around the *Bellerophon;* they greeted him, they cheered him, they threw him flowers and presents. He had fascinated Maitland, won over his officers . . .

'You can say what you like about this man,' concluded the crew when questioned by their officers, 'but if the English people knew him as we know him, they would not touch a hair of his head.'

'He's a fine fellow,' the men of the *Northumberland* said later. 'He doesn't deserve his fate . . . '—just as the crew of the *Undaunted,* ordered to take him to Elba, had on leaving him wished him 'long life and prosperity on the island and better luck next time'!

Admiral Hotham's prejudices against him had vanished after his reception on the *Superb.* 'All the old animosity has gone,' wrote Senhouse, his flag-captain. For all the sailors of the *Bellerophon* he was 'the Emperor' and regarded as such. The prestige, the charm, the magnetic influence which he had had over his soldiers, the Paris Federals, the Niort Hussars, the veterans and recruits of the 14th Marines, the men and women of all countries, had captivated the English. Lord Keith, the old Scotsman, the popular and distinguished veteran of Egypt, of the American war and of Toulon, who had vowed undying hatred of Republican France and of everything under its flag, none the less expressed his respect. He was to say to Cockburn, impatient to get Napoleon on board the *Northumberland:* 'Far bigger men than you or I have waited longer for him . . . Let him take his time.'

And after his final meeting, he was to write: 'What a devil of a man! If he had obtained an interview with His Royal Highness the Prince-Regent they would have become the best friends in the world after half-an-hour!' Very likely!

This popularity exasperated the ministers; a jealous fear drove them to take odious, puerile and idiotic precautions. The Allies, who had knelt on the steps of his throne, contested his title of Emperor, belittled all that he had done, everything that had surrounded him, the very air he breathed—without realizing that the more they tried to denigrate him the greater they made him and the more they dishonoured themselves. 'I never think of the proceedings which I then witnessed,' wrote the midshipman Home with shame, 'without feeling my blood boil up with indignation, and my face blush crimson for my degraded country'.

*   *   *

Half-past one in the morning of July 26th. An order was brought by Sartorius from London: go at once to Plymouth with the *Myrmidon* and the *Slaney*.

They set sail at three o'clock.

The Irish sentry, on guard before the Emperor's door, crossed himself and whispered to Marchand: 'Not good for the Emperor. Saint Helena.' Maitland's chief steward, sent ashore, told him the same on his return.

Why this move westward? The Emperor's entourage became more and more uneasy. Saint Helena? . . . Madame Bertrand in great agitation tackled Maitland, who excused himself and slipped away. A violent squabble broke out between Las Cases and Lallemand. The chamberlain put his trust in English hospitality, even as he still believed in the reign of Napoleon II! The general remarked that his forebodings were coming true and treated Las Cases brusquely and discourteously.

What had Lord Liverpool meant by 'very delicate legal questions could be raised on this matter which would be particularly embarrassing'?

Four o'clock in the afternoon. The anchors were dropped in Plymouth roadstead in the shelter of the breakwater. Maitland went ashore.

'I would very much like to see the admiral,' said the Emperor. 'I ask him to come without any sort of ceremony. I have no objection to being treated as a private individual until the British government has decided the manner in which I must be treated.'

More and more drastic orders came from the Lords of the Admiralty. Frigates, seventy-four-gunners, the *Eurotas* and the *Liffey*, moored close to the *Bellerophon*: the sentries were doubled everywhere. There was a formal prohibition against anyone boarding or leaving the ship. Coasting vessels were forbidden to approach. An anchor watch was permanently on duty; an armed longboat, always at the ready, lay alongside, to act as a guard-boat. At night a pinnace under the command of a first lieutenant rowed around the ship and was relieved every hour.

Despite all these precautions the bay was crammed with boats, some of which had been hired for sixty pounds. The Emperor watched them through his pocket-glass, smiled at the ladies who waved their handkerchiefs, raised his hat to them . . . He never wholly uncovered but bowed with satisfaction . . . At times there were from eight to ten thousand people on the water; some came even from Scotland! They took a trip round the *Bellerophon* as if it were a trip on the continent! Here and there, shouts could be heard. Heavy dockyard boats, ordered to keep the sightseers at a distance, manoeuvred roughly, bumping into the boats and capsizing some of them . . . The women shrieked and the men swore!

'We were handsomely guarded too, for no sooner had we come to anchor in the Sound, than three or four seventy-fours and frigates were ordered to take up their position on our bows and quarters, with the charitable intention, I suppose, had any rumpus occurred, such as Napoleon taking unto himself wings and flying to the uttermost parts of the sea or by the use of a diving-bell getting back to France, or any other such probable movement, of sending our good old ship, "with all she did inherit", to the bottom of the Sound,' wrote Home, a precursor of science-fiction. All these precautions were intended to forestall the seizure or flight of the giant who was not even dreaming of escape. Napoleon even protested to Maitland: 'All afternoon the guards have been firing rifle-shots to keep the boats away,' he said. 'That worries and grieves me. I would be glad if you could stop it.' The Emperor was obeyed.

*　　　*　　　*

In Paris the King had promised that no one would be molested for his opinions, but the witch hunt had begun.

The *Moniteur* of July 26th wrote:

'Those generals and officers who betrayed the King before March 20th or who attacked France and the government with armed force, as well as those who seized power by violence, will be arrested and brought before competent courts-martial in their respective military divisions.

'To wit: Ney, La Bédoyère, the two brothers Lallemand, Drouet d'Erlon, Lefebvre-Desnoëttes, Ameil, Brayer, Gilly, Mouton-Duvernet, Grouchy, Clausel, Laborde, Debelle, Bertrand, Drouot, Cambronne, Lavallette, Rovigo.

'The individuals whose names follow, to wit: Soult, Allix, Exelmans, Bassano, Marbot, Félix Lepelletier, Boulay (de la Meurthe), Mehée, Fressinet, Thibaudeau, Carnot, Vandamme, Lamarque (General), Lobau, Harel, Piré, Barrère, Arnault, Pommereul, Regnault (de Saint-Jean d'Angély), Arrighi (of Padua), Durbach, Dejean fils, Garrau, Réal, Bouvier, Dumolard, Merlin (de Douai), Dirat, Defermont, Bory de Saint-Vincent, Félix Desportes, Garnier (de Saintes), Mellinet, Hullin, Cloys, Courtin, Forbin-Janson (eldest son), Le Lorgne d'Ideville, will leave Paris within three days and will withdraw into central France to such place as the Minister of Police shall indicate and shall remain there under surveillance and wait there until such time as the Chambers shall determine which of them must leave the kingdom and which shall be brought before the courts.

The lists were drawn up. In three months 12,371 officers, non-commissioned officers and men would be expelled from the capital.

Copies of the proscription orders reached Davout by chance on July 27th. Davout was astounded, indignant and in despair. The officers threatened with death or banishment were his victims. Dupe of Vitrolles, of Fouché, of Gouvion-Saint-Cyr, he had pledged them to renounce the defence of Paris and to submit to the King. Twice disarmed, they were now handed over to the courts. The same day he wrote from Bourges to Gouvion-Saint-Cyr: 'If I can place any trust, Sir, in all that you have told me and written to me, then I can only suppose that these lists are false . . . '

Having assumed responsibility for the actions imputed to these generals and officers under his command, he went on: 'They have done no more than obey the orders which I gave them. My name should take the place of theirs. If only I could take upon myself alone the whole effect of this proscription! It is a favour that I demand in the interest of both King and country. I call upon you, in the name of the King and of all France, to place this letter before the eyes of His Majesty.' For sole response, Gouvion-Saint-Cyr was to appoint Macdonald in his place!

*   *   *

On board the days passed slowly in anxiety and boredom. The *Bellerophon* rolled in the swell. The creaking of the rigging was maddening. The Emperor stayed longer than usual in his cabin, went on deck about five in the afternoon and was then the object of endless ovations, while forebodings of disaster and irritating restrictions became more and more frequent. On the 27th all those who were not in the personal service of the Emperor were transferred to the *Liffey*. It seemed that Gourgaud would have to go too.

Saint Helena as a destination became more and more certain. A letter from Lady Clavering, a friend of Madame Las Cases, and a secret report received by Savary dispelled all illusions. Maitland went ashore daily, returning in the evenings sombre and impenetrable. The newspapers were full of threats. Saint Helena became an obsession. The admiral announced that he would pay them a visit the next day. Perhaps he would bring news.

Not yet. Lord Keith, very amiable and very respectful, paid a courtesy visit to His Majesty, excusing himself for having been so late in coming. The instructions from the commissioners had not yet reached him. The officers who had been transferred to the other ships would be sent back to the *Bellerophon*. He showered courtesies on Madame Bertrand and Madame Montholon. On his departure the Emperor's entourage felt less depressed; but His Majesty remained unmoved.

Savary had been able to establish a secret correspondence with the English lawyer Sir Samuel Romilly, and had received from him, wrote Montholon, 'sundry notes and documents to further the legal process which would place His Majesty under the protection of the English laws and make any refusal to receive him in England impossible'.

The Emperor at once dictated to Las Cases (July 28th) a protest and a memorandum 'for the lawyer to use as a basis for discussion and to defend his political position'. A sailor who was a good swimmer took the document to Plymouth during the night; it would be in the lawyer's hands in London the next day.

At table Montholon said that a light yawl, decorated with flowers and with a pretty young woman on board holding her child up to show him to the Emperor, had approached the ship, but one of the guard-boats had brutally capsized it. A midshipman and several of the *Bellerophon* sailors had leapt overboard and had saved the mother and child.

A turbot was served. The Emperor talked about fishing and the English fishermen who had given him information to help the French prisoners interned at Plymouth, Norman Cross, etc. Thanks to one of them, Lefebvre-Desnoëttes had been able to get back to France—and so had many others. In the evening there were fresh anxieties. Rumours abounded. The Cabinet at St James' had reached a decision.

That very day, at Paris, Castlereagh had submitted the Cabinet's proposals to the plenipotentiaries of Austria, Russia and Prussia :

'Napoleon Buonaparte is considered by the Allied Powers which signed the treaty of March 25th last as their prisoner. Since the guard over him has been especially entrusted to the British government, it has chosen as his place of deportation the island of Saint Helena, the most suitable place in the world for the isolation of such a person. There is a fine citadel there where he may live. The situation is healthy. There is only one place in the circumference of the island where ships can anchor and we can, if necessary, forbid all neutral vessels access to it.

'Moreover Lord Bathurst, Minister of War and of the Colonies, has arranged with the directors of the East India Company, the owners of Saint Helena, that the island shall be, for

K

the term of Buonaparte's detention, under the sole authority of the British crown . . . At such a distance and in such a spot all intrigues will be impossible and, being thus removed from the European scene, he will quickly be forgotten.'

These gentlemen paid no attention to this last phrase, but insisted that each one of the Great Powers should have a commissioner on Saint Helena 'so that they may be able to reply to ill-intentioned rumours'. The British Foreign Minister raising no objection, there was added to the protocol 'what Great Britain has undertaken to do, in order to take Napoleon Buonaparte to a safe place and keep a guard over him, will ensure the gratitude of Europe'.

The newspapers brought the news to the *Bellerophon* on July 30th. Apparently indifferent to everything, the Emperor stayed in his cabin, read, now and again took a short stroll, and slept. Meanwhile fresh problems arose: it seemed that His Majesty could take only three or four officers with him. Who would they be?

Monday, July 31, 1815, at eleven-fifteen in the morning. Lord Keith and General Harry Bunbury, his Secretary of State for War and a well-known historian, came to see the Emperor. Bunbury, sent by Lord Melville, one of the Lords of the Admiralty, bore a letter from the Ministry with instructions to let Napoleon know its contents:

'My Lord, since it is suitable to inform General Buonaparte without further delay of the instructions of the British government concerning him, Your Lordship is at liberty to give him the information contained in this letter. It would be incompatible with our obligation towards the country and towards His Majesty's allies for us to leave to General Buonaparte the means or the possibility of once more disturbing the peace of Europe and renewing the miseries of war. It is, therefore, inevitable that his personal liberty be restricted as long as it may be necessary to assure our first and sovereign object.

'The island of Saint Helena has been chosen for his future residence. The climate is healthy and local conditions will permit him to be treated with greater leniency than in any other spot, yet with equal security . . . '

Silence. The Emperor listened patiently. 'His expression was serious and almost melancholy, but he showed no trace of temper or violent feeling,' wrote Bunbury who, himself impassive, went on with his reading.

'General Buonaparte is permitted to choose, from those persons who have been brought to England with him, three officers (with the exception of Generals Savary and Lallemand) who, with the surgeon, will be granted permission to accompany him to Saint Helena. Twelve servants, including those of the officers, will also be permitted. It must be clearly understood that these individuals will be subjected to restrictions during their service with him and their residence on Saint Helena, and that they will not be allowed to resign their posts without the permission of the British government.

'Rear-Admiral Sir George Cockburn, appointed commander-in-chief of the Cape of Good Hope and the seas adjoining, will transport General Buonaparte and his suite. He will receive instructions.

'Sir George Cockburn will probably be ready to embark in a few days; it is much to be desired that General Buonaparte will designate without delay those persons who are to accompany him.'

Calmly and without apparent emotion, the Emperor spoke. Bunbury, according to his own account, recalled every word, uttered with mildness and dignity:

'I came to place myself under the protection of the British government. I am not a prisoner of war. I must be treated according to the law of nations. I was like a passenger on a ship. On board this ship, I was as if in a city. To deport me to Saint Helena is my death sentence.'

He then spoke of America, and of Moreau whom he had authorized to reside overseas . . . then, once more taking up the thread: 'How long does it take to become an English subject? How many years are necessary to establish domicile?'

'Four years, I think,' replied Bunbury.

'Very well,' he replied. 'Be so good as to tell the Prince-Regent that he should put me in central England under his surveillance; if he asks for my word of honour, I shall give it to him. I want only as much liberty as a studious literary man requires. At Saint Helena I should not live three months. I need to walk ten leagues a day. How am I to do that on a little rock at the end of the world? I am no longer a sovereign. What danger could there be in leaving me in the centre of England? . . .

'From the time when I was freely received on the *Bellerophon* I was under the protection of the laws of your country. The government is, as far as I am concerned, violating the sacred right of hospitality. I appeal from its decision to British honour.'

Lord Keith, embarrassed and ashamed, asked Napoleon to address his protest to him in writing. The meeting had lasted three-quarters of an hour.

* * *

In the afternoon the Emperor walked on deck as usual and that evening, at dinner, he was in good humour. A great man does not bear malice; his anger and his ill-humour do not last beyond the moment. He no longer sees persons, he sees only events, their significance and their consequences.

Chapter IX

HYPOCRISY AND BREACH
OF FAITH

Outside, the admiral tried in vain to calm Madame Bertrand and Madame Montholon. Then he vanished in his barge, while the Emperor summoned his officers. Crammed into his cabin, they listened to the decree. Then, suddenly, the storm broke.

The Emperor vehemently denounced the treatment meted out to him. A prisoner! Saint Helena! They called him 'general'! Why not archbishop! Formerly their King had written to him 'My brother'! . . .

Gourgaud wanted to die fighting, to defend himself sword in hand, to set fire to the powder magazines of the *Bellerophon*! Lallemand and Savary, condemned to the scaffold, invoked Maitland's promises that they would find an inviolable sanctuary under the British flag. The Emperor had been dishonoured! Better death! He would commit suicide!

Las Cases stretched out maps, said that on Saint Helena there were tropical fruits, vegetables, cattle—exasperating his companions.

Outside the cabin there were angry and confused outbursts. Madame Bertrand insulted Maitland in French end English. Losing all dignity, this great lady, this charming, wayward woman, forced her way into the captain's cabin, said that the Emperor was 'a monster of egoism who could see women and children perish without lifting a finger'. Furious and suppliant at the same time, she implored him to see that her husband would not be on the list of persons who were to accompany him. And as Montholon, who witnessed the scene, told his comrades and the Emperor of her conduct, she threw herself at His Majesty's feet, raged, pleaded, threatened to throw herself overboard . . . luckily in front of her husband who caught her round the waist.

273

'Let her get on with it!' Savary advised laughing, without pity for this spoiled and insupportable child, English in taste and feelings, who had only married her 'unobtrusive general' out of boredom.

Alone with the Emperor, Las Cases wrote under his dictation a letter that Maitland was to forward to Lord Keith:

'My Lord, I have studied with care the extract from the letter that was read to me. I have told you of my protest. I am not a prisoner of war, I am England's guest. I came to this country on the English ship *Bellerophon*, after having told the captain of the letter that I had written to the Prince-Regent and having received from him the assurance that his orders prescribed that he should receive me on board and transport me and my suite to England if I should ask him.

'Admiral Hotham afterwards repeated similar assurances. From the time when I was freely received on board the *Bellerophon* I was under the protection of your country's laws. I wish to live freely in the central part of England under the protection and surveillance of the laws, assuming all the obligations which may be deemed suitable. I do not wish to have any connection with France, nor to become involved in any political affairs. Since my abdication, my intention has been to reside in the United States or in England. I assume, My Lord, that you and the Under-Secretary of State of your government will make an accurate report of these facts. It is in the honour of the Prince-Regent and the protection of the laws of your country that I have put, and still put, my trust.

'NAPOLEON'

In the roadstead the crush of boats increased. As on other days, the Emperor appeared at his usual time, loudly cheered by men wearing red carnations. His expression betrayed no emotion. 'His spirit,' wrote Marchand, 'rose above this monstrous decision which made Saint Helena a calvary and the Emperor a martyr . . . ' He showed great pity on seeing some boats filled with the wounded from Waterloo, then withdrew into his cabin and ordered Marchand to bring him 'some boxes filled with silver and jewels', undressed, lay down and, with curtains drawn, told his valet to take 'the book on the table there and read where it is marked'. It was Plutarch: *The Death of Cato.*

Outside, Maitland, convinced by Savary and Lallemand that his honour was involved, wrote to Lord Melville that these officers had placed themselves under the protection of the British flag and that he, in its name, had guaranteed this protection. Once again he failed to understand that what he wrote about the two generals was equally valid for the Emperor, and ended: 'I earnestly beg Your Lordship to use your influence to prevent two men who have asked and obtained from me the protection of the British flag from being sent to the scaffold . . .'

Savary and Lallemand were to be sent to Malta with the other officers who were not authorized to follow the Emperor. They were freed in April 1816, whereas Maitland, whose actions were severely criticized in England, was to be deprived of his command and was only to be reinstated in 1818. He died in Bombay in 1839 as a rear-admiral and is buried in the cathedral there.

*   *   *

The protests and the outbursts of anger continued, though less vehemently. Had the Emperor ever contemplated suicide? Marchand, on reading Plutarch, feared it. But Napoleon had always despised suicide and was to say on Saint Helena: 'In my eyes it is the most revolting of crimes.'

He summoned the Marshal of the Household, ordered him to draw up the list of those who were to follow him, chatted with Las Cases, pondered their occupations in that deserted spot.

'We shall live in the past,' said the chamberlain. 'Sire, you will re-read it.'

'Very well, we shall write our memoirs,' replied Napoleon, always a realist. 'Work is also the scythe of time . . . After all, one must fulfil one's destiny . . . Let mine be accomplished.'

Little by little, calm was restored among the Frenchmen.

Meanwhile, there were alarums and excursions among the English. On August 3rd an embarrassing article appeared: 'An Act of Parliament is needed to make the detention of Buonaparte in England legal; another act is no less necessary to intern him in a colony . . .'

'Buonaparte is causing us a pack of trouble at Plymouth,' wrote Liverpool.

The 'fear of legal problems, very delicate and particularly embarrassing' expressed to Castlereagh was raised by the liberal lawyers. Had the memorandum dictated to Savary by the Emperor and taken by 'the sailor who was a good swimmer' to Sir Samuel Romilly had some effect?

In any case the radical M.P. Sir Francis Burdett and several liberals intervened with the Lord Chancellor. A writ of *habeas corpus ad testificandum* was obtained, served and signed by the Lord Chief Justice, Lord Ellenborough. It demanded, in the name of the King's Bench, the person of 'Napoleon Bonaparte' and ordered him to appear on November 10th next before the said court to give evidence in a trial. This trial involved Antony MacKenrot, a former judge at Tortola (two hundred miles northwest of Guadeloupe) and Rear-Admiral Sir Alexander Cochrane, accused of not having fought a fleet inferior to his own commanded by Admiral Willaumez and in which Prince Jérôme Bonaparte was commanding the *Vétéran*. 'Napoleon is summoned to give details of the state of the French navy at the time.'

This was not a joke; it was the law and the most efficient method found by the liberals and Bonaparte's friends to save him from exile. To Latin eyes, the procedure lacked nobility and poetry but it was what Liverpool feared and considered 'embarrassing'. So in fact it was. The serving of the writ would force the authorities to let Napoleon land 'free henceforward' on English soil until November 10, 1815. It was sufficient to hand the writ to Lord Keith who had the former Emperor in his custody.

MacKenrot was entrusted with this simple mission . . . or at least so it seemed.

In fact, warned of what to expect, Keith disappeared. When the server came to his house on August 4th, he slipped out by the tradesman's entrance, fled to the port with MacKenrot on his heels, leapt into a boat, climbed the starboard ladder of the *Tonnant* from which he could see the man of law get into another boat whose oarsmen rowed frantically. Then he clattered down the port-ladder, crossed the deck of the *Eurotas* and set off at all speed for Cawsand Bay. With ruses worthy of a Sioux he just managed to avoid his pursuer. He did not return home but went into hiding on the *Prometheus*.

That evening MacKenrot, drenched, dog-tired, filled with doubts about the efficacy of the English laws, was obliged to forego the pursuit. Lord Keith, aged sixty-eight, had had a narrow escape.

'All day I have been chased by a lawyer with a *habeas corpus*,' he wrote to Maitland. 'He is at Cawsand and will perhaps take a sailing boat from there tonight. Keep any boat, of whatever sort, well away. I will do the same, from aboard the ship where I can now be found.'

In a confidential letter addressed the following day to his wife, published in London in 1925 and cited by M. Jules Dechamps who has devoted a remarkable article in the *Bulletin de l'Académie royale de Belgique* to this matter, Lord Keith recognizes that 'if the order had been served he would have had to appear before the court with his prisoner, for whom he would have been responsible until November'! MacKenrot only managed to achieve his purpose on August 9th. It was then too late!

On the 31st he was to send to the Empress Marie-Louise a letter, discovered by Jules Dechamps in the British Museum Archives. In an evil moment the writer thought that Napoleon's wife would be interested to hear of the most recent attempts by Napoleon's friends in England to have the Emperor freed. But Marie-Louise did not reply and, wittingly or not, showed the letter to Metternich who, on September 29th, sent a copy of it to Castlereagh. Having lost the game, MacKenrot, charged with fraud, was tried, acquitted and then handed over to the commissioners of lunacy. He was found in the Bedlam Hospital in 1821 but, as Jules Dechamps says, 'the last word in this shady affair has still to be written'.

The whole thing so alarmed Lord Keith that on the night of August 4th he gave orders to the *Bellerophon* and her escort to leave Plymouth at once and cruise off Start Point, while at Portsmouth a ship capable of replacing the veteran of Aboukir, too old to undertake the voyage to Saint Helena, was being hastily fitted out.

This was the *Northumberland*, a seventy-eight, under Captain C. B. H. Ross. In a veritable scuffle they crammed into her stores of all kinds, the staff, a company of the 53rd Regiment, its commander, Colonel Sir G. R. Bingham, and a company of artillery.

The fitting out was done at all speed; to avoid the watchful MacKenrot the transhipment was carried out at sea.

Rear-Admiral Sir George Cockburn was to take command of the ship together with several other units composing the escort. His flag was hoisted on the *Northumberland*. He had been appointed on July 26th. During the war with the United States, it had been he who had given the order for the burning of the Capitol and the White House on August 24, 1814. His reputation for forcefulness had won him a K.C.B. and the mission of transporting Buonaparte.

Admiral Fleming had declined the honour. As president of the Naval Club he was to say in 1846, during a dinner in London in honour of Prince Napoleon, the future Napoleon III, that when he received the government's order to take the Emperor to Saint Helena he had replied: 'I am ready to die in the service of my sovereign, but I do not wish to take part in a deed that dishonours my country.'

During the night the *Bellerophon* and her escort had set sail in heavy weather, fleeing from MacKenrot who had tried to get on board and who had seen and saluted the Emperor. Where were they going? Everyone was sick. It seemed that the Marshal of the Household was hesitant to link his fate with that of the Emperor. Had his pest of a wife succeeded in winning over the English? Gourgaud was not on the list; his name had been scratched out and replaced by Planat's; was it possible? Perhaps the government had modified its regulations? Certainly not! The newspapers announced that Sir George Cockburn had had his farewell audience with the Lords of the Admiralty. All arrangements had been made to send Buonaparte and his very small suite to Saint Helena. They were right.

On August 2nd, at Paris, identical treaties were signed between Great Britain and Austria, Great Britain and Russia and Great Britain and Prussia:

'In the name of the Most Holy and Indivisible Trinity, since Napoleon Buonaparte is now in the custody of the Allied Powers, Their Majesties have agreed, in accordance with the terms of the Treaty of March 25, 1815, on the most suitable measures to make impossible any undertaking on his part against the peace of Europe.

'1. Napoleon Buonaparte is regarded by the Powers which signed the treaty of March 25th last as their prisoner.

'2. His custody is entrusted especially to the British government. The choice of location and the measures best calculated to ensure the aim of the present stipulation are reserved to His Britannic Majesty.

'3. The Imperial Courts of Austria and Russia and the Royal Court of Prussia will appoint commissioners who will go to, and reside at, the spot which the government of His Britannic Majesty shall assign for the residence of Napoleon Buonaparte and who, without being responsible for his person, shall assure themselves of his continued presence there.

'4. His Most Christian Majesty shall be invited, in the name of the four courts above-mentioned, also to send a commissioner to the place of detention of Napoleon Buonaparte.

'5. His Majesty the King of the United Kingdom of Great Britain and Ireland shall pledge himself to fulfil the obligations arising out of this agreement.'

Such was the law of Europe, imposed without other right than that of force, without expressly stating that Napoleon was the guest and not the prisoner of the English and without avowing that the treaty of March 25th had never been put into effect except by Napoleon.

But Napoleon was 'outlawed, placed outside all political and social relations', 'a declared enemy and disturber of world peace' who had been handed over to 'public obloquy'.

Meanwhile, to the great scandal of the newspapers, the King, appearing that day at the Tuileries, had been greeted with shouts of 'Long live the Emperor!' Macdonald, having taken Davout's place in order to disband the army, received the bodyguards in civilian dress, bearing the warrants of arrest to the gendarmerie commanders. 'Take care not to let yourselves be seen,' he told them. 'I will take no responsibility. Tomorrow, we shall see . . . In the meantime, stay here and I will see that you have somewhere to sleep and something to eat.'

And when the guards protested that they were not afraid:

'Then why have you changed your clothes?' the marshal asked.

Rushing at once to Davout, the Duke of Taranto told him to

send messages to the cantonments to warn the threatened officers, who could thus get away during the night.

Lefebvre-Desnoëttes cut off his moustaches and said he was a commercial traveller. Delaborde, suffering from gout, hid in a farm where the farmer passed him off as his invalid grandfather and finally managed to get out of France. La Bédoyère, Piré, Boulay de la Meurthe, etc. were arrested; Drouet d'Erlon, Brayer and Vandamme fled.

In the cantonments the young men awaited their liberation, and the old ones dreaded it. They knew that their days were numbered. It was better so. Since the Emperor, betrayed, a prisoner of the English, was to be exiled to Saint Helena, it was better to disappear and hand over the eagles than to serve under colours that had never been seen on a battlefield. On the lowest rung of military greatness, but often first in the breaches, having spilt their blood for the glory of France and the triumph of the Emperor, the veterans of the Old Guard awaited their fate without a murmur.

Still in their heart of hearts they hoped; one never knew with 'Old Baldy'! Perhaps he would come back . . .

*   *   *

Shut in his cabin on the *Bellerophon*, rolling gunwales under in the storm, Napoleon felt that he had seen his last hours in Europe. Expecting nothing of the present, he launched a message to the future and dictated to Las Cases the protest which branded England with eternal dishonour and was to echo so widely throughout the world:

'I solemnly protest, before God and man, against the violence done to me, against the violation of my most sacred rights, by disposing of my person and my liberty by force. I am not a prisoner, I am the guest of England. If the government, by giving orders to the captain of the *Bellerophon* to receive me and my suite, wished only to set a trap for me, then it has forfeited its honour and stained its flag . . .

'I appeal to history. It will say that an enemy who for twenty years has waged war on the English people came freely, in his misfortune, to seek asylum under its laws; what more striking proof could he give of his esteem and trust? But how has England responded to such magnanimity? She pretended to hold out her hand in hospitality to her enemy and, when he had surrendered in good faith, she sacrificed him.

'NAPOLEON
'August 5, 1815. At sea, on board the *Bellerophon*.'

From August 1st Fouché had been the husband of Ernestine de Castellane, pretty and poor, of high Provençal nobility, allied, so it was said, to the Bourbons. She was twenty-one and he was fifty-six; despite which he had let it be known that he had made a sacrifice by marrying her. Cardinal Maury had sent his blessing from Rome to this deserter from the Church, co-religionist of Père Duchesne, persecutor of the Oratorian Fathers, sacrilegious and homicidal. For ambition's sake, he had voted for the death of the King whose brother had appointed him a minister and, for twenty-five years, had betrayed all those who had come into contact with him, employed him or loaded him with honours. Rich to the tune of twenty millions, one of the greatest landowners of the kingdom, a duke as had been Richelieu and Rochefoucauld, he had overthrown Napoleon and been elected deputy in the Chamber which was to become known as the *introuvable*. But his victims accused him; two thousand Lyonnais whom he had had massacred had by now finished rotting in the Plaine des Brotteaux.

The old Jacobin was lost and his fall precipitous. Spurned by his new colleagues, disgraced by Louis XVIII, 'Monsieur Fouché', Minister at Dresden, was to leave Paris on October 4th, a few days before the Emperor arrived at Saint Helena . . . never to return. Exiled by the King, cast out, continually asseverating that it had been he who had saved Paris, the Revolution, the Bourbons, France and Europe, but henceforth ignored by Wellington and Metternich, despised and forgotten, he died at Trieste on December 26, 1820, four months before the Emperor.

*   *   *

Monday, August 7, 1815. Dull, windy weather. The day before, the list of persons who were to accompany the Emperor had been drawn up: Bertrand, Montholon and their families. Gourgaud, Las Cases and his son, Marchand, Saint-Denis, and ten servants.

They had hidden some jewels and a little gold. Then, the

odious competing with the imbecile, they submitted to a search of their luggage, the confiscation of all firearms and the generals' swords. Stopped by a steely look, Keith left Napoleon's on one side. In the scurry, the confusion, the fear of the *habeas corpus*, of some violent manifestation of the opposition or of an abduction, the triumvirate, Liverpool, Castlereagh and Bathurst, had urged on the departure even though the *Northumberland* was not yet ready. They did not even have the time to procure on land the indispensable materials for a long voyage and an undetermined residence at the end of the world!

Eleven o'clock in the morning. The Emperor made his farewells to those of his companions who were not to follow him into exile, kissed Savary and Lallemand, both in tears; then all filed before him in order of rank. Some clasped his hand or touched the skirts of his grey coat. He shook hands with Maitland and talked with him for about ten minutes, a red-letter day in the Scotsman's life. He raised his hat and with a smile thanked the officers for all that they had done for him; with calm dignity he saluted the assembled crew standing, caps off, on the maindeck. The guard presented arms. He wanted to speak but emotion prevented him; he made a few gestures with his hand and walked towards the poop-ladder, followed by 'the Household' and Admiral Keith, whose steps hammered on the deck.

'You will observe, My Lord, that those who weep are those who stay behind,' said Las Cases.

'One could have heard a pin drop from the mast,' noted Midshipman George Home, who concluded on seeing the longboat carry Napoleon away to his destiny: 'It will be a vile stain on our name for centuries to come.'

It was about one o'clock in the afternoon, just outside Torbay, that Napoleon boarded the *Northumberland*.

Chapter X

THE SUPREME VICTORY

Received like a general on the retired list, he was henceforth to be known, by government decision, as 'General Buonaparte, prisoner of state'.

What did it matter to him! 'Let them call me what they like,' he was to say later. 'I shall still be myself!' It was a cry from the heart, born of immense pride! For, as Bourrienne wrote, 'he scorned consular fripperies and imperial masquerades'.

'What is the name Emperor? It is a word like any other. If I had no other title than that to show before the bar of history, I would be a laughing stock.'

He knew that better than those three insular puritans who begrudged him that title and were trying to wrest it with all its outward trappings from him. Nevertheless Maitland and Hotham, from whom he had asked the hospitality of the British flag, had received him, welcomed him and treated him as a guest. The signatures of three individuals, even if they were ministers, could not alter that.

'What I admire most in the world,' he once said, 'is the impotence of force to organize anything. In the long run, the sword is always conquered by the spirit.'

It was in the name of the spirit that he had protested against the use of force to class him as a prisoner and impose upon him an illegal captivity. It was in the name of the spirit that he rejected the incognito that he had wished to adopt, that he abandoned the name of his aide-de-camp Muiron, which he had chosen in order to live in peace in the English countryside. It was in the name of the spirit that he had haughtily affirmed his rights as sovereign, as head of the French government and, with the title of First Consul, had been recognized by the King of England. The imperial sovereignties, dignities and titles conferred by the French people had been consecrated by the indelible unctions of the Holy Father and ratified by the sovereigns of Europe who had bent the knee before him and would have worshipped him like a god if he had been pleased to order it'.

He had united in his person the totality of the religious, civil and political titles which existed among men and which none of the reigning princes of Europe could show 'piled by destiny upon the head and founder of his dynasty'.

To renounce the title of Emperor would mean to recognize the unique condition imposed on him by force, to countenance Britannic phariseeism, to become the accomplice of Europe whose leaders pretended to act in the name of the Holy Trinity. It would mean to consider illegitimate the régime of the Rights of Man, the Code and all that France had acquired in twenty years. It would be the final downfall and he was 'a man whom one kills but whom one does not insult'.

By the power of the people's right and by his conscience, he was and will remain the Emperor for ever. And it was the Emperor who, on August 7, 1815, at two o'clock in the afternoon, went on board the *Northumberland*.

ARMY COMMUNIQUE

published in the Special Supplement to the *Moniteur Universel*
of June 21, 1815

Laon, June 20, 1815

BATTLE OF LIGNY, NEAR FLEURUS

On the morning of the 16th the position of the army was as follows:

The left wing, commanded by Marshal the Duke of Elchingen, and made up of the 1st and 2nd Infantry Corps and the 2nd Cavalry Corps, occupied positions at Frasnes.

The right wing, commanded by Marshal Grouchy, made up of the 3rd and 4th Infantry Corps and the 3rd Cavalry Corps, occupied the heights behind Fleurus.

The Emperor's headquarters were at Charleroi, where were the Imperial Guard and the 6th Corps.

The left wing was ordered to march on Quatre-Bras and the right wing on Sombreffe. The Emperor went to Fleurus with his reserves.

Marshal Grouchy's column, while on the march, came into contact with the enemy army beyond Fleurus. The enemy army was commanded by Field-Marshal Blücher and was on the flat country by the Bussy Mill. Its left was at the village of Sombreffe and its cavalry was advancing for a considerable distance along the Namur road; its right was at Saint-Amand and occupied this large village in force. A ravine in front protected its position.

The Emperor reconnoitred the strength and positions of the enemy and decided to attack at once. A change of front had to be made, the right wing moving forward and pivoting on Fleurus.

General Vandamme marched on Saint-Amand, General Gérard on Ligny and Marshal Grouchy on Sombreffe. The 3rd Division of the 2nd Corps, commanded by General Girard, marched as a reserve behind General Vandamme's corps. The Guard drew up abreast of Fleurus, as did the cuirassiers of General Milhaud.

These dispositions were completed by three o'clock in the afternoon. General Lefol's division, which was a part of General Vandamme's corps, was the first to be engaged and took possession of Saint-Amand, chasing the enemy out at the point of the bayonet. Throughout the fighting, it held firm at the cemetery and bell-tower of Saint-Amand. This village, which covers a considerable area, was the scene of various combats during the early evening; the whole of General Vandamme's corps was engaged there and the enemy too made use of considerable forces.

General Girard, held in reserve for General Vandamme's corps, outflanked the village on the right and fought there with his usual valour. The forces engaged, on both sides, were supported by about sixty guns.

On the right, General Gérard was engaged with the 4th Corps at the village of Ligny, which was taken and re-taken several times.

On the extreme right, Marshal Grouchy and General Pajol were fighting at the village of Sombreffe. The enemy had between eighty and ninety thousand men and a large number of field-pieces.

By seven o'clock we were masters of all the villages situated on the edge of the ravine that covered the enemy's position. But the enemy still held, in full force, the plateau of the Bussy Mill.

The Emperor with his Guard moved to the village of Ligny : General Gérard brought up General Pécheux with what remained of the reserves, almost all the troops having been engaged in this village. Eight battalions of the Guard then made a bayonet charge and, behind them, the four squadrons attached to them, General Delort's cuirassiers, those of General Milhaud and the mounted grenadiers of the Guard. The Old Guard charged the enemy columns on the Bussy heights with fixed bayonets and in a moment the whole field of battle was covered with dead. The squadrons then attacked and broke a square and the cuirassiers drove the enemy out pell-mell. By half-past seven we had taken forty guns, many carriages, some flags and many prisoners, whilst the enemy sought safety in precipitous flight. By ten o'clock the battle was over and we were masters of the entire field.

General Lützow, leading irregular troops, was taken prisoner.

We were told by prisoners that Field-Marshal Blücher had been wounded. The élite of the Prussian army has been destroyed in this battle. Its losses cannot be less than fifteen thousand men, whereas ours were three thousand men killed or wounded.

On the left, Marshal Ney had marched on Quatre-Bras with a division which had routed an English division in position there. But, attacked by the Prince of Orange with twenty-five thousand men, partly English, partly Hanoverians in English pay, he withdrew to his position at Frasnes, where there were several engagements. The enemy attempted to storm it, but without success. The Duke of Elchingen was waiting for the 1st Corps, which did not arrive until nightfall. He limited himself to holding fast in his positions. In a square attacked by the 8th Cuirassier Regiment, the colours of the English 69th Infantry Regiment fell into our hands. The Prince of Brunswick was killed and the Prince of Orange wounded. We were told that the enemy had lost several of their leaders, killed or wounded, including a number of generals. The English losses are estimated at between four and five thousand men; on our side too there were very heavy losses, amounting to about four thousand two hundred men killed or wounded. The fighting ended at nightfall. Wellington then evacuated Quatre-Bras and moved towards Genappe.

On the morning of the 17th the Emperor went to Quatre-Bras, whence he advanced to attack the English army. He forced it to retreat to the outskirts of the Soigne forest, with the left wing and the reserve. The right wing moved on Sombreffe, in pursuit of Field-Marshal Blücher who was making his way towards Wavre where, it seemed, he wanted to take up position.

At ten o'clock in the evening, the English army, whose centre had occupied Mont-Saint-Jean, was in position in front of the Soigne forest. We would have needed three hours to attack it. We had, therefore, to postpone this until the next day.

The Emperor's headquarters were set up at the Caillou farm near Plancenoit. It was raining heavily. Thus, during the day of June 16th, the left wing, the right wing and the reserve were all engaged, over a front of about two leagues.

THE BATTLE OF MONT-SAINT-JEAN

At nine o'clock in the morning, the rain having slackened a

little, the 1st Corps moved and took up fresh positions, its left on the Brussels road opposite the village of Mont-Saint-Jean, which appeared to be the enemy centre. The 2nd Corps based its right wing on the Brussels road and its left on a little wood within gunshot of the British army. The cuirassiers were kept in the rear as a reserve and the Guard as a reserve on the heights. The 6th Corps, with General Domon's cavalry, under the orders of Count Lobau, was to move behind our right wing to face a Prussian corps which seemed to have evaded Marshal Grouchy and which intended to attack our right wing, an intention we had become aware of through our own reports and through a letter from a Prussian general which was carried by an orderly officer captured by one of our scouts. The morale of the troops was high.

The English army was estimated to be about eighty thousand men strong; the Prussian corps which might be considered to become effective before evening was estimated at about fifteen thousand men. The enemy forces were therefore more than ninety thousand men. Our forces were less numerous.

By midday everything was ready and Prince Jérôme, commanding a division of the 2nd Corps intended to form part of the extreme left wing, moved towards the woods, a part of which was held by the enemy. The cannonade began; the enemy supported with thirty guns the troops sent to keep watch on the wood. We too, on our side, carried out some artillery movements. By one o'clock Prince Jérôme was master of the entire wood and the whole English army withdrew under cover of fire. Count d'Erlon then attacked the village of Mont-Saint-Jean and supported his attack with eighty guns. He opened a terrific cannonade which must have caused great havoc in the English army. All the shots fell on the plateau. A brigade of Count d'Erlon's 1st Division captured the village of Mont-Saint-Jean; a second brigade was charged by an English cavalry corps and suffered great losses. At the same time an English cavalry division charged Count d'Erlon's batteries from the right and put several guns out of action. But General Milhaud's cuirassiers charged this division, three regiments of which broke and were smashed to pieces.

It was three o'clock in the afternoon. The Emperor ordered the Guard to advance and take up position on the plain, on the ground that the 1st Corps had occupied at the beginning of the action. This corps was now in the front line. The Prussian division, whose movements had been foreseen, then became engaged with Count Lobau's tirailleurs, keeping the whole of our right flank under fire. It was therefore best, before undertaking anything elsewhere, to await the issue of this attack. For this reason, all the available reserves were in readiness to go to the assistance of Count Lobau and to smash the Prussian corps when it should advance.

This done, the Emperor had the idea of launching an attack on the village of Mont-Saint-Jean which, it was hoped, would lead to a decisive success; but, by a movement of impatience so frequent in our military annals and which has so often been disastrous to us, the cavalry reserve, having perceived a retrograde movement by the English to keep out of range of our batteries from which they had already suffered greatly, occupied the high ground at Mont-Saint-Jean and charged the infantry. This movement, which had it been made at the right time and supported by the reserves could have decided the day, was made independently and before the dispositions of the right wing had been terminated and was therefore disastrous. Having no way of countermanding it, and since the enemy threw large masses of infantry and cavalry into the battle, the two cuirassier divisions became engaged and all our cavalry rushed to support their comrades. For three hours several charges were made which resulted in several squares being broken and six British infantry colours captured, advantages out of proportion to the losses sustained by our cavalry through grape-shot and rifle fire. It was impossible to make use of our infantry reserves until the flank attack by the Prussian corps had been beaten off. This attack was still going on at right angles to our right flank. The Emperor sent General Duhesme there with the Young Guard and several reserve batteries. The enemy was held, driven back and forced to retreat; it had expended its forces and there was no more to fear. This was the suitable moment for an attack on the enemy centre.

As the cuirassiers had suffered heavily from grape-shot, four battalions of the Moyenne Garde were sent to cover the cuirassiers, to hold the position and, if possible, to disengage and allow some of our cavalry to withdraw into the flat country. Two other battalions were sent to attack at right angles on the extreme left of the division which had been manoeuvring on our flank, so that we should not have any further anxiety on that score. The rest was placed in reserve, a part to support the flank attack behind Mont-Saint-Jean, a part to remain on the plain behind the field of battle which formed our line of retreat.

In these circumstances, the battle was already won; we occupied all the positions which the enemy had occupied at the beginning of the action; but as our cavalry had been made use of too soon and had been badly deployed, we could not hope for a decisive success. But Marshal Grouchy, having been advised of the movements of the Prussian corps, marched on its rear, thus ensuring us a brilliant success for the following day. After eight hours under fire and having sustained infantry and cavalry charges, the whole army saw with satisfaction that the battle had been won and that the field of battle was in our hands. At half-past eight, the four battalions of the Moyenne Garde which had been sent to the plateau beyond Mont-Saint-Jean to support the cuirassiers, being harassed by the enemy grape-shot, advanced to take the enemy batteries at the point of the bayonet. The day was coming to an end. A charge by several English squadrons on their flank threw them into disorder. The fugitives recrossed the ravine. The nearby regiments, who saw a number of men belonging to the Guard in rout, thought that it was the Old Guard which had given way and wavered. There were cries of 'All is lost! The Guard has been driven back!' The soldiers even claim that ill-disposed persons stationed in various places shouted '*Sauve qui peut!*' However that may be, a panic terror spread suddenly over the whole battlefield. Everyone rushed in great disorder along the lines of communication. Soldiers, gunners, limbers, all crowded to get away. The Old Guard, which was in reserve, was caught in the rush and was itself swept away.

In a few moments, the army was one confused mass. All types of men were mixed together and it was impossible to re-form a corps. The enemy, seeing this astonishing confusion, launched its cavalry columns in pursuit. The disorder increased. The confusion of the night prevented the troops from rallying and realizing their mistake.

Thus a battle over, a day ended, false measures repaired,

greater successes assured for the morrow, but all was lost through a moment of panic terror. Even the squadrons drawn up near the Emperor were overrun and disorganized by these tumultuous waves of men and were forced to go with the current. The reserve parks and supply trains which had not re-crossed the Sambre, and in fact everything that remained on the battlefield, fell into enemy hands. There was no possibility of awaiting the arrival of the troops on our right wing. The bravest army in the world was thrown into utter confusion. Nothing of its organization remained.

At five o'clock in the morning of the 19th the Emperor crossed the Sambre at Charleroi. Philippeville and Avesnes are to be the rallying points. Prince Jérôme, General Morand and the other generals have already rallied a part of the army. Marshal Grouchy, with the corps of the right wing, is making good his withdrawal along the lower Sambre.

Judging from the standards which we have captured and by the retreats which the enemy has been forced to make, its losses must have been very great. Ours can only be estimated after the troops have been re-formed. Before the disorder broke out, we had already suffered considerable losses, above all in the cavalry, so disastrously and yet so courageously engaged. Despite these losses, the valorous cavalry continued to hold the positions they had taken from the English and only abandoned them when forced to do so by the tumult and confusion on the battlefield. In the middle of the night and amid all the obstacles blocking the roads, it has not been able to preserve its formations.

The artillery, as always, covered itself with glory.

The carriages of the general staff remained where they were, no retreat having been considered necessary. During the day, they fell into enemy hands.

Such has been the issue of the battle of Mont-Saint-Jean, so glorious and yet so disastrous for the French armies.

BIBLIOGRAPHY

Archives nationales : F 7 3774.
AF IV 1933, 1934, 1935, 1936, 1937, 1938.
AF IV 908.
Archives du ministère des Armées: C 14. 24 à 37. 59. 60.
C 16. 28 à 45.
Armées du Nord, du Rhin, du Jura, des Alpes, de la Loire.
Registres de correspondance du major général.
Archives de la Marine : B B3. 426.
Journal de bord de la Saale.
Archives du comte EXELMANS.
Le Moniteur, Journal de l'Empereur, Journal des Débats, Revue des Etudes Napoléoniennes, Revue de l'Institut Napoléon, Revue Historique de l'Armée, Neptunia, etc.
ALI (Mameluk): Souvenirs sur l'Empereur Napoléon.

BARANTE : Souvenirs.
BEKER (General): Relation de ma mission auprès de Napoléon.
BEUGNOT : Mémoires.
BONAPARTE (Lucien): La vérité sur les Cent-Jours.
BONNEFOUX (Baron de): Mémoires.
BORJANE (Henry): Napoléon à bord du Northumberland.
BOURGUIGNON (Jean): Mémoires de Valérie Mazuyer.

CARNOT (H.): Mémoires sur Carnot.
CHANLAINE (Pierre): Napoléon à l'île d'Aix.
CHASTENET (Jacques): Wellington.

CLAUSEWITZ: Der Feldzug von 1815.
COCHELET (Mademoiselle): Mémoires.
CONSTANT (Benjamin): Journal.
CURELY (General): Souvenirs.

DAVOUT (Marshal): Mémoires manuscrits.
DOHER (Marcel): Charles de La Bédoyère.
DUMAS (Mathieu): Mémoires.

ERNOUF: La capitulation de Paris.

FLEURY DE CHABOULON : Mémoires sur les Cent-Jours.
FOUCHÉ: Mémoires.

GANIÈRE (Dr Paul): Napoléon à Sainte-Hélène.
GOURGAUD (General): Campagne de 1815, Journal de Sainte-Hélène.
GROUCHY (Marshal): Souvenirs, Relation succincte des événements de 1815.

HOBHOUSE: Letters.
HORTENSE (Queen): Mémoires.
HOUSSAYE (Henry): 1815, Waterloo, la Seconde Abdication.
HYDE DE NEUVILLE : Mémoires.

JAL : Souvenirs.
JOSEPH (King): Mémoires.
JOURDAN DE LA PASSARDÈRE : Relation, Revue rétrospective, 1er oct. 1897.

LACHOUQUE (Commandant Henry): Mémoires de Marchand, Général de Tromelin, le Secret de Waterloo.

Bibliography

LA FAYETTE (General): *Mémoires, Lettres inédites.*

LAS CASES: *Mémorial de Sainte-Hélène.*

LAVALLETTE (Comte de): *Mémoires et Souvenirs.*

MACDONALD (Marshal): *Souvenirs.*

MACIRONE: *Faits intéressant la mort du roi Murat.*

MADELIN (Louis): *Fouché.*

MAITLAND (Captain) and George HOME (Ensign): *Napoleon on the Bellerophon.*

MASSON (Frédéric): *Le général comte Flahaut.*

MIOT DE MELITO: *Mémoires.*

METTERNICH: *Mémoires.*

MONTHOLON (Madame de): *Souvenirs.*

MONTHOLON (General): *Récits de la captivité, Mémoires.*

NAPOLEON: *Correspondance.*

PASQUIER (Chancellor): *Mémoires.*

PEYRUSSE: *Mémorial et Archives.*

PONTECOULANT (de): *Souvenirs.*

REVUE DE CAVALERIE: *La brigade du colonel von Sohr.*

ROVIGO (Duc de): *Mémoires.*

SILVESTRE: *La Malmaison, Rochefort, Sainte-Hélène.*

SISMONDI: *Notes sur les Cent-Jours.*

TOUCHON (Charles): *L'île d'Aix.*

VALÉE (General): *Journal.*

VERNON (Guy de): *Gouvion-Saint-Cyr.*

VILLEMAIN: *Souvenirs contemporains.*

VITROLLES (de): *Mémoires.*

WELLINGTON (Duke of): *Dispatches.*

WELSCHINGER: *Procès du maréchal Ney.*

INDEX